Heading Out

A Celebration of the Great Outdoors
in Calgary and Southern Alberta

ORARIO

Heading Out

A Celebration of the Great Outdoors
in Calgary and Southern Alberta

Bruce Masterman

Johnson Gorman Publishers

The Publishers
Johnson Gorman Publishers
3669 – 41 Avenue
Red Deer Alberta Canada T4N 2X7

Credits
Cover design by Boldface Technologies.
Text design by Full Court Press.
Front cover photographs (main) and backcover (spine) courtesy of Eye-
Wire Studios. All other cover photographs by Bruce Masterman.
Photograph page 158 courtesy of Clive Schaupmeyer. All other pho-
tographs by Bruce Masterman.
Printed and bound in Canada by Friesens for Johnson Gorman Publishers.

Acknowledgments
Financial support provided by the Alberta Foundation for the Arts, a ben-
eficiary of the Lottery Fund of the Government of Alberta.

COMMITTED TO THE DEVELOPMENT OF CULTURE AND THE ARTS

Canadian Cataloguing in Publication Data
Masterman, Bruce, 1952–
Heading out
Includes bibliographical references.
ISBN 0-921835-52-3
1. Calgary Region (Alta.)—Guidebooks. 2. Outdoor recreation—Alberta—
Calgary Region—Guidebooks. I. Title.
FC3697.18.M37 1999 917.123'38043 C99-910101-3
F1079.5.C35M37 1999

5 4 3 2 1

To the special loves of my life—Sarah, Chelsea and Karen—for being there to share all those "slight inclines," literally and figuratively. And to God the Creator, with thanks for the gift of nature and the opportunity to enjoy and praise its beauty.

Though every care has been taken to ensure accuracy at the time of publication, laws, regulations and conditions are constantly changing. The material in this book is therefore intended to provide general information only. This book is sold with the understanding that the author and publisher are not engaged in rendering professional travel, legal or other advice. Readers are encouraged to consult local authorities to obtain the most recent information about road, trail, weather and water conditions that may affect their experience in the regions described in this book.

Contents

Foreword 11
Acknowledgments 15
Introduction 17

Chapter 1
Wild Calgary:
The City's Natural Environment Parks 22
Outdoor Activities and Courses 27
Calgary's Pathways 31
Calgary's Wildlife 37

Chapter 2
Urban Getaways:
Getting Away from It All Without Leaving Calgary 49
Nose Hill Natural Environment Park 51
Fish Creek Provincial Park 54
Inglewood Bird Sanctuary 59
Weaselhead Flats Natural Environment Park 64
Glenmore Reservoir 68
Beaverdam Flats Natural Environment Park 71
Carburn Natural Environment Park 74
Edworthy Natural Environment Park 78
Sam Livingston Fish Hatchery 82
Best Cross-Country Skiing in Calgary 87
Best Cheap Skating in Calgary 92
Best Tobogganing in Calgary 94
Best Winter Picnicking in Calgary and Area 95

Chapter 3
Day-Trip Destinations:
Great Escapes Within Forty-Five Minutes of Calgary 97
Big Hill Springs Provincial Park 99
Ann and Sandy Cross Conservation Area 102

Ghost Lake 107
Brown Lowery Provincial Park 110
Frank Lake Conservation Area 114
Wyndham–Carseland Provincial Park 118
The Middle Bow River 121

Chapter 4
Weekend Destinations:
Great Escapes within Three Hours of Calgary 125
Head-Smashed-In Buffalo Jump 127
Chain Lakes Provincial Park 132
Drumheller Badlands 136
Dinosaur Provincial Park 141
Kinbrook Island Provincial Park 146
Waterton Lakes National Park 151
Cypress Hills Provincial Park 156
Writing-On-Stone Provincial Park 160

Chapter 5
On the Rocks:
The Beckoning Mountains 165
Cross-Country Skiing 167
Hiking 169
Outings with Children 173
Lake Hikes 178
Autumn's Gold Rush 183
Best Cross-Country Skiing 187
Banff National Park 188
Pipestone Creek 188
Lake Louise Shoreline/Telemark/1A Highway 189
Spray River Picnic Site Loop 190
Cascade 190
Johnson Lake 191
Kananaskis Country 192
Peter Lougheed Provincial Park 192

West Bragg Creek 192
Sandy McNabb Recreation Area 193
Ribbon Creek 193
Canmore Nordic Centre 194
Banff's Triple Crown 195
Johnston Canyon 196
Lake Minnewanka 199
Plain of Six Glaciers Trail 202

Chapter 6
Kananaskis Country:
The Natural Playground at Calgary's Doorstep 206
Peter Lougheed Provincial Park 208
The Big Spawn—A Very Bullish Hike 213
Elbow River Valley 217
Sibbald Recreation Area 222
Eagle Fever: The Migration 227
Sheep River Valley 231
Highwood–Cataract Region 236
Kananaskis Country Circle Driving Tour 241

Chapter 7
Playing it Safe in the Rocky Mountains 246
Bears and Other Critters 249
Avalanches 253
Staying Warm 254
Water Warning 256
On Thin Ice 257
Ticked Off 260

Recommended Reading 261
About the Author 264

Foreword

WHEN I WAS 12 OR 13, my older brother, Gordon, and I were fascinated by the wild. We lived in a smaller Calgary then; downtown was full of squat, smoky buildings and in winter the streets were full of the blue sparks and hiss of passing trolley buses. From anywhere in the city, we could look past the rooftops and see the swelling rise of prairie and the blue line of the Rockies on the western horizon. It was possible to imagine bears out there and big trout in secret streams.

We hungered for outdoor adventure. On weekends we took turns crossing the Bow River to a used bookstore in Hillhurst, where we bought back issues of the Big American outdoors magazines: *Field and Stream, Sports Afield* and *Outdoor Life*. Later, at home, we pored over each issue with loving thoroughness, drinking in the authors' tales of hunting in Alaska and Colorado or fishing in famous trout streams like Montana's Big Hole and Madison rivers. There were so many great places out there and so much scope for adventure. We tried to prevail upon Mom and Dad to take us to those faraway places during our short family vacations, but they didn't share our fantasies.

Instead, we had to make do with fishing trips into the foothills of the Rockies, pheasant hunting along irrigation ditches near Strathmore and—later in our teenage years—backpacking in Banff or pursuing big game in the Porcupine Hills. When Dad couldn't spare time from work to take us afield, we had to make do with fishing along the Bow River.

Edmonton ecotourism expert Dr. Jim Butler talks about a phenomenon he calls "parochial myopia." He describes it as the inability of local people and communities to recognize the spectacular natural value of their own backyard. The city fathers of my childhood, who treated the Bow River as a handy place for dumping unwanted old sidewalks and construction fill, were victims of this affliction. So, too, were my brother and I as we glumly fished for big brown trout and plentiful rainbows, dreaming of some day being able to fish a truly great river.

It took visiting anglers, visionary local business people and great outdoor writers like Bruce Masterman to startle us all out of our parochial myopia into the realization that the Bow River is, in fact, one of the very finest trout streams in the whole world.

And it doesn't stop there. Southwestern Alberta's big game populations and the wild landscapes they inhabit are second to none. The finest high country hikes in the Rockies are just an hour's drive from downtown Calgary. No less than four World Heritage Sites are within a half day's travel from Calgary. Spectacular waterfowl migrations darken the prairie skies within sight of the city. Cougars, elk, sage grouse, tiny salamanders, pure white orchids—the natural diversity of our home landscapes is beyond the ability of most of the worlds' people to imagine.

Southern Alberta is not a land of second bests. It is one of the last great places on Earth. And Bruce knows it.

Grown up, I began to recognize the unique and vulnerable nature of my home landscape and became active in the environmental movement. It began with the loss of small places I loved—an aspen forest where I once hunted deer bulldozed to make way for alfalfa; a secret mountain paradise peeled away to reveal the coal seams underneath; a much-loved river dammed to store water for irrigation farming. Increasingly, as the years have passed, I've come to realize that in being an Albertan one cannot help but be defined by the landscapes in which one passes one's life. What always struck me as profoundly self-defeating was the way I and my fellow Albertans blithely imposed permanent changes on the face of this place we choose to name ourselves after. How could we continue to chase prosperity at any price without considering how much we could afford to squander before finding that we had sacrificed our identities and failed utterly in our duty to our home place?

Many of us railed—and continue to rail—with a passionate but futile rage at the forces of change. We staged campaigns to protect wilderness and undammed rivers, published newsletters to try to educate our neighbors and lobbied inattentive governments. In our desperation we sometimes resorted to name-calling and other unworthy tactics. And still the irreplaceable beauty of wild Alberta continues to erode.

Alberta's conservation history is not always a happy story. On reflection I suspect that this is because the environmental community often failed in a basic way. We told Albertans what was being lost, but we rarely showed them. I suspect that Bruce Masterman — who has never chosen to describe himself as an environmentalist — may do more with this book than has been achieved by half a century of conservation advocacy.

Caring, commitment and change come from encounters with the wild. It was our childhood experiences along the trout streams, pheasant coulees and mountain ridges of wild Alberta that built the foundation for Gordon's and my conservation activism. By the same token it is the sheer joy and wonder of discovering the living wild that Bruce offers to a whole new generation of Albertans. In an urban society, in a young city peopled mostly by families that have moved here from afar, finding contact with wild nature is a daunting challenge. Bruce removes the barriers by introducing his readers to the many wild places he has come to know and love with his own family. He also introduces us to a great variety of Southern Albertans who have come to care for these special places. We aren't alone out there.

This book is a love story — a story of the love many Albertans feel for places both spectacular and subtle, wild and near-urban, familiar and bizarre. It is written by a man who knows the wild well, a seasoned and well-rounded outdoorsman who lives the simple truth that the finest gift a parent can give his or her children is the opportunity to experience the real world that lies out there just beyond the pavement's edge.

If each Alberta family owned a copy of this book — and I sincerely hope that in the not-too-distant future every family will — and used it only five or six times a year to explore and discover the wonderful places Bruce describes so well, then I believe there would be little need for conservation advocacy campaigns to defend the last of the wild. If enough of us simply discover for ourselves the sheer joy and beauty of wild Alberta, we will become, inevitably, a society of real Albertans who consciously choose to cherish and protect our shared heritage.

This is a fine book, written by a fine outdoors writer—and it hasn't come a moment too soon. Alberta will be the better for it; and as Bruce shows in the pages that follow, Alberta is already pretty darn fine.

See you out there.

–Kevin Van Tighem
Waterton Lakes National Park

Acknowledgments

A book like this doesn't happen without a great deal of help from others. My sincere thanks to:

Dennis Johnson of Johnson Gorman Publishers for sharing my belief in this project and for being one of the best editors I've known in 26 years of writing professionally.

Members of my family and many friends for believing in me and encouraging the completion of this book. You know who you are.

Kevin Van Tighem for writing the eloquent foreword and for keeping me on track.

Andy Russell, Sandra Foss and Kevin for their kind words on the back cover.

Mike Sturk for his darkroom work and Clive Schaupmeyer for use of the Elkwater Lake photo in the section on Cypress Hills Provincial Park.

Dave Elphinstone, Ellen Gasser, Kendy Bentley, Jacquie Gilson, Mairi Babey, Sue Cunningham and Jeff Gruttz for checking sections of the manuscript for accuracy. All surviving mistakes are strictly my own.

Jim Stelfox, Ron Chamney, Kym McCulley, John McFaul, Stephen Herrero, Jerry Brunen, Jim McLennan, George Freeman and Alasdair Fergusson for sharing their knowledge and passion.

Colin Weir of the Alberta Birds of Prey Centre at Coaldale for providing willing models for the sections on bald and golden eagles.

Charles Dee, of Toronto, whose eloquent words delivered on a bench beside Elbow Lake reflected the special feelings of many for Kananaskis Country.

A succession of publishers, editors, copy editors, reporters and editorial assistants and other colleagues at the *Calgary Herald* for their support in the past two decades.

Finally, my thanks to the hundreds of people who have had the misfortune of encountering this pesky notepad-wielding writer — especially those bothered in remote locations where they thought they were away from it all. Thank you for sharing your experiences. The outdoors needs more friends like you.

Introduction

CALGARY IS PARADISE for lovers of the outdoors. People from all over the world come to explore the city's natural areas, the famous Bow River and the nearby mountains, prairies and foothills. Within city limits more than 800,000 Calgarians escape the pressures of urban living by visiting over 100 natural areas, including one of Canada's easternmost stands of Douglas fir trees. Residents picnic, hike, bike, jog, fish, watch wildlife and cross-country ski without ever leaving the city. They relax urban-weary muscles on or beside the Bow and Elbow rivers, which run through the most spectacular urban valleys in Canada and are home to hundreds of species of wildlife. They enjoy more than 330 km (205 mi) of city-maintained paved pathways and another 46 km (29 mi) of trails in Fish Creek Provincial Park, a unique treasure in its own right. School teachers and parents use Calgary's natural areas as living classrooms to help kids learn about the fragile relationship between humans, flora and fauna.

Within an hour's drive of the city are small, secluded provincial parks as well as more popular spots offering some of the best hiking and fishing anywhere. Farther afield is the magic of Waterton Lakes National Park and the mysterious hoodoo-studded terrain of Writing-On-Stone and Dinosaur provincial parks. To the west are the Rocky Mountains, creating a spectacular view and offering endless opportunities for outdoor enthusiasts. Banff National Park and Kananaskis Country, a provincial mountain-and-foothills recreation area of 4,156 km^2 (1,605 mi^2), have much to offer, from lazy afternoon picnics and scenic drives to vigorous backpacking trips that last several days.

Sometimes the city's lively economy and bottom-line attitude make it too easy for residents to ignore the natural treasures just past the pavement, to let their lives revolve solely around jobs and family. But heading out to the world of forests, prairie, rivers and wildlife helps soothe the soul. Being outdoors is like installing a governor on the psyche—it slows down the pace of life and encourages enjoyment of life, friends and family. It can also be invigorating, stimulating and enlightening. The choice is yours.

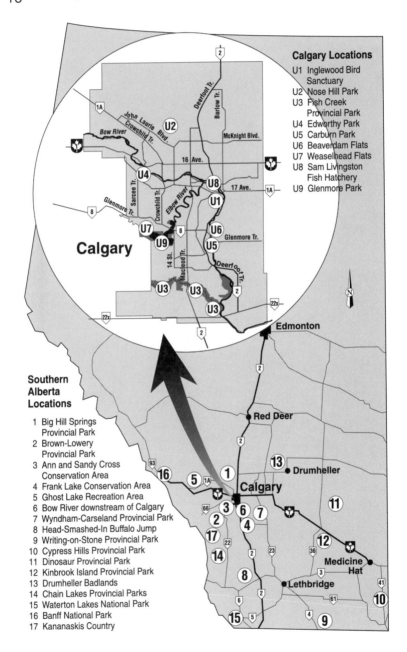

Calgary Locations

U1 Inglewood Bird
     Sanctuary
U2 Nose Hill Park
U3 Fish Creek
     Provincial Park
U4 Edworthy Park
U5 Carburn Park
U6 Beaverdam Flats
U7 Weaselhead Flats
U8 Sam Livingston
     Fish Hatchery
U9 Glenmore Park

**Southern
Alberta
Locations**

 1 Big Hill Springs
     Provincial Park
 2 Brown-Lowery
     Provincial Park
 3 Ann and Sandy Cross
     Conservation Area
 4 Frank Lake Conservation Area
 5 Ghost Lake Recreation Area
 6 Bow River downstream of Calgary
 7 Wyndham-Carseland Provincial Park
 8 Head-Smashed-In Buffalo Jump
 9 Writing-on-Stone Provincial Park
10 Cypress Hills Provincial Park
11 Dinosaur Provincial Park
12 Kinbrook Island Provincial Park
13 Drumheller Badlands
14 Chain Lakes Provincial Parks
15 Waterton Lakes National Park
16 Banff National Park
17 Kananaskis Country

Many longtime residents already know how lucky they are to live in this region. Witness the thousands of people who stay within the city to enjoy its natural areas every day, the steady stream of traffic out of the city each Saturday morning and the lineups at local outdoor equipment shops. Other residents are late converts to the outdoors. They wake up one morning and realize they've missed something important, or they suddenly find themselves retired with time on their hands. If you fit this description this book is for you.

Calgary's population, estimated at about 820,000 in early 1999, is growing by about 20,000 people annually. Over the past three years more than 70,000 people moved to the city. Many newcomers have transferred to Calgary with their companies as the city competes for bragging rights to head office capital of Canada. Others have moved on their own, seeking opportunity in a city that hates to use the B-word (boom) but can't deny that things are looking pretty good, economically speaking. Whatever their reason for moving, once here, they soon discover Calgary's outdoors. Newcomers also will discover plenty of breathing room, even at the most popular outdoor destinations. If you are a newcomer to Calgary or you are visiting and want to head outdoors, this book is for you, too.

Some people, especially when they're just getting into outdoor activities, are intimidated by potential hazards such as bears. Overcoming fears, however, is simply often a matter of learning more about, and gaining respect for, the natural world. If you're new to wilderness outings or have similar fears, turn to Chapter 7 "Playing it Safe in the Rocky Mountains," which covers several common concerns ranging from bear country safety to avalanche awareness and cold weather preparations. The information will help reduce your level of anxiety and point you in the right direction for more help if needed.

Heading Out celebrates the outdoors. It is not an all-inclusive hiking trail or tourism guide. Many excellent detailed guides already exist for that purpose. Some are listed in the recommended reading section at the back of this book. Instead *Heading Out* offers snapshots of the best the outdoors has to offer in this region. They're humbly offered by a transplanted Manitoban who's spent 21 years heading out in Calgary and Southern Alberta, and a lifetime enjoying the outdoors from New Brunswick to British Columbia.

I have written about the outdoors in the *Calgary Herald* since I was hired in 1979, six years after I started making a living writing for newspapers. The hundreds of "Outdoors" and "Heading Out" columns I've written were intended to raise Calgarians' awareness of natural places, wild creatures and the issues facing both. I've been fortunate to spend many days out and about, savoring the sights, inhaling the sweet air and talking to people with similar interests and concerns. This book includes information gleaned from some of my columns as well as the many experiences I've had outdoors over the years.

All locations covered in this book are perfect for family outings. Some of you will cringe to discover I've revealed a secret spot; others will wonder why I've left out a favorite. My selections were purely subjective, the main criteria being whether I thought you would find a place interesting to read about and visit, and whether further exposure would threaten its future. Cost also was a criterion. Families on tight budgets don't have a lot of spare cash to spend on outings. Of the dozens of destinations covered in this book, only a handful—Canmore Nordic Centre, Canada Olympic Park, the Royal Tyrrell Museum of Palaeontology, Head-Smashed-In Buffalo Jump, and Banff and Waterton Lakes national parks—charge visitors a daily fee at the time of this writing. This may change as the Alberta government proceeds with promised plans to privatize various operations in parks and day-use areas—something that has already resulted in higher camping fees and firewood charges in many provincial parks and recreation areas. In the meantime you should make liberal use of what you already pay for as a taxpayer.

To help your planning, each destination includes directions, a list of available activities, hours, fees and seasons of operation, if applicable, a description of the terrain and telephone numbers for additional advice. Detailed maps show the routes to particular locations.

With this information in hand, you may find your biggest problem is choosing where to go. If you could hike every weekend from now to the end of your life, you wouldn't cover more than a fraction of the hiking trails available in this region. Ditto for fishing and almost any other activity. But that's the beauty of the outdoors here: you're all dressed up, and there are too many places to go. So without further ado, let's get packed and hit the trail. It's time to head out.

Chapter 1

Wild Calgary

The City's Natural
Environment Parks

N ATURAL AREAS have become as much a part of Calgary as the Calgary Tower and the Calgary Stampede. "Calgarians don't want a city without art or schools, and they don't want a city without natural environments," says Dave Elphinstone, the city's natural area management coordinator. "It's one of the things that makes the city good."

Calgary's natural areas, now officially known as natural environment parks, are people magnets. Replete with greenery and open spaces, natural areas don't discriminate. They offer everyone places to walk, hike, cycle, cross-country ski and watch birds and other wildlife. They offer respite from hectic lifestyles. They encourage time to relax, bond with friends and family, educate children and keep life in order.

Calgary is blessed with more than 100 natural areas covering almost 2,900 ha (7,166 acres). In addition to land under the city's jurisdiction, there are another 1,189 ha (2,938 acres) at Fish Creek Provincial Park, Canada's largest urban park, which is managed by the provincial government. Calgary's natural areas vary considerably in size. They range from just a few hectares to a popular 1,127-ha (2,785-acre) grassland plateau known as Nose Hill Park. This park in northwest Calgary is the largest city-run natural area in Canada. In mid-April 1999 the Calgary Parks Foundation announced the creation of 11 new parks covering about 200 ha (494 acres). The new parks include a 92 ha (227 acre) spruce-studded natural area just west of Weaselhead Flats along the Elbow River in Calgary's southwest corner. Worth $3.5 million, the land was donated by 96-year-old Wilbur Griffith, a retired oilman. The parks foundation also unveiled plans for another 10 parks under the Millennium River Valley Legacy plan, which will expand green space along the Bow and Elbow rivers, Nose Creek and Fish Creek.

To many Calgarians, natural areas not only make the city good, they make the city. Period. And residents' passion for natural areas runs deep. Several years ago, city council considered a plan to develop a golf course on a small parcel of city-owned land on the west side of the Bow River near Southland Drive. To residents, this area was a

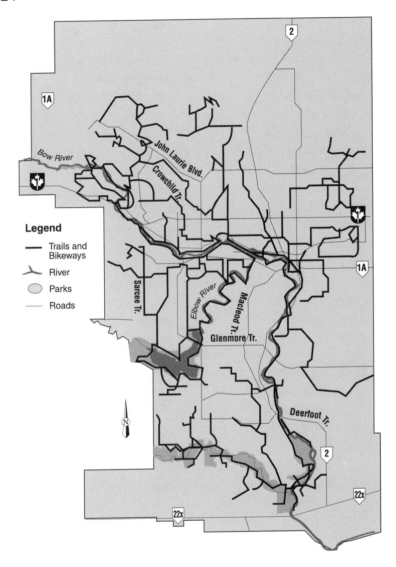

haven for running their dogs, traveling the bike path, watching wildlife and fishing for trout in the river. They were so opposed to the private golf course proposal that they crammed the Acadia Recreation Centre's Rose Hall to fight it. The golf course proposal never left the drawing board.

A few years ago the city considered a $3.8 million expansion of the Shaganappi Point Golf Course in southwest Calgary. The golf course is adjacent to Edworthy Natural Environment Park, which includes Edworthy Park, Lawrey Gardens and the Douglas Fir Trail, a 4-km (2.5-mi) route featuring a unique stand of Douglas fir trees. The expansion project would have meant the development of a 4.9-ha (12-acre) natural parcel of land containing native fescue grassland and willow. Local residents were up in arms immediately. They chose to live near Edworthy Park because of the Bow River Valley, the wildlife and the natural vegetation. "I'm not against golfers, but I'm for natural areas," proclaimed resident Joan Beck, herself a golfer. After heated public outcry, the project was reworked to avoid the natural area.

Under the city's natural parks management plan, approved by city council in 1994, staff have been assigned day-to-day administration, operation and maintenance. Some have been designated as operational specialists. But the real strength of Calgary's natural areas isn't in facilities and services provided by people. It's in the wildlife and terrain. These natural elements combine to create living classrooms where residents can learn about their wild environment. City naturalist John Riddell says classroom-based natural history courses and reference books are a good start. But natural areas are the best places to learn about Calgary's outdoors.

The management plan also recognizes the importance of considering natural areas in future development and planning processes. It establishes the need for planning, resource management, education, interpretation and marketing of natural areas to ensure long-term viability, *and* it creates the parameters for appropriate public use. Under the plan, a classification system has been developed that gives special designations to natural areas based on their size, ecosystems and public use. The plan takes a landscape ecology approach based on the understanding that by protecting the viability of the resource—vegetation, topography, soil and related ecology—the wildlife habitat will remain intact.

Dave Elphinstone's beard, tousled dark hair, blue jeans, sneakers and wool sweaters are the uniform of an outdoors lover, not a paper pusher. Elphinstone is a committed naturalist, photographer and writer. In 1990 he wrote *Inglewood Bird Sanctuary: A Place for All Seasons*, the definitive book on this special place in southeast Calgary. He was a naturalist–educator at the sanctuary for eight years before leaving to oversee development of Calgary's new natural area management plan. Calgary became one of the first Canadian cities to have such a policy.

As the plan evolved, some Calgarians resisted having their activities restricted. Many users of natural areas share a common environmental interest, but they have different personal philosophies about how that interest is best served. Some decried the city's decision to stop people from feeding birds in natural areas in order to keep wildlife wild. For years, well-intentioned Calgarians had religiously stocked feeders in the Weaselhead natural area. In 1996 city crews removed tin cans, cardboard milk containers and other artificial feeders according to the plan's objective to discourage bird feeding. "They don't need feeding if the habitat is healthy," Elphinstone says. "If we encourage feeding structures all over the place, it doesn't look like a natural area anymore." Feeding birds also attracts undesirable species, such as house sparrows, and can introduce harmful, nonnative weeds. Feeding also concentrates birds, making them more susceptible to disease and predation. Some users, such as mountain bikers banned from all but paved trails in the Weaselhead natural area, accused the city of being exclusionary. Through many public meetings and letters, Elphinstone stuck to his guns.

While working at the Inglewood sanctuary, Elphinstone had dreamed that one day the natural areas he loved would be officially recognized as a crucial component of Calgary—and given the protection they needed to survive. The plan is a vision come true for Elphinstone. "Management of natural areas is more than protection, maintenance and loving it," Elphinstone points out. "It's doing what has to be done in the long term to make it viable."

Outdoor Activities and Courses

IT IS A TYPICAL SUMMER AFTERNOON in Calgary's outdoors. Hundreds of sun-seekers frolic on the beach and cool off in the sparkling water of Sikome Lake in Fish Creek Provincial Park. Beside the lake's parking lot, a family in a compact car has stopped to watch a herd of mule deer feeding quietly at the edge of a poplar stand. A video-camera lens protrudes from the driver's side window. Strolling along a red-shale trail, a couple of senior citizens with binoculars and notepad search for the downy woodpecker they've heard rat-a-tatting on a dead tree trunk. On a paved trail a young mother in tights and T-shirt jogs steadily, pushing a large-wheeled cart that carries her sleeping baby. A group of teenaged boys on mountain bikes ring their bells as they pass the woman. Not far behind, a helmeted teenaged girl with sparkling braces on her teeth glides along on in-line skates, her knees and hands protected by padded guards. A man in khaki-colored shorts and hiking boots takes a swig from a plastic water bottle as he steps onto the pavement from an adjoining dirt trail.

In Hull's Woods day-use area, two families are enjoying a picnic. A small fire crackles in the steel pit. The smell of burning tube steaks wafts in the light south breeze. In the park upstream of the Highway 22X Bridge, anglers line the west bank of the Bow River. An elderly man in a lawn chair flips a silver-bladed spinner far into the current. Farther upstream, a wading fly-fisher casts a tiny Parachute Adams dry fly toward a dimple on the water that she knows is caused by a feeding trout. A pair of fishers in flight—orange-billed American white pelicans—silently drifts by overhead. A scarlet canoe with two middle-aged paddlers floats down the river close to the opposite bank. About 14 km (8.7 mi) to the west, near the Shannon Terrace Environmental Education Centre, several riders on horseback are enjoying a trail ride.

Ah, summer. Ah, Calgary.

The city has much to offer if your idea of a good time is heading out to enjoy nature and fresh air. Calgary is an active city, a four-season center of outdoors excellence. Without going beyond city limits, you can participate in almost every outdoors activity imaginable. You can cast a line in the Bow or Elbow rivers, and in Glenmore Reservoir and Carburn Park ponds. You can hike, in-line skate, jog or cycle. You can compete in orienteering, a sport combining running and walking while finding your way to various checkpoints in the woods. It's like a car rally on foot. You can watch birds and other wildlife, and go on picnics, summer and winter. You can kayak and canoe in flowing rivers or peaceful still water. In winter, you can skate, toboggan, snowshoe, sleigh ride, cross-country ski and downhill ski. Blessed Chinook winds in midwinter allow many of the same activities available in the other three seasons.

If you're not already involved in Calgary's outdoors scene, don't despair. Help is just a phone call away. The city boasts dozens of clubs with membership lists full of like-minded people eager to help. Some clubs are listed in the telephone book, but the easiest, most direct way to contact them is through the Calgary Area Outdoor Council (CAOC) at 403 270-2262. Based in an old brick firehall on the banks of the Bow River in downtown Calgary (1111 Memorial Drive NW), the council is a nonprofit umbrella organization of about 110 local groups involved in outdoor recreation, conservation, education and leadership.

In addition to dispensing information about local outdoor groups and activities, the council helps kick start new clubs and provides workshops on organizational planning and leadership training. It publishes a handy booklet, *The Guide to Outdoor Recreation In and Around Calgary*, listing names and phone numbers of all the clubs it represents. The guide is aimed at all ages, from senior citizens seeking company for hiking and cross-country skiing to youths interested in programs such as Junior Forest Wardens. Several groups are for people facing mental or physical challenges.

Launched in 1983, CAOC is operated by a volunteer board. It is funded by membership fees, special fundraising events, city grants, corporate donations and a modest contribution from the province. CAOC informs members about pressing recreation and conservation issues, such as the Special Places 2000 program and user fees in national parks. It also connects with members through its quarterly newsletter, *The Odyssey*. Although not a lobby group, CAOC provides information members can use as lobbying ammunition.

CAOC is not, however, the only game in town when it comes to learning about the local outdoor scene. Several places offer courses on subjects ranging from backcountry hiking for beginners to spring bird-watching. Top bets include the University of Calgary Outdoor Program Centre at 403 220-5038, the city's Outdoor/Nature Services at 403 268-1311 and Inglewood Bird Sanctuary at 403 269-6688.

The University of Calgary offers the most extensive outdoors program, with more than 1,500 courses. It also operates North America's largest university rental shop, featuring more than 7,000 pieces of gear, from canoes and cross-country skis to sleeping bags and climbing ropes. The university's mountain-related courses include hiking, map and compass navigation, bear safety, backpacking, rock and mountain climbing, caving and spring skiing. For wheelies, there's in-line skating, cycle touring and mountain biking. For riding the wind, there's paragliding, hang-gliding, sky-diving and ballooning. Water-based courses include canoeing, kayaking, river rafting, windsurfing, sailing and scuba diving. Wilderness first aid and horseback riding also are offered.

Calgary's Outdoor/Nature Services offers about 150 outdoor-related courses annually. They include mountain biking, fishing, kayaking, canoeing and snowshoeing. "The testimonials we get are wonderful," says Sue Cunningham, outdoor coordinator. "They speak of the importance of lifelong learning and active living." Many people who sign up for courses, she says, had a passive interest in the outdoors, but family or job commitments prevented them from becoming active sooner. They needed the support of a group to become involved.

At Inglewood Bird Sanctuary, city naturalists teach a wide selection of natural history programs. They include free Walks on the Wild Side at city natural areas and seasonal courses on birds, animals, wild flowers, gems, mushrooms, geology and natural history.

The sanctuary's hiking and cross-country skiing courses, both in and out of Calgary, are popular.

Inglewood also offers the city's most extensive outdoor programs targeted at kids. These include free family nature walks in local natural areas and a course exploring how nature copes in winter. City naturalists host nature-based birthday parties and nature hikes custom designed for the age of the birthday child. The sanctuary also runs a summer Nature Study and Discovery program. Kids aged six to nine can spend a week exploring nature with an Inglewood naturalist.

Kym McCulley, the sanctuary's natural history programmer, says it's important that children gain an appreciation for nature early in their lives. "Attitude starts at a young age," she says. "Kids should learn they don't have to leave the city to see some beautiful flowers, birds and animals. . . . If you know about something, you'll appreciate it and you'll value it."

Some courses are for women only. "It's a real spiritual, bonding type of thing," says Kendy Bentley, a mother of two and local health promotion consultant who teaches hiking with children and leads hikes for women. Most of her clients are women over 30. Many have spent their lives raising children or working outside the home. Often they sign up for a course after deciding to do something for themselves.

The provincially operated Sam Livingston Fish Hatchery (403 297-6561) offers basic fishing courses and environmental education programs for school children. The Conservation Education Centre for Excellence (403 252-7387) teaches hunting and fishing education courses that cover everything from fish and wildlife identification and outdoor ethics to firearms safety and wilderness survival.

The *Calgary Herald* provides updated information about fishing conditions each Friday in the Sports section and on the TELUS Talking Yellow Pages. Call 403 521-5222, Local 1288.

Calgary's Pathways

IT'S CALGARY'S LARGEST outdoor recreation facility. It's used by joggers, dog walkers, in-line skaters, cyclists, wheelchair users, commuters and people out for a leisurely stroll. It runs for more than 330 km (207 mi) through the scenic Bow and Elbow river valleys, passes through peaceful natural areas and sits in the shadow of downtown office towers. It helps bring Calgarians closer together (it's hard not to nod hello as you approach another user). It's the envy of many other Canadian cities.

Calgary's pathway system is the city's pride and joy, linking neighborhoods like a network of nerves in a body. A study conducted in 1994 (21 years after pathway construction began) revealed that up to 75,000 people a day use the system in summer. It's definitely the busiest season, but the pathway system is well used by Calgarians year-round. A city survey a few years ago found that 43 percent of pathway users do it for exercise, 28 percent for recreation, 20 percent to commute and 7 percent to enjoy nature.

Chris Valentine is a frequent pathway user. He lives in the southwest community of Riverdale, just minutes away from the pathway along the Elbow River. On a cool Wednesday afternoon in late fall 1996, I encountered Valentine and his dog, a blue heeler–border collie cross named Tommy. Valentine, then 23, had a day off from his job as a junior land administrator for a downtown oil company. He was spending the afternoon taking Tommy and himself out for some exercise at River Park. A biting north wind didn't slow them down a bit. Stopping on a footbridge spanning the Elbow, Valentine peered around him at the leafless poplars and inhaled the crisp autumn air. "This is a great area to have," he said. "It's kind of hard to think it's right in the middle of the city."

Senior citizens May and John Upton were 68 and 73 years old respectively when I caught up to them later that afternoon. The Altadore residents had been hiking through the area for almost 50 years, long before the pathways concept was ever considered. John and May were averaging four hikes of several kilometers each week.

In-line skating on the Calgary pathway system.

"It's so handy and close to home," John says. Even winter doesn't usually slow them down. The valley seldom has heavy snow cover, and high cliffs along the Elbow River provide protection from the wind.

The Elbow River pathway starts at Glenmore Reservoir, which is fed by the Elbow River as it flows eastward from an alpine lake of the same name in Kananaskis Country. Running northeasterly toward downtown, the Elbow valley extends all the way to the confluence with the Bow River at Fort Calgary. Along the way the system takes in several attractive, user-friendly parks: River, Sandy Beach, Princess Obolensky, Stanley, Woods, Elbow Island, Lindsay and Stampede. From Sandy Beach it's about 9 km (5.6 mi) to Fort Calgary and 7 km (4.3 mi) to the Weaselhead natural area. The pathway's link to the Bow River system is just over 9 km (5.6 mi).

The Bow River pathway starts at Fish Creek Provincial Park in south Calgary and runs north through the Carburn Park and Beaverdam Flats natural areas en route to Inglewood. It skirts the bird sanctuary to the west, then proceeds through Pearce Estate Park before swinging west. You can stay either on the south side of the river or cross at St. George's Island and hook up with a pathway leading north to Nose Hill Park. If you keep heading west on the river's south side, you'll pass through Prince's Island Park, Lawrey Gardens and Edworthy Park. Then you can follow the signs to the northwest to reach Bowmont Park in northwest Calgary.

The Calgary Parks and Recreation Department operates a 24-hour Play Line (403 268-2300) that provides current information about the pathways system and other recreation facilities and programs. Users can report concerns or obtain the latest scoop on pathway openings, closures and detours, bylaws and safety tips. A detailed map showing pathway routes is published annually. It's available each spring for one dollar at city hall, local bike shops and outdoor equipment stores.

Several times each winter, snow can be a problem on the pathways along the Bow and Elbow rivers. It makes traction difficult for cyclists and joggers, especially when it melts and refreezes after a warming Chinook wind. Particularly bothersome are ice build-ups at the bottoms of slopes or on curves, where meltwater collects. City crews clear several pathway sections throughout the city, including a 12.5-km (8-mi) loop downtown. This extremely busy section is used by the noon-hour fitness crowd of joggers, strollers, in-line skaters and cyclists, in addition to active residential commuters who live nearby. Community associations and clubs remove snow from other sections. Several years ago a select group of ardent cyclists opted not to sit around and complain about snow on the pathways. They decided to do something about it. They developed special snow plows that could be pulled along behind mountain bikes. Volunteers pedaling to and from work regularly maintain several busy sections of city pathways.

Dubbed Operation Share Plough, the project is believed to be unique to Calgary. Colynn Kerr, a graphic artist, started the project in 1990 after moving to Parkdale. Wanting to commute to city hall on his bicycle, he chose a home within spitting distance of the pathway. But after the first snowfall, Kerr encountered rough going. He bounced and pounded his way along the snow-covered, footstep-pocked pathway until he hit easier going on the maintained downtown stretch. Kerr vowed to remove the snow on the initial stretch.

His first handcrafted plow was crude, but it worked. The snow-clearing blades were made of inversely cut sections of a large plastic pail. With a plywood deck, the plow was weighted with sand-filled pop bottles and pulled by ropes attached to Kerr's bicycle carrier. He started using the contraption to plow the section after each snowfall. He'd do one side of the path on the way to work, the other side going home.

Soon, Kerr was joined by several other volunteers, including Jeff Gruttz, a year-round cyclist who works at city hall as the city's outdoor recreation specialist. In winter Gruttz installs traction-enhancing sheet metal screws in the front tire of his 21-speed mountain bike. He says pulling a plow with a bike is a great workout. "People might think it's wasted time," Gruttz laughs, "but look at all that wasted energy with people using stationary exercise bikes in downtown sweat centers. Plowing the pathway has a heck of a lot more benefit for the community."

Not surprisingly, the pathways' popularity contributes to a few other problems: littering and user conflicts. Garbage strewn along the pathways makes its way into the underbrush and stands of cottonwood trees lining the riverbanks. Each spring thousands of Cal-

garians give up the better part of a Sunday to participate in a pathways and river valley cleanup organized by the Calgary Canoe Club
and Calgary Parks and Recreation. Since the volunteer effort started
in 1968, Calgary senior citizen John Dicey has missed only one
cleanup. He gets involved for one big reason: "I hate junk and litter.
Unless we do something about it, it's going to get worse, not better."
Dicey says he would love the annual cleanup to become obsolete.
For now, however, the event attracts conservation and recreation
groups, corporate employees and families and individuals. While
they search the land for litter, members of local scuba clubs, the
Calgary fire department and the canoe club handle a water-based
assault on garbage.

In addition to the usual candy wrappers and cigarette packages,
volunteers pick up old tires, shopping carts and animal carcasses. One
year, cleanup crews retrieved a suitcase containing a handgun and
map highlighting the locations of several city banks. Riverbanks also
can become cluttered with discarded fishing tackle packages, beer
cans and monofilament fishing line, which birds such as geese, ducks
and gulls can get caught up in, sometimes with fatal consequences.

The city's Jeff Gruttz explains that "the majority of pathway users
are responsible, but there's always a few rotten apples." He's used the
system for commuting and recreation since 1980. He knows user
conflicts increase each spring when winter-weary Calgarians venture out of their domestic cocoons. But most conflicts, Gruttz says,
can be avoided. "Pathway rights mean sharing responsibility and
that means communicating." Gruttz prescribes a dose of common
sense and normal traffic awareness. This means always being alert
for other users, shoulder checking and signaling where you plan to
go before moving.

Joyce Patten, former chairman of the Calgary Pathway Advisory
Council, notes that pedestrians who walk three or four abreast run
the risk of interfering with other users. Another problem arises when
cyclists and in-line skaters who use the pathways for serious physical
training become so focused that they forget about people in wheelchairs, baby strollers, seniors using walkers and kids learning to ride

bicycles. Pathways should be used for recreation, not training, says Patten, who has jogged, walked and cycled the system for more than 30 years. "Nobody should look at how fast they can go and how many people they can mow down."

To help reduce the number of encounters of the painful kind, the city has established a bylaw that sets out pathway operating rules listed below. Breaking the rules can result in a $50 fine. But with enforcement almost impossible because of the size of the pathways system, Patten advises users to police themselves.

Using Pathways Responsibly

◆ Do not use poles when in-line skating and roller skiing.
◆ When cycling, yield right of way to other users and do not ride double unless the bike is designed for more than one person.
◆ Cycle in single file except to pass another cyclist traveling in the same direction.
◆ Do not cycle with an animal on a leash.
◆ Equip bicycles with a bell or horn, a head lamp and tail lamp for night riding and a red reflector mounted on the back end.
◆ Adhere to the speed limit, which is 20 km (12 mi) per hour unless otherwise posted. Also consider factors such as the condition of the pathway, weather, visibility and numbers of users.
◆ Obey posted signs and signaling devices.
◆ Travel with care and attention to avoid collisions.
◆ Be considerate of other users.
◆ Stay in the right lane when passing other travelers going in the same direction or when turning left off pathways onto intersecting roads.
◆ Give advance warning of your intentions to pass by calling out or using a bell, horn or other device.
◆ Use caution and yield right of way to others when entering pathway.

- Yield right of way to slower moving users.
- Keep out of prohibited areas.
- Stay to the right, using only your side of the pathway.
- During winter, when only one lane is free of snow and ice, share the pathways.
- When the center line is obscured by snow or ice, stay to the right at all times.
- Ski adjacent to the pathway, not on it.
- When walking or jogging in winter, wear suitable footwear to guard against slipping.
- When cycling in winter, beware of ice patches, especially on slopes or curves.
- Watch for snow-clearing equipment, either city-operated machines or plows pulled by bikes or vehicles.
- Take time to thank a volunteer snow cleaner (hot chocolate, tea, coffee, cookies or brownies speak volumes).

Calgary's Wildlife

SEEING WILDLIFE in any natural setting is rewarding. Being able to enjoy it in a hectic urban environment is doubly so. It has a therapeutic effect. It calms city-frayed nerves and provides simple reassurance that things are right in the world. It's a rare schedule that is too busy to allow a few seconds to admire a deer standing in a field beside the road or a flight of geese from an office window.

A study released in 1994 by the Canadian Wildlife Service reveals Canadians' keen interest in wildlife. It showed that 18.9 million Canadians—which was then 90 percent of the population—participated in one or more wildlife-related activities in 1991. These included hunting, fishing, wildlife photography and just plain viewing. In the process, Canadian wildlife buffs spent a staggering $8.3 billion. The study also concluded that Canadians are spending more time than ever on wildlife-related activities. Although hunting has declined, participation has increased in nonconsumptive outings to view, feed, study or photograph wildlife. More locally, the study

Canada geese and inverted mallard duck at Inglewood Bird Sanctuary.

found that in 1991 1.8 million Albertans spent almost $835 million participating in wildlife-related activities.

Wild birds and animals can be viewed in virtually every Calgary natural area. Some places are considered prime viewing areas. These include Fish Creek Provincial Park, Nose Hill Park, Weaselhead Natural Environment Park, Inglewood Bird Sanctuary, Beaver

Dam Flats and Edworthy Park. The best times for seeing wildlife are just after dawn and before dusk. Wildlife also tends to be more active immediately before or after a major weather change, such as a blizzard or rainstorm. A good set of binoculars or a spotting scope will provide close-up views of animals from a distance and reduce the risk of harassing them with your presence.

"We're pretty lucky," says city naturalist John McFaul. "Green areas and wildlife are what makes Calgary such a special place to live." Wildlife lives in Calgary because it offers plenty of habitat. It's that simple. The city has two major river valleys, the Bow and Elbow, and Fish Creek. All three waterways flow from the foothills to the west, providing natural travel corridors for wild critters. Adjacent to the rivers and creek, the city and province have preserved thousands of hectares as natural areas, which provide diverse cover for wildlife to live and feel safe in.

Calgary's steel and concrete monuments to prosperity and progress share the downtown skyline, for instance, with more than 200 bird species, from bald eagles and peregrine falcons to warblers and ring-necked pheasants. Calgary is ornithologically advantaged because it's situated on major bird migration routes, has plenty of green areas and parts of the Bow River remain ice-free all winter — an open invitation to thousands of ducks and geese that refuse to follow nature's script and fly south. The city also is surrounded by various bird-friendly terrains, from eastern prairie grassland to northern aspen parklands and mountain forests.

Bird-watching is the fastest growing outdoor activity in North America, a trend that is abundantly evident in Calgary, where people take their bird-watching very seriously. Several specialty shops have existed in the city since the early 1990s. About one in four city houses has a feeder or birdbath in the yard. Registrations for bird-watching, identification and feeding courses at the Inglewood Bird Sanctuary generally fill quickly. The sanctuary, a 29-ha (72-acre) piece of heaven beside the Bow River, attracts up to 30,000 human visitors annually (and many more of the feathered variety). "Bird-watching is a way of plugging into nature and the natural flow of the seasons," notes John McFaul, a veteran Inglewood naturalist and a longtime member of the Calgary Field Naturalists' Society.

The term *bird watcher* has certain connotations. It suggests a rabid passion for spotting and identifying bird species. It conjures up images of binocular-toting, Tilley-hatted keeners who drop everything at the mere hint of a rare bird being spotted somewhere, even on the other side of the world. But this breed of bird watcher represents the minority. Most of us, whether we want to admit it or not, are bird watchers of a more casual nature. We stop our busy lives to watch in awe as a hawk draws circles in the sky and stand transfixed when we hear the *har-onk* of migrating Canada geese overhead. We are entertained by the antics of saucy blue jays at the backyard feeder.

Calgarians' passion for bird watching is evident in the city's annual Christmas bird count. The one-day event is part of a North American program, started in 1900, and coordinated by the National Audubon Society. About 1,800 individual bird counts are held in Canada, the United States and Mexico each year between December 20 and January 5. Results are sent to the Audubon Society, which compiles them. Scientists, wildlife managers and bird experts use the reports to track changing bird populations. Sharp drops or increases sometimes indicate severe environmental changes. A sharp decline in hawks, for example, could be an early sign of an environmental problem affecting small rodents on which hawks feed.

In Calgary, from dawn to dusk on the last Sunday before Christmas, about 200 volunteers forsake shopping malls and other holiday destinations. Wielding binoculars, notebooks and bird identification guides, they bundle up against the cold to tally birds in river valleys and natural areas. Some volunteers stay home, watching and recording chickadees, blue jays, red polls and other visitors to backyard feeders. The Calgary count set a western Canadian record in 1987 by identifying 69 different bird species and tallying almost 28,000 birds.

The local effort doesn't cover the entire city. When it was started in 1952, organizers mapped out a 12-km (7.5-mi) area around the Louise Bridge over the Bow River in the heart of Calgary. As the city expanded, the count area remained unchanged, resulting in exclusion of many bird-rich areas, including Fish Creek Provincial Park. Regardless, volunteers are out at dawn to count great grey, great horned and barred owls before they vanish to their daytime roosts deep in the thickest forests. Counters also are out at first light along the Bow River, tallying ducks and Canada geese before they take flight to feed in nearby fields. In 1995, 1,260 geese and 18,000 ducks were counted. That included 10,000 mallards, 4,000 goldeneyes and an assortment of other species.

Ian Halladay, a retired city geologist who coordinated 30 annual counts up to 1997, says the event has revealed some real surprises. Blue jays seem to have invaded the city since 1966, when only one was counted. In 1995 there were 156, perhaps due to the increase in backyard feeders and ornamental, berry-producing trees. Ravens increased from only one or two in 1975 to 92 in 1995. They have an interesting habit of spending days in the city, then leaving at night to roost in the adjacent foothills.

Halladay says Christmas bird counters take the job seriously. Many have a deep-rooted interest in ecology, natural history, the environment and the biodiversity of the planet. "People who do it recognize the value of what we're doing," Halladay says. "It's all part of trying to understand this planet."

Many people enjoy bird watching so much they design their yards to attract birds. Trees such as spruce, pine, mountain ash and crab apple provide shelter and food. Thick shrubbery and piles of brush in the corner of a yard provide protection from the weather and predators. Water in artificial ponds or free-standing ceramic birdbaths attracts birds year-round. Transforming a backyard into a bird haven might sound like a lot of work, but thousands do it because it's worth it.

Most people aren't aware that Calgary has one of Alberta's largest populations of overwintering bald eagles. Up to 20 have been reported in a winter. The enthusiasm of anyone lucky enough to spot one of these mighty, 1-m (3.2') -long birds is understandable. Bald eagles affirm the majesty of the natural world. Whether effort-

Bald eagle.

lessly circling in the sky on powerful wings spanning more than 2 m (6.6') or standing guard on a skeletal cottonwood along the Bow River, these regal birds evoke a sense of wonder in many. Mairi Babey, naturalist–ranger at Inglewood Bird Sanctuary, receives dozens of calls each winter from people eager to report bald eagle sightings. They're often bursting with exuberance more befitting the

Second Coming. "Some of them start off by saying, 'You're not going to believe what I just saw,'" Babey says. "They're really surprised when we tell them it's not that unusual." She tries to let them down easy.

Bald eagles have thousands of tasty reasons to stay in Calgary all winter. They are attracted by ducks, mainly mallards, which frequent ice-free stretches of the Bow River. Some people are shocked to learn that the noble national bird of the United States is an opportunistic scavenger. Bald eagles prefer to feed on dead waterfowl and animals rather than kill their own food. When it comes to Calgary's ducks, eagles usually will opt for one that is dead or near death from cold, injury or sickness. Sometimes eagles will kill a duck that's become frozen in the ice.

Several years ago I witnessed a bald eagle swoop down and kill a duck that appeared to be healthy. It happened near Strathmore during a winter when more than 45,000 mallards inexplicably stayed in the area rather than heading south. When Tom Sadler of the Strathmore office of Ducks Unlimited Canada and I first spotted them, the ducks looked like a swarm of locusts. They were trying unsuccessfully to cram into a baseball-diamond–sized piece of open water on a frozen lake. Thousands of ducks were on the water and the ice, while thousands more were in the air.

After getting out our spotting scopes and binoculars, Sadler and I saw that not all the birds in our field of view were ducks. About a dozen white-headed bald eagles were in the area, standing on the ice, perched on fence posts and circling like vultures. Suddenly an eagle swooped down and struck an ice-bound duck with its strong, razorlike talons. As so often happens in nature, one creature's misfortune had translated into another's good luck. The circle of life goes on.

In the foothills it's not unusual to see bald eagles feeding on dead wildlife or frequenting cattle calving fields, where they can devour fresh afterbirth and calves that have died. But you don't have to go that far to see eagles. They're regularly seen in fall and winter by motorists driving along Deerfoot Trail between Southland Drive and Calf Robe Bridge. Do yourself and other Deerfoot roulette players a favor, however, and keep your eyes on the road, not on the sky or trees. Carefully pull over onto the shoulder, or better yet, visit a river park to view eagles in a more relaxed atmosphere. Take along a camera with a telephoto lens, binoculars or a spotting scope mounted on a tripod. Watch for dark round shapes sitting in trees.

The best parks and natural areas for viewing eagles are Carburn Park, Inglewood Bird Sanctuary, around the Calgary Zoo, Beaverdam Flats, Edworthy Park and the south end of Fish Creek Provincial Park off Bow Bottom Trail SE. It's not known where the eagles come from each fall or where they disappear to in spring. It's believed some breed and raise young in the Calgary region, possibly even along the Bow River downstream of the city.

If you wish to have a closer look at eagles than that afforded by binoculars or spotting scope, travel a couple of hours southeast of Calgary to the Alberta Birds of Prey Centre at Coaldale (403 345-4262). This is the largest facility of its kind in North America. It features many kinds of birds of prey, from burrowing owls and ferruginous hawks to great grey owls and eagles. It also houses the Western Canada Eagle Centre, Canada's biggest aviary for injured eagles. Alberta Ecotrust, a Calgary-based organization, is a leading funding partner.

If you see an eagle without a white head and tail, don't automatically assume it's a golden eagle, which are common in the Rockies but rarely seen in Calgary. Chances are it's an immature bald eagle. Baldies don't develop the trademark white markings until their fourth year. Immature bald eagles are dark brown with mottled white wing linings. Their beaks are a dusky shade, not yellow like the adults, and their legs are feathered halfway down. Goldens' legs are feathered all the way down to the talons.

Naturalist Dave Elphinstone is a devoted eagle watcher. He studies them closely, identifying individual birds by feather variations and other distinguishing markings. Although Elphinstone admires their size and power, what really fires his imagination are their bright yellow eyes. "They glare, almost like a flashlight." While working at the Inglewood sanctuary several years ago, Elphinstone enjoyed creeping underneath an eagle perched in a tree. He loved to watch it take off with a powerful yet graceful rush of wings.

Calgary also boasts dozens of animal species. The more common include mule and white-tailed deer, moose, skunk, coyote, red fox, mink, beaver, muskrat, short- and long-tailed weasel, badger, various mice and voles, red squirrel, Eastern gray squirrel, Richardson's ground squirrel (aka gopher), porcupine and white-tailed jack rabbit.

Several years ago, while driving along the south end of Deerfoot Trail, I spied thousands of mallard ducks swarming over a barley stubble field. After carefully pulling over onto the shoulder and activating the car's four-way flashers, I crept up the embankment and peered at the field. That's when I saw the coyotes. Two of them were lying flat on their grey bellies. Their eyes were riveted on the ducks overhead and those already on the ground stuffing themselves with grain. The coyotes' tails twitched. Every few minutes, one of the coyotes would dash toward the feathered smorgasbord, causing them to billow up and fly a few feet away. Finally, the coyotes lit out in search of easier pickings, bushy tails planted firmly between their hind legs.

Calgarians eager to see wildlife seldom have far to go. Beaver and muskrat are commonly spotted swimming at dusk in the Elbow and Bow rivers. If you walk quietly in a natural area or along the rivers in early morning or evening, chances are very good you'll spot a deer, coyote or maybe even a mink or weasel. A clump high in the branches of a tree, which looks at first glance like a bird's nest, might actually be a porcupine.

From my window seat in the *Calgary Herald* newsroom several years ago, I used to watch a red fox at its den, which had been dug into a creek bed on the west side of Deerfoot Trail. The scene was backdropped by office towers and the Rocky Mountains behind them. Flocks of ducks and geese, and the occasional eagle, would fly past the window, often in the shadow of a giant 747 jet preparing to land at Calgary International Airport. Looking over the balcony, I often saw a white-tailed jack rabbit hopping alongside a set of railroad tracks beside the building. The contrasting images were amazing, and uniquely Calgarian.

Mule deer in a Calgary natural area.

Sometimes wildlife in Calgary can be a nuisance. Deer raid gardens and chomp ornamental trees. Several times annually deer are killed or injured in collisions with vehicles, sometimes resulting in injury to people. Deer also have died after crashing into windows of buildings, a fate that befalls hundreds of birds each year. Unleashed dogs and cats can be mauled or killed by coyotes defending their territory or looking for an easy meal. Badgers cornered by aggressive dogs almost always come out the winners, leaving pets hurt and bleeding. Beavers relentlessly destroy hundreds of stately old cottonwoods along river valleys, leading to bank erosion and an unsightly mess. Gophers dig holes in lawns. Gophers and other wildlife on local freeways and highways cause accidents when drivers swerve to avoid them. Coyotes, skunks and increasingly raccoons (once rare in the city) raid garbage bins, forcing residents to resort to solid metal or plastic cans (spraying ammonia around cans helps deter wildlife). Squirrels can get into attics and crawl spaces of houses. The big, black-colored Eastern gray squirrel, which has flourished since it was imported from Toronto by the Calgary Zoo in the 1930s, attacks birds' nests and wreaks havoc on bird feeders. Even Canada geese, those noble symbols of the Canadian wilderness, can be pests. With populations thriving in the last several years, geese leave messy droppings where they congregate in parks, and on golf courses and river pathways. They hiss aggressively and rush anyone who dares approach. Feeding the geese only compounds the problem.

Occasionally, cougars and black bears wander into the city, sending residents into a tizzy and wildlife officers into action. If the larger animals are deemed a threat to people, they are shot or tranquilized and relocated out of the city; otherwise they are left alone in the hope that they will leave of their own accord.

Wildlife officer Ed Pirogowicz says the key to living in harmony with wildlife in an urban setting is to treat animals with respect. "They require their space. You must remember they are wild animals." Dave Elphinstone, the city's coordinator of natural areas management, calls urban wildlife a sign of a healthy city. Most problems with wildlife occur when people interfere with them in some way. Removing or otherwise altering natural habitat can disrupt animals' traditional travel corridors, says Elphinstone.

Problems can be reduced by not feeding, approaching, touching, chasing or otherwise harassing wildlife. When traveling in natural areas, stay on established trails or viewing platforms to avoid surprising animals and pushing them out of their favorite habitat. Bird nesting or wildlife bedding areas should be avoided too. Dogs should be kept under control at all times to avoid conflicts.

Problems with wildlife can be reported to Alberta Fish and Wildlife (403 297-6423). For general questions about wildlife, contact the Inglewood Bird Sanctuary (403 269-6688). The sanctuary and Calgary Field Naturalists' Society jointly operate a 24-hour hotline (403 237-8821). You can phone the line to learn about or report unusual bird sightings. The TELUS Talking Yellow Pages and the Inglewood Bird Sanctuary provide free 24-hour information by calling 403 521-5222, then pressing extension 8937 for information about natural areas and nature notes or extension 8944 for information about the sanctuary.

Using Natural Areas Responsibly

ALTHOUGH MOST PEOPLE respect natural areas, some don't. The more popular areas are littered with garbage. Initials and proclamations of love are carved into picnic tables. Dogs are allowed to run free in areas where leashes are required. Flowers are picked and plants are dug up for gardens at home. Trees are sometimes cut for firewood, or deadfall is hauled out to burn. Hiking or mountain biking occurs off established trails.

Not everyone realizes that each plant, flower, tree, animal and bird plays a key role in maintaining a healthy habitat. The following are suggestions for helping you play a key role.

◆ Leave plants and wildlife alone.

◆ Stay on established hiking trails or footpaths.

◆ Place garbage in containers provided, or bag and carry it out.

◆ Respect public property.

◆ Use supplied firewood if available and bring your own wiener sticks.

◆ Confine recreational sports to game areas and facilities where available.

◆ Do not drive motor vehicles, minibikes, motorcycles or snowmobiles in natural areas. They are prohibited.

◆ Keep horses on designated equestrian trails.

◆ Keep dogs on a leash unless signs indicate otherwise.

Chapter 2

Urban Getaways

Getting Away from It All
Without Leaving Calgary

49

URBAN GETAWAYS are those special places that tempt Calgarians away from hectic lifestyles. They are places that define Calgary as much as the oil and gas industry, ranching and the Calgary Stampede. They are places people seek when they need solitude, when they long for the sweet song of a meadowlark or the glimpse of a sleek mink weaving through tree roots lining the riverbank. They are places people go to cast a line, spend quiet time with loved ones or escape from the pressures of living in a city that never stops. They are places where people learn the lessons of nature, study a bald eagle resting on a bare cottonwood or stoop to smell a wildflower in spring. They are places untouched by developers, areas that deer and moose call home despite housing and industrial subdivisions that lick at their boundaries.

Calgary's natural areas offer important lessons. One of the most important concerns the delicate balance that exists between flora and fauna, and the people who enjoy them. The more time people spend in natural areas, the more they come to know and appreciate them. If a major road or theme park is proposed for development in a natural area, many Calgarians who've learned this lesson are quick to rise to its defense. The places described in this chapter are natural environment parks such as Nose Hill, Fish Creek and Inglewood Bird Sanctuary, and facilities such as Sam Livingston Fish Hatchery. In these places, Calgarians take their lessons and reconnect with the natural world.

Nose Hill Natural Environment Park

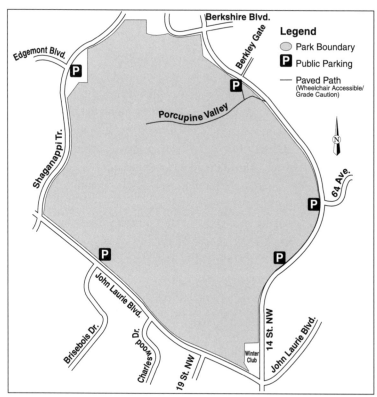

Access: Between 14 Street and Shaganappi Trail NW, north of John Laurie Boulevard. Park at 64 Avenue and 14 Street NW, Berkley Gate and 14 Street NW, Quarry Road and 14 Street NW or Brisebois Drive and John Laurie Boulevard NW.

Terrain: Hills, sheltered ravines, glacial erratics, willow and aspen woodlands, shrub thickets, fescue and introduced grasslands, old gravel pits and archaeological sites.

Activities: Hiking, cycling, in-line skating, picnicking, wildlife watching, dog walking (off-leash allowed only on top of plateau), cross-country skiing, tobogganing.

Hours: Open 24 hours.

Contact: 403 268-2300.

NOSE HILL PARK is Canada's biggest city-operated urban park. The 1,127-ha (2,785-acre) natural area also is one of the city's last surviving natural prairie areas. It's a study in contrasts. Looking inward, you'll see an expanse of native fescue grasslands, aspen groves and dozens of secretive coulees choked with wolf willow, snowberries, saskatoon bushes and choke cherries. You might spot a red-tailed hawk circling overhead, a coyote scrambling for cover, deer, moose or even a prairie long-tailed weasel hunting mice and a variety of hares. A total of 91 bird species have been sighted on the hill, including the red-tailed hawk, Swainson's hawk and great horned owl.

In late spring you'll be amazed by an explosion of mauve prairie crocus, Canada anemone, three-flowered avens and other wild flowers. "The wealth of flowers and wildlife on the hill is truly remarkable, especially now that it is almost surrounded by houses," the late Mary Dover wrote in 1988 in the introduction to *Nose Hill: A Popular Guide*, a Calgary Field Naturalists' Society labor of love.

This is a perfect place to close your eyes and let your mind wander. You might imagine aboriginal people camping here as early as 8,000 years ago, leaving tepee rings, cairns and stone artifacts that excited archaeologists could uncover centuries later. You might imagine thousands of buffalo grazing, some rubbing their thick hides on truck-sized boulders deposited by receding glaciers that came from as far away as today's Jasper National Park. You might picture explorer David Thompson resting at the top of the hill before he continues his 1808 overland journey. You might imagine the Blackfoot hunting bison here each winter until the mid-1800s. You might even hear early settlers cutting hay and harvesting crops or herding sheep and cattle that graze on the hillside.

Now open your eyes and look around. Things are a little different. The glacial erratics are still here, but they've been defaced with graffiti and markings that have nothing to do with Nose Hill's rich history. The hill is surrounded by residential communities with names like Huntington Hills, Foothills Estate and Sandstone Valley. It's obvious what the fate of the rest of the hill would have been if it hadn't officially been designated a park in 1992.

From atop the plateau (maximum elevation 1,213 m / 3,980'), you can behold one of the most spectacular views you'll ever get in an urban setting. To the east, giant silver jets take off and land at Calgary International Airport. To the south, downtown office towers stretch toward the clouds. The west offers a panoramic north–south view extending more than 100 km (62 mi) along the Rockies. To the north, a steady stream of vehicles along Highway 2 look like ants scurrying to a picnic.

Weekends can get busy here, but if you get away midweek, early in the day, only a few visitors will be scattered through the park. Numbers increase as the *après*-work crowd gets home, changes and comes to the park to ease workaday tensions and exercise dogs. Regardless of numbers of people, Nose Hill truly is a place to gather your thoughts.

Fish Creek Provincial Park

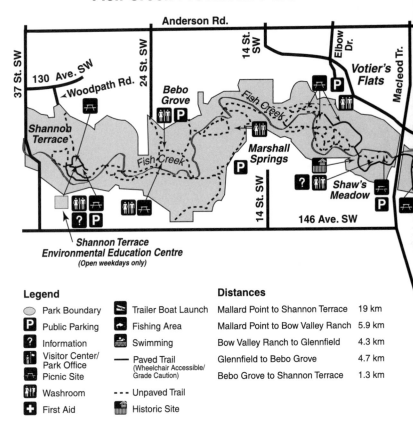

Shannon Terrace
Environmental Education Centre
(Open weekdays only)

Legend

- Park Boundary
- **P** Public Parking
- **?** Information
- Visitor Center/ Park Office
- Picnic Site
- Washroom
- First Aid
- Trailer Boat Launch
- Fishing Area
- Swimming
- — Paved Trail (Wheelchair Accessible/ Grade Caution)
- - - - Unpaved Trail
- Historic Site

Distances

Mallard Point to Shannon Terrace	19 km
Mallard Point to Bow Valley Ranch	5.9 km
Bow Valley Ranch to Glennfield	4.3 km
Glennfield to Bebo Grove	4.7 km
Bebo Grove to Shannon Terrace	1.3 km

Access: Shannon Terrace Environmental Education Centre off 37 Street SW; Bebo Grove off 24 Street SW; Votier's Flats off Elbow Drive SW; Shaw's Meadow west off Macleod Trail; Glenfield east off Macleod Trail; Bow Valley Ranch Visitor Centre, Sikome Lake, Hull's Woods, Burnsmead, Bankside and Mallard Point all off Bow Bottom Trail SE.

Terrain: West end features spruce trees and aspen stands. Eastern areas near Bow River have balsam poplar woodlands and open mixed grasslands.

Activities: Hiking, cycling, in-line skating, picnicking, fishing, swimming, wildlife watching, horseback riding, playground, cross-country skiing, skating, snowshoeing, tobogganing.

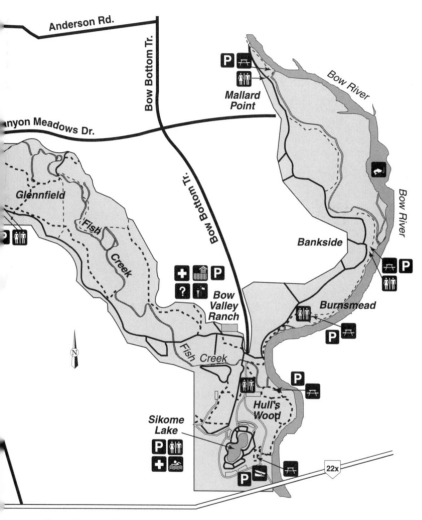

Hours: Bow Valley Ranch Visitor Centre open weekdays 8:15 A.M. to 12:00 P.M. and 1:00 P.M. to 4:30 P.M.; open weekends and holidays 11:00 A.M. to 4:00 P.M. Day-use areas open daily 8:00 A.M. to 11:00 P.M.

Contact: Park office and visitor center at 403 297-5293. Shannon Terrace Environmental Education Centre at 403 297-7827. Fish Creek Environmental Support Society at 403 297-7849.

GETTING TOTALLY WRAPPED UP in nature is an inherent danger for anyone who falls under the spell of 1,189-ha (2,938-acre) Fish Creek Provincial Park. Calgary's largest and most popular natural area also qualifies as Alberta's only urban provincial park and as the largest city-based park in Canada. Opened in 1975 Fish Creek spans 19 km (12 mi), the entire width of southwest Calgary.

About two million people visit the park annually. Wild visitors and residents include more than 150 species of birds, among them great blue herons and peregrine falcons. There also are more than 15 types of mammals along with 46 archaeological sites telling of human life dating back 8,000 years.

The more recent history of this area includes key people from the latter half of the last century: John Glenn, Sam Livingston, Samuel Shaw, William Roper Hull and Pat Burns, who later became a senator. Hull purchased the Bow Valley Ranch in 1895. Shortly after, he built a luxurious ranch house that stands to this day. It can be toured on weekends. Hull sold the ranch to Pat Burns in 1902. The Burns family owned the ranch and house until the province purchased them in 1973 to develop the park. The Bow Valley Ranch Visitor Centre is the park's administrative and visitor information headquarters.

For many visitors, especially those living in south Calgary, Fish Creek Provincial Park is an integral part of who they are. Along with jobs and families, it helps define their lives. They ride their bikes here after work and school, picnic, hang out at the beach and generally regard it as their own private resort.

The diversity of recreational activities—from cycling and hiking to swimming and fishing—and the natural layout of the trails are two big reasons for the park's popularity. Stretching from the Bow River to the east all the way to Calgary's west limits, Fish Creek offers 16 km (10 mi) of paved trails, 30 km (18.6 mi) of red-shale trails and 6 km (3.7 mi) of horseback riding trails. A private riding stable is located in the park's west end. There isn't a more perfect place in Calgary for families who enjoy the outdoors.

Every season is special at Fish Creek, but autumn has a particular appeal. The bustling crowds of summer are gone, Sikome Lake is closed and Mother Nature has swept her paintbrush of rich browns and golds across the landscape. Mule deer gather into herds in preparation for winter. Beavers and squirrels stockpile food. Canada geese and ducks noisily join migrating flocks. Brown and rainbow trout rise to feed on tiny insects in quiet side channels of the Bow River.

The park's east end is the busiest. The main visitor center is located there, as is the Bow River and Sikome Lake. Many Calgarians take years to discover the park's west end. Indeed, the section adjacent to Fish Creek, west of Macleod Trail to 37 Avenue, features several day-use areas, extensive trails and the Shannon Terrace Environmental Education Centre. It annually attracts almost 20,000 school kids who learn about nature in a natural setting.

Fishing is popular in Fish Creek park. The Bow River, which ranks among the world's top trout fishing waters, borders the park's east end. Several access points are available, from Mallard Point to the north to the Highway 22X Bridge to the south. Small spinners, spoons, jigs, weighted nymphs, streamers and dry flies are good bets for trout in the Bow River. While fishing is permitted year-round, there are regulations concerning seasonal closures of short sections and special fishing rules. To help preserve the trout population, the use of bait such as worms, minnows and corn is prohibited on the Bow, except for several weeks each autumn, when maggots can be used.

Many anglers believe they must cast in the river's middle, where the current is strongest. But it's more productive to fish closer to shore, focusing on areas where the current is broken by a log, boulder or indentation in the shoreline. Trout generally avoid deeper, faster water in midriver because it takes too much energy to maintain position in the current. Trout often hold in the slower water, waiting to gobble any tasty morsels that drift along. Seams separating fast water from slow water also are good places to cast.

Another mistake some anglers make is to fish in Sikome Lake. The lake contains no fish. But it is the only public lake with a beach within 90 minutes of the city. On hot summer days, thousands of people pack the 8-ha (19.8-acre) lake area.

Wayne Meikle, the park's chief ranger, cautions parents to vigilantly watch their kids at Sikome. Children 12 and under must be accompanied by an adult, a regulation designed to stop parents from dropping kids off and leaving them there all day for park staff to baby-sit. Unsupervised kids have drowned in the 2-m (6.5') -deep lake. Meikle also worries about the threat of human predators who sometimes lurk in public places.

Traditionally lake visitors haven't been charged a day-use fee. That could change under a provincial government plan to expand privatization of services in Alberta's provincial parks. Lake Sikome is touted as one of the first places on the government's hit list for privately administered admission charges.

Inglewood Bird Sanctuary

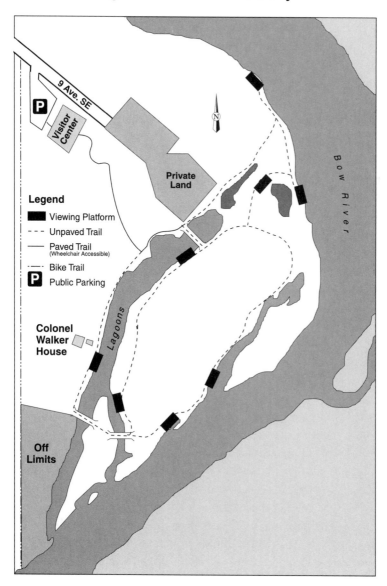

Access: Sanctuary Road off 9 Avenue SE.

Terrain: Riparian vegetation with balsam poplar, riverine tall shrub, non-native grassland.

Activities: Hiking, wildlife watching, educational programs.

Prohibited: Dogs, bicycles, fishing, feeding wildlife, picking vegetation.

Hours: Sanctuary open dawn to dusk. Visitor center open weekdays 9:00 A.M. to 4:00 P.M. and weekends 9:00 A.M. to 3:30 P.M.

Contact: For general information about nature courses, guided hikes and Calgary wildlife, call Inglewood Bird Sanctuary at 403 269-6688. To report or learn of unusual bird sightings, call the 24-hour Bird Alert Hotline at 403 237-8821.

ON AN EARLY SPRING MORNING the Inglewood Bird Sanctuary resounds with a virtual symphony of contrasting sounds—natural and otherwise. Canada geese aggressively chase and hiss at each other in a flurry of feathers and splashes. In the willows, black-capped chickadees flit about, singing cheery high-pitched tunes of *fee-be-ee*. Concealed in thick undergrowth, a cock ring-necked pheasant crows for a mate. Overhead, screaming American kestrels compete with roaring jumbo jetliners making their final approach to Calgary International Airport. Train whistles toot, steel couplings clank and brakes squeal, like fingernails raked on chalkboard, at the nearby CPR shunting yard. To the east traffic hums steadily on Deerfoot Trail. Listen closely, some say, and you can hear frustrated golfers swearing at lipped-out putts and hooked drives from the Inglewood Golf Course across the Bow River.

If you number among the 60,000 annual visitors to the bird sanctuary, however, you don't have reason to be frustrated. Quite the contrary. When you park your vehicle in the spacious parking lot, you also can park your worries. Passing through the gate to the 37-ha (91-acre) sanctuary, you slip into the natural world of ducks, geese, songbirds, deer and dozens of other types of wildlife that call this special place home. Just 5 km (3.1 mi) from downtown office towers, the Inglewood Bird Sanctuary is a natural oasis in one of Calgary's oldest industrial sections.

Volunteers Weldon Vickers (left) and David Lumley at Inglewood Bird Sanctuary.

Early one afternoon I encountered a man and his two-year-old son on a trail leading to the sanctuary's main spring-fed lagoon. They were bundled up against the late October chill. The boy was silent in his father's arms as he contemplated a raft of Canada geese and mallard ducks paddling on the water. The son didn't have much to say, but his face reflected his happiness. The father spoke for them both. "We like the quiet, the remoteness," he said. "This is one of the few places in Calgary with natural habitat that you can actually get away to."

The sanctuary is steeped in a rich and colorful history. The area was first settled by Colonel James Walker, who came West from Ontario in 1880 as superintendent of the North-West Mounted Police. He established a homestead and sawmill in 1882 at the present sanctuary site. In 1910 he built a stately red brick mansion, which he named Inglewood, and it was the envy of the town.

The area's designation as a federal migratory bird sanctuary came in 1929 thanks to the efforts of James Walker's son, Selby, a devoted conservationist in an era when it wasn't trendy to be one. The city acquired the site in 1970. The house stands proudly today as a designated provincial historic site. Up to the summer of 1996, the mansion housed administrative offices and classrooms for natural history courses.

Harold Pinel, Calgary's first city-employed naturalist, was hired in 1972 to operate the sanctuary and offer courses in the old Walker house. He says the facility traditionally has ridden "a teeter-totter between recreational use and preservation." All developments, including the new $750,000 interpretive center that opened in 1996, were designed to respect and preserve wildlife.

The single-story visitor center is cross-shaped. Its 743 m^2 (8,000 ft^2) provide almost eight times more space than the old Walker house. You can enter the sanctuary through the public information wing of the center during regular hours or via an outside gate. The wing features a reception area, washrooms, disabled-friendly facilities and season-related educational interpretive displays. You can learn about bird migration flight paths, see real bird nests and study mounted birds common to the area. A live-action television monitor connected to a remote-controlled video camera was donated by Ducks Unlimited Canada and features ducks and geese in the main lagoon. The educational wing offers two large classrooms for the sanctuary's popular nature courses and for renting to private groups.

Stepping outside, you take a path over a wooden bridge toward the lagoons and 3 km (1.8 mi) of tree-lined pathways. Eight wildlife viewing platforms are provided. Across Sanctuary Road just west of the visitor center is the Inglewood Wildlands Park, a 30-ha (74-acre) natural area developed as additional wildlife habitat.

Kym McCulley, the sanctuary's natural history programmer, says many first-time visitors are surprised because they expect to see birds in cages. Instead, they view wildlife in natural settings. The city, she says, tries to keep the area as natural as possible. Feeding wildlife was prohibited in 1988 to keep the behavior of birds and animals wild. Educational programs, both on-site and in city schools, are a big part of the sanctuary's operation. "We want to prepare people to be good stewards of the land and to have good ethics," McCulley says. "That message starts here."

The sanctuary gets help from about 150 dedicated volunteers. Wearing distinctive green vests, they watch wildlife, note unusual sightings, keep visitors on established paths and answer questions. Volunteers Weldon Vickers and David Lumley traditionally take Christmas morning duty. "We have great philosophical discussions," notes geophysicist Lumley. Vickers loves being at the sanctuary anytime, but especially on Christmas morning. He's amazed at the number of visitors that day: strolling singles, senior citizens, couples and families. "It seems a lot of people are using it as a stress reliever," notes Vickers. "It gives a little meaning to your life to get in tune with your real ties to the land."

More than 270 bird species, 300 plant species and several types of mammals have been identified in the sanctuary. Year-round residents include mallards, black-capped chickadees, downy woodpeckers, white-tailed and mule deer, coyotes and assorted hares. The sanctuary also is considered one of the best places in Alberta to see wood ducks. The busiest times of year are spring and autumn, when dozens of migrating species stop here. In summer, you're likely to see ducklings doing their best imitation of little downy fluff balls as they follow their mothers around the lagoon. Binoculars and a camera are a must.

Although visitor numbers drop in winter, there's still plenty to see. Great horned owls, bald eagles, flickers, white-breasted nuthatches, redpolls and magpies are common winter residents. Deer browse in the underbrush. Tracks in the snow chronicle travels of coyotes, squirrels, rabbits and weasels. No matter the season, Inglewood is perfect if you're in need of solitude for quiet reflection.

Weaselhead Flats Natural Environment Park

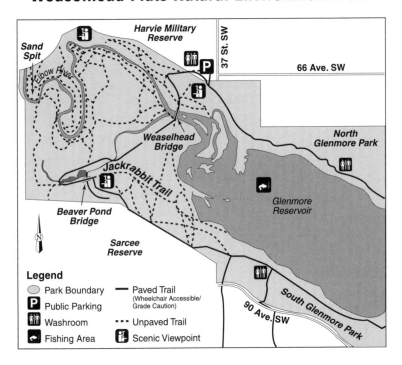

Access: South Glenmore Park, turn north at 24 Street from 90 Avenue SW to southwest corner of Glenmore Reservoir. Park at 37 Street SE or 66 Avenue SE.

Terrain: Low hills and wetlands with seven of Calgary's 10 habitat types, including white spruce, aspen, balsam poplar, riverine tall shrub, upland tall shrub, cattail and sedge wetland.

Activities: Hiking on interpretive trail, cycling on paved pathway only, picnicking, fishing, wildlife watching, horseback riding on designated 6-km (3.7-mi) trail, cross-country skiing, snowshoeing,.

Hours: Open 5:00 A.M. to 12:00 A.M.

Contact: 403 268-2300.

THIS 405-HA (1,001-ACRE) AREA is considered Calgary's most environmentally significant natural environment. Its location within the Elbow River delta and its variety of habitat types combine to create prime conditions for birds and mammals. The Weaselhead adjoins the Glenmore Reservoir, which is fed by the Elbow River.

White-tailed and mule deer, coyotes, beaver and, yes, even weasels are regular residents. Other animals more common to the western foothills and mountains—moose, Canada lynx, cougar and black bear—make regular appearances. The best times to spot wildlife are early morning and evening. More than 480 plant species also have been reported here, and it's believed that up to 71 species of birds breed in the area because of the variety of vegetation.

Named after a Sarcee Indian who lived on the flats in the late 1800s, the Weaselhead was used before World War II as a military training ground. Remnants of foxholes and trenches are still evident. Modern use is a little tamer. Now it's a favorite destination for Calgarians, especially for those living in the neighboring communities of Lakeview, Oak Ridge and Lincoln Park.

The Weaselhead can be busy on weekends. Early mornings and weekday evenings are better times to visit if you want to avoid crowds. "I think it's fantastic to have this so close," says Jim Sherren, a semiretired home renovator who has lived in nearby Glamorgan for more than 30 years. He enjoys walking in the area for 90 minutes a day, sometimes twice a day.

One February afternoon I encountered a grey-haired woman stepping gingerly along an ice-encrusted trail in Weaselhead. She clutched a white grocery bag. A tiny black-capped chickadee flitted onto a branch next to the trail and chirped. "You're hungry, aren't you?" the woman asked. Reaching into her bag, she sprinkled a small pile of sunflowers and assorted birdseed on the frozen grass. The chickadee landed and started to eat. Declining to give her name—"Just call me an old lady with her own ideas"—the woman stopped to fill a homemade wooden bird feeder. Then she continued on her rounds, shuffling down the trail and disappearing around a bend.

Bird feeding has since been stopped in Weaselhead and Calgary's other natural areas. City crews try to remove bird feeders as fast as people put them up. The idea is to keep birds wild and maintain the natural integrity of these special places.

A few years ago the city also was forced to restrict mountain bikers and horseback riders. The area was being severely bisected with unofficial trails—shortcuts through the trees created by thrill-seeking mountain bikers. An official said at the time that the area was being "loved to death." The city blocked off some of these trails with orange snow fence, deadfall and closure signs. Hikers and mountain bikers continued using them as shortcuts, so bikers now are restricted to the paved regional Glenmore pathway, slowing but not completely eliminating them from blazing their own courses through the terrain. Horses are limited to a 6-km (3.7-mi) designated trail.

The paved pathway through the Weaselhead can be included in an enjoyable 16-km (10-mi) loop around Glenmore Reservoir. If you don't want to go the entire stretch, start instead at the parking lots for North or South Glenmore parks, then head west into the Weaselhead. Coming from the north, you'll drop down into the valley and soon encounter the Weaselhead Bridge across the Elbow River. You'll have to walk your bike across. It's too narrow for riding, especially if the bridge is being used by another cyclist or hiker. If you're near this bridge in evening or early morning, keep a close watch for beavers swimming in the broad section of Elbow River as it enters the Glenmore Reservoir.

Follow the trail southwest to the Beaver Pond Bridge, another great place to see beavers, muskrats and other wildlife. The paved trail then rises out of the valley and heads east, where it hooks up with South Glenmore Park. After finishing the climb out, stop for a breather and enjoy the scenery at one of several viewpoints.

The Weaselhead also offers a network of trails restricted to hiking or cross-country skiing, including the Jackrabbit Trail. It's named for Norwegian cross-country skier Jackrabbit Johanssen, who brought the sport to Canada at the turn of the century and died in 1988 at the age of 112. The Jackrabbit Trail also leads to South Glenmore Park, running adjacent to the paved pathway. A new interpretive trail several kilometers long has been developed in the valley bottom. It features signs explaining the area's rich and varied flora and fauna, and a boardwalk bridge over a wonderful wetland. A natural getaway for most people, the Weaselhead can be delightfully therapeutic.

Glenmore Reservoir

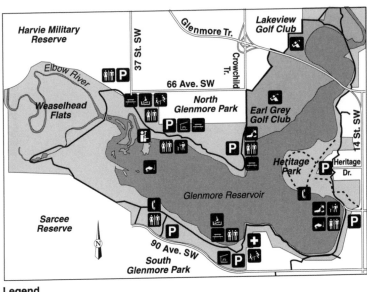

Legend

⬭ Park Boundary	📞 Telephone	🛶 Hand Boat Launch	••• Unpaved Trail (no cycling)
🅿 Public Parking	🚻 Washroom	🎠 Playground	📷 Scenic Viewpoint
🍱 Picnic Site	✚ First Aid	🎣 Fishing Area	🪧 Interpretive Plaque
🏠 Picnic Shelter	Barbeque Pit	— Paved Trail (Wheelchair Accessible/ Grade Caution)	⛳ Golfing

Access: To South Glenmore Park turn north at 24 Street from 90 Avenue SW. To North Glenmore Park head south on 37 Street SW from Glenmore Trail or east on 54 Avenue from Crowchild Trail. To East Glenmore Park head west on Heritage Drive off 14 Street SW.

Terrain: Rolling hills, poplar stands and grassy plains.

Activities: Hiking, cycling, in-line skating, tennis, picnicking, fishing, canoeing, rowing, sailing, heritage park, playground.

Prohibited: Pets, motorboats, boats longer than 8 m (26'), inflatable craft or rafts, wading, swimming, sail boarding, fishing from docks, boating before sunrise or after sunset.

Hours: Open 5:00 A.M. to 12:00 A.M.

Contact: 403 268-2300.

THE RESERVOIR is one of Calgary's most popular recreational facilities. Perhaps it's the novelty of a huge, publicly accessible water body in the middle of a landlocked metropolis. Or maybe it's the range of recreational activities available here. Maybe it's the combination of the two. For whatever reason, Glenmore Reservoir draws people from all over the city.

Covering 2.4 km² (1.5 mi²), the reservoir went into operation in 1933, four years after a Toronto consulting firm recommended a dam on the Elbow River. When the reservoir was filled, it covered part of the land owned by colorful Calgary pioneer Sam Livingston. His old house still stands in Heritage Park, an historical western village that is the featured attraction in East Glenmore Park. With a total capacity of 16.4 million l (4.3 million gal), the reservoir provides two-thirds of Calgary's water supply.

It also provides a big share of the city's outdoor recreation. The reservoir is ringed by a 16-km (10-mi) paved pathway for cycling, in-line skating and hiking. Tennis courts are available in South Glenmore Park. A city-run sailing club in South Glenmore Park offers sailing lessons for landlubber Calgarians. The Calgary Canoe Club, in North Glenmore Park, offers lessons and rentals. Heritage Park features a variety of activities, including tours of the reservoir aboard an old paddle-wheeler steamship, the SS *Moyie*. Picnic tables are provided in North, South and East Glenmore parks. Playgrounds provide a diversion for young families.

If you desire less active pursuits, you'll enjoy watching the wildlife, especially the shorebirds and waterfowl in the reservoir. Deer and coyotes are seen regularly at the reservoir's west end. Dozens of bird species live in the area. Your enjoyment of viewing wildlife from a distance will be enhanced by using a good set of binoculars or a spotting scope. Trying to sneak closer isn't a good idea because it usually results in birds and animals fleeing once they know they're being stalked.

To protect this important repository of drinking water, the city has implemented strict rules for public use. The prohibitions listed at the beginning of this section are enforced. You also are warned to keep off the ice in winter because dangerous air pockets form under the ice as water is drawn out. Ice above and below air pockets is brittle.

Many Calgarians seeking fishing action without having to leave town find Glenmore a welcome break. They fish in the Elbow River, using spinners and flies, or try their luck in the reservoir itself, either from shore or from canoes and rowboats. Glenmore Reservoir is one of the few fisheries in Alberta that regularly offers a diverse catch of northern pike, yellow perch and brown trout. Vance Buchwald, a provincial fisheries biologist, calls the piscatorial mix "not common at all."

Government test netting one night in 1989 caught 32 northern pike, 25 yellow perch and 6 brown trout. The biggest pike topped 4 kg (9 lb), the largest perch about .5 kg (1.1 lb). The heaviest brown trout, believe it or not, was almost 4 kg (9 lb). Anglers also have caught chunky mountain whitefish and big, silver-sided rainbow trout.

For catching trout, many anglers have success on small spoons, spinners and minnow-shaped plugs. Olive-colored weighted nymphs and black streamer flies also work. Perch can be fooled on an earthworm worked on a No. 6 hook placed 2 m (6.5') below a small bobber. Pike will take smelts, big spoons and plugs. Late one evening a few years ago, Calgary angler Zdzislaw Lelek caught a 4.8-kg (10.6-lb) burbot—freshwater ling cod—on a frozen smelt in about 10 m (33') of water. The biggest burbot he'd ever seen fell short of the 5.4-kg (12-lb) provincial record set in 1992 at Swan Lake.

Jeff Gruttz, city outdoor recreation specialist, says Calgarians are lucky to have easy access to a large municipal water storage reservoir. Many cities erect fences around their reservoirs to keep out visitors. Gruttz says continued recreational use of Glenmore Reservoir depends on Calgarians treating it responsibly and following the rules.

Beaverdam Flats Natural Environment Park

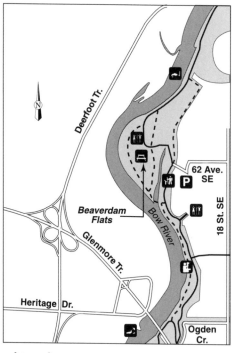

Legend

⬭	Park Boundary	····	Unpaved Trail (No Cycling)
P	Public Parking	⬛	Hand Boat Launch
🛏	Picnic Site	⬛	Scenic Site
🚻	Washroom	🛕	Interpretive Plaque
⬛	Fishing Area		
—	Paved Trail (Wheelchair Accessible/ Grade Caution)		

Access: Glenmore Trail east to 18 Street SE, follow signs north for 1.5 km (.9 mi), turn west on 66 Avenue SE, then right on Lynnview Road for .4 km (.2 mi) to parking lot.

Terrain: River valley, balsam poplar, riverine tall shrubs, cattail slough, mixed and native grassland.

Activities: Hiking, cycling, picnicking, fishing, dog walking, wildlife watching, playground, cross-country skiing.

Hours: Open 5:00 A.M. to 12:00 A.M.
Contact: 403 268-2300.

APTLY NAMED for the large and industrious buck-toothed rodents that have wreaked havoc on the poplars lining the riverbank, Beaverdam Flats is a reclaimed industrial site. A popular spot for local residents, it's particularly busy in summer, but city naturalist Olga Dropp likes the area in winter, when she can trace the movements of small mammals, coyotes and deer in the snow. Old bird nests stand out more in winter, when the branches on which they sit are free of obstructing leaves.

Unless you arrive by boat on the river or bike along the paved pathway, you face a 10-minute walk from the parking lot down a relatively steep path to the natural area. The walk is invigorating, whether you're heading down or returning to the top. Either way, you should stop frequently to enjoy the different views. Wild flowers in spring on the west-facing escarpment are spectacular. They're a good reason to stay on the trails and tread carefully. Watch for wildlife too. Beaverdam Flats' grassy hills, towering poplars, understory of bushes and famous Bow River provide homes for many different species of birds. Waterfowl (mallards, common goldeneyes and Canada geese), great horned owls and bald eagles can be seen all winter. Double-crested cormorants, American white pelicans and kingfishers hang out in late spring and summer.

Beaverdam Flats also is popular with people. Just ask Len Nixon, who was visiting Calgary from his rural home north of the city a few winters ago. After a few days of cooling his heels at his sister's house in nearby Lynnwood, Nixon longed for the serenity of his country home. "My idea of a fast time is a nice brisk sit," Nixon, then 25, told me. He found his "fast time" in Beaverdam Flats on a solid wooden bench with a great view of the river valley, downtown office towers and the Rocky Mountains. Wearing shirt sleeves on the Chinook-warmed February afternoon, Nixon watched people wandering the trails below him, while Canada geese and ducks buzzed over the water. "It's a little bit of quietness in the whole center of confusion," he observed.

*Len Nixon takes a break on a bench overlooking Beaverdam Flats
Natural Environment Park.*

Carburn Natural Environment Park

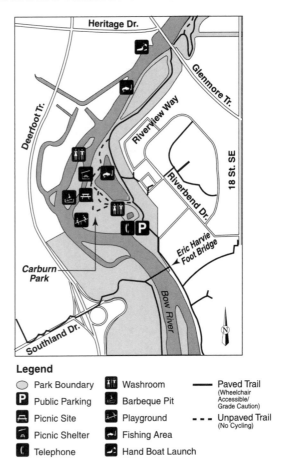

Legend

⬭ Park Boundary	🚻 Washroom	▬▬ Paved Trail (Wheelchair Accessible/ Grade Caution)
🅿 Public Parking	🍖 Barbeque Pit	
🪑 Picnic Site	🛝 Playground	▪ ▪ ▪ Unpaved Trail (No Cycling)
🏠 Picnic Shelter	🎣 Fishing Area	
📞 Telephone	🚤 Hand Boat Launch	

Access: East on Glenmore Trail, south on 18 Street SE, then follow the signs to Riverview Drive SE. From Southland Drive walk across the Eric Harvie Bridge spanning the Bow River.

Terrain: Floodplain with three manufactured lagoons, balsam poplar, riverine tall and low shrubs, chokecherries, saskatoons, willow, cattail slough, mixed and native grassland.

Activities: Hiking, cycling, in-line skating, picnicking, fishing, canoeing, wildlife watching, dog walking (on leash only), playground, cross-country skiing, tobogganing, wheelchair accessible (limited in winter).

Prohibited: Swimming in or ice skating on the lagoons.

Hours: Open 5:00 A.M. to 12:00 A.M.

Contact: 403 268-2300.

THE TROUBLE with secret refuges in Calgary is that they don't stay secret very long. That's the story of Carburn Park. After it opened in 1986, the park's main users were Riverbend residents who walked the trails after work, fished the three lagoons and played there with their families on weekends. That all changed when the 61-ha (151-acre) park was discovered by the rest of Calgary. Now people from all over the city, and even some from the country, flock in droves to enjoy the park's laid-back atmosphere.

On a sun-washed pathway, Jacqueline Mill pulls a sled carrying her dozing 10-week-old son, Justin. Proud grandparents Vern Mill and Carla Wold walk alongside. Although Jacqueline and her family live in the southwest community of Braeside, they favor Carburn Park over the closer and larger Glenmore Park, which has longer stretches of remote pathway. Jacqueline says she feels safer in Carburn Park. "And the trails are shorter. If you don't want to do a lot of exercise, you don't have to."

Therein lies the essence of Carburn Park: set your own agenda, follow your own pace and be as active as you want. It might mean just sitting on a log watching the river flow by. It might mean speed walking along the trails.

Although use has increased, the park retains its magic. It's still a little piece of quiet natural beauty tucked away in the midst of a city in a hurry. During the day bushy-tailed squirrels frolic in the grass, searching for food, chasing one another and chattering saucily at people who get too close. Bald eagles cruise at treetop level, eyeing their next meal of *mallard canard de Bow*. White-tailed deer tentatively pick their way through the poplars. The deer become bolder as they approach adjacent houses, where some residents have been known to offer them grain, though this practice is mis-

Carburn Park Pond is a great fishing hole for kids.

guided entertainment. Deer survive quite well on their own without handouts.

In late evening, beavers emerge from their dens and begin their tireless cruising of the Bow. Where beavers slide in and out of the water onto shore, runs are slick with mud. Bases of big poplars are ringed with wire fencing, a reminder that beavers may be fun to watch, but they're also beasts of destruction. Coyotes still wander freely, their howls hauntingly mournful in the black of night. Magpies squawk while great horned owls hoot eerily from the treetops. If you look closely enough on a late clear evening, you can see the large ear-tufted birds on their cottonwood perches silhouetted by moonlight.

Carburn Park is an angler's delight. It provides easy access to a long stretch of the Bow River, famous around the world for its great rainbow and brown trout fishing. Spinners, spoons, jigs, streamers, weighted nymphs and some dry flies can be very effective on this reach. Anglers must wade carefully because the rocky bottom is slippery underfoot.

The three lagoons, easily located by sight or sign, have a checkered piscatorial past. The provincial government used to stock them with rainbow trout. That stopped several years ago with the discovery of yellow perch. Perch, according to fisheries biologists, had been illegally stocked by persons unknown. The city tried to drain the lagoons and net out the perch. That didn't work because many fish avoided nets by hiding among the rocks. Crews were shocked during the attempt, however, to discover a 6.3-kg (14-lb) brown trout that apparently had grown fat on a perch diet. The trout, jokingly dubbed Moby Dick, was left in the lagoon to feed on perch. Today the main catch in the lagoons is perch and the odd northern pike. Nobody knows where the pike came from either. And nobody's seen Moby Dick since.

Perch make the Carburn Park lagoons a perfect spot to bring kids just learning to fish because the fish aren't huge and they're fun to catch. A tiny lead-head jig tipped with maggots or a small worm hooked a few meters under a small torpedo-shaped casting bubble are time-proven perch foolers.

Carburn Park is a good fishing spot for kids for other reasons. When they get bored—as most kids tend to do when they're learning to fish—you can take them on a nature walk along the river or cycle along the pathway. Or you can burn energy in the playground after sharing a picnic lunch of hot dogs roasted over a fire in one of the camp stoves provided.

Edworthy Natural Environment Park

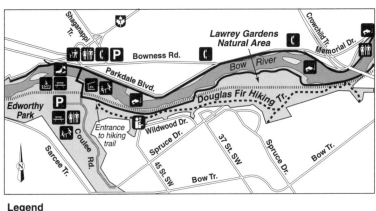

Legend

○ Park Boundary	🚻 Washroom	— Paved Trail (Wheelchair Accessible/ Grade Caution)
P Public Parking	🔥 Barbeque Pit	
Picnic Site	Hand Boat Launch	▪▪▪ Unpaved Trail (No Cycling)
Picnic Shelter	Playground	Scenic Viewpoint
Telephone	Fishing Area	Interpretive Plaque
ⅲⅲ Railway Track		

Access: From the north, park at 16 Avenue NW and Montgomery View and cross Harry Boothman Bridge (pedestrians and cyclists only) over the Bow River. From the south, exit Bow Trail to 45 Street SW and Spruce Drive.

Terrain: Aspen woodland, mixed coniferous forest, white spruce and Douglas fir forest (unique to Calgary) on south escarpment, mixed shrubland, sedge wetland, native grassland.

Activities: Hiking, cycling, picnicking, fishing, wildlife watching, dog walking (off-leash on top of valley only), playground, cross-country skiing and tobogganing.

Hours: Open 5:00 A.M. to 12:00 A.M.

Contact: 403 268-2300.

THE APPEAL of Edworthy Natural Environment Park is that it's full of surprises. One day a bald eagle flying along the river will veer south and perch with mighty talons on a cottonwood limb directly overhead. Another day might bring a colorful burst of wild flowers on the hillside, or a sleek mink weaving in and out of sight through the rocks along the riverbank. Or you might see fresh deer tracks in the snow, making you wonder how long ago the animal passed by.

Sandwiched between the Bow River and the Sarcee, Crowchild and Bow trails, Edworthy Natural Environment Park encompasses three natural areas running 6 km (3.7 mi) along the Bow River in northwest Calgary: 77-ha (190-acre) Edworthy Park itself, 33-ha (82-acre) Douglas Fir Trail and 17-ha (42-acre) Lawrey Gardens. Each area by itself is truly special; together, they comprise one of the city's richest, most diverse natural zones, which includes woodland, shrubland, wetland, grassland and a centuries-old Douglas fir forest.

The Douglas Fir Trail, arguably Calgary's best hiking trail, looks like it should be in the mountains, not in the middle of a city. Four-hundred-year-old Douglas firs and balsam poplars tower over the trail. The Douglas firs are some of the farthest found east of the Rockies. The ground alongside it is blanketed with lush green vegetation and brightly punctuated with a rainbow of wild flowers such as wild roses, Virginia bluebells, western wood violets and twining honeysuckle. Hawks scream overhead and nuthatches hop upside-down on trunks of fir trees. A pretty spring trickles down the hill toward the Bow River.

Feelings for the park area run so high that residents are quick to rally to its defense when it needs help the most. They opposed a planned $3.8 million expansion of Shaganappi Point Golf Course because it threatened 4.9 ha (12 acres) of native fescue grassland and willow. The plan was scaled back to reduce residents' concerns. They fought a proposed traffic overpass that would have sliced through the park's western edge. That proposal died, partly due to public pressure.

Residents participated heavily in a major wetlands restoration project in Lawrey Gardens. With labor supplied by the John Howard Society, the ambitious project reclaimed one of the city's most important breeding bird habitats. Chunks of concrete and other fill material from the old Robin Hood Mill downtown were dumped in

Dog-walking in the off-leash area at Edworthy Park.

the wetland almost 30 years ago. The fill was removed and the surrounding native grassland replanted.

Residents also came to the rescue of the Douglas Fir Trail, a vic-
tim of many years of user abuse since it was first built in 1972. Calgarians participated in a $200,000 restoration program funded by the
city, province and several nonprofit foundations. The city contributed much of the technical labor, and 1,000 hours of grunt work
were donated by volunteers coordinated by the Edworthy Park Heritage Society. Volunteers came from several groups, including the
Woodcliff Scout Troop No. 83, LDS Scout Troop No. 211, Al-Azhar
Youth Group and Wildwood Community Association.

Seven new bridges were built. Steps and railings were replaced.
Eight truckloads of tread mix—clay, gravel and sand—were meticu-
lously spread by hand along the 4-km (2.5-mi) trail. A sandstone
viewpoint, known as Dead Man's Lookout, was erected, providing
hikers with a spectacular view overlooking the Bow River and Point
McKay. Volunteers also planted 5,000 wild flowers with seeds col-

lected from private yards and a field near Edworthy Park that was destined to be bulldozed.

Bob Beamish, a retired petroleum engineer who's lived in Wildwood for more than 35 years, contributed a dozen Saturdays to work on the project. He's been a fan of the Douglas Fir Trail for years. Volunteering gave him a chance to contribute to its future. "When you see something like this, you want to preserve it," Beamish says. "It's not just a nice walk. It's a botany and bird sanctuary."

The park's area was homesteaded in 1883 by Thomas Edworthy, an English immigrant who built a log cabin using Douglas fir trees on the south side of the Bow River. He ranched and operated three of the area's four sandstone quarries. Now abandoned, the quarries provided much of the building material for Calgary's historical buildings. In the early 1880s pioneer John Lawrey started market gardening in an area along the river now known as Lawrey Gardens. Early archaeological evidence includes campsites, tepee rings and buffalo jumps used by paleo-Indians and, later, the Plains Indians. Between 1905 and 1931 the area was heavily used to produce bricks for houses.

Sam Livingston Fish Hatchery

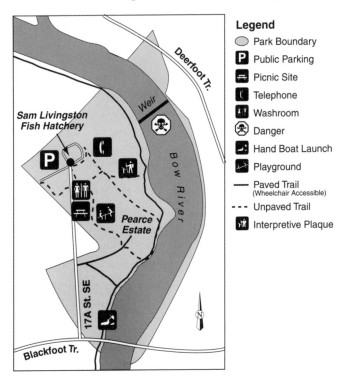

Legend

- ⬤ Park Boundary
- 🅿 Public Parking
- 🍴 Picnic Site
- ☎ Telephone
- 🚻 Washroom
- ☠ Danger
- 🚣 Hand Boat Launch
- 🛝 Playground
- — Paved Trail (Wheelchair Accessible)
- - - - Unpaved Trail
- 🧍 Interpretive Plaque

Access: West of Deerfoot Trail, at 1440 – 17A Street SE in Pearce Estate Park.

Activities: Interpretive tours (self-guided or volunteer-led), hiking, fishing, playground.

Hours: April 1 – September 30 open weekdays 10:00 A.M. to 4:00 P.M., weekends and holidays 1:00 P.M. to 5:00 P.M. October 1 – March 31 open weekdays 10:00 A.M. to 4:00 P.M. Evening tours can be arranged.

Contact: 403 297-6561.

NAMED AFTER a Calgary pioneer who homesteaded in the area now occupied by Glenmore Reservoir, the Sam Livingston Fish Hatchery is the city's only publicly operated trout hatchery. It is visited by about 30,000 people a year. Most are Calgarians eager to learn more about Alberta's fish species, fisheries and the sport of fishing. In the process, they witness the high technology involved in raising millions of trout to be stocked for fishing.

John Enns, the fisheries technician, delights in making his friends envious. He spends his days surrounded by trout in the provincially operated hatchery, which opened in 1973. His buddies have to wait until they're off work to try to get close to a fish via a fishing rod. Enns, who has been at the hatchery since 1977, says he feels lucky: "I like working with the fish, seeing them swim around and grow."

Sometimes, during his lunch hour, Enns likes to fish in the Bow River, which flows behind the hatchery. He has been known to haunt some places stocked with trout raised at the hatchery (fishing rod at the ready). Enns figures he's handled more than 50 million trout during his career. That's the stuff of dreams for ardent anglers.

The hatchery annually raises more than three million rainbow, brook, brown and cutthroat trout for stocking in Southern Alberta lakes, ponds and reservoirs. (Trout are rarely stocked in Alberta rivers and other flowing waters; the Bow River is never stocked.) Growing trout is a complex process. Employees must carefully monitor a number of factors: water quality, feeding rates, water flow and even fish behavior. A few years ago, hatchery officials introduced wild Bow River rainbow trout genes into hatchery rainbows to make them more hardy, wary and feisty when hooked.

The Sam Livingston hatchery is an ideal family destination for a rainy or winter day, or on a nice one when the outing is combined with a picnic in 6-ha (15-acre) Pearce Estate Park located just off the facility's parking lot. Guided hatchery tours with trained volunteers can be arranged for schools and other groups. Otherwise a brochure, available on-site, outlines a self-guided tour.

Upon entering the front door, you are immediately struck by the strong odor of fish, which isn't too surprising in a place that grows them. The smell, not entirely unpleasant, doesn't come from live fish. It comes from ground fish, an ingredient of the trout feed. Next

Young rainbow trout at the Sam Livingston Fish Hatchery.

you'll notice the dim lighting, especially on the lower and upper levels. Lights are kept low to simulate natural conditions. Bright lights could panic trout fry of 5–10 cm (2–4") causing them to crowd together and smother one another while seeking shelter from the light.

The hatchery's inner workings can be viewed through glass windows. The rearing areas include several kilometers of overhead pipes and dozens of holding tanks. Viewers are kept behind glass windows to reduce the risk of disease and disruption of the fish. The tour also features several interactive displays, including a large plastic trout with body parts that light up when buttons with corresponding names are pressed.

Live trout swim in tanks set into walls in the dark cavernous basement. Another display features mounted Alberta fish, including a snub-nosed rainbow trout alleged to weigh 5.4 kg (12 lb) when it was caught in 1969 at Chain Lakes Provincial Park in southwestern Alberta. Now, a rainbow one-fifth that size at Chain Lakes comes with bragging rights.

The best time to visit the hatchery is between January and early June, the most active growing period. The process begins with fertilized eggs gathered from several locations, including the provincially operated Raven and Allison Creek brood trout stations. Some eggs come from wild fish. From eggs of about 1 cm (.4"), trout grow to alevin of about 2.5 cm (1"). After 30 to 60 days in the incubation room, alevin are relocated into troughs, where they are fed up to 20 times daily. Each trough holds about 25,000 trout. Their next stop is circular tanks, where the trout double their size in two months. The final rearing area is the Burrows ponds, where fingerlings of 10–15 cm (4–6") rest before they are stocked.

As a precaution against bringing in fish diseases from the river, the hatchery uses well water instead of drawing from the nearby Bow. The Bow's water is too warm in summer and too cold in winter for rearing fish. Silt and other pollutants in the Bow are another concern.

Hatchery officials will never forget the disastrous viral disease, infectious pancreatic necrosis, that hit the facility in 1989. The disease originated from the province's hatchery at Cold Lake. About 2.6 million infected rainbow trout were destroyed. The Calgary hatchery was closed for three years during the $2-million cleanup operation. Every piece of equipment and pipeline was disassembled, then scrubbed at least twice with chlorine to kill bacteria.

Since those dark days, the situation has brightened considerably. Employees and the hatchery volunteer society have developed programs to attract more Calgarians to the facility. New visitor and educational programs have been developed. An ambitious project just getting underway will enlarge the hatchery's role to include a major environmental education center. Formed by the Sam Livingston Fish Hatchery Volunteer Society and Alberta Environmental Protection, the Bow Habitat Station is designed to develop a world class visitor and interpretive/education center at the hatchery.

One of the hatchery's newest programs involves providing fertilized trout eggs to 21 Southern Alberta schools. Students learn to care for the eggs until they hatch, then babysit the young trout for several months before they are released in Kananaskis Country. Environmental stewardship is the lesson here.

As government budgets have tightened in recent years, the importance of the Sam Livingston Fish Hatchery Volunteer Society has increased. Devoted volunteers assist with visitor reception services, conduct guided tours and lend a hand in the field when trout are being stocked. They also teach the Alberta Fishing Education Course to Calgarians new to fishing or to newcomers eager to learn the sport's local nuances.

Best Cross-Country Skiing in Calgary

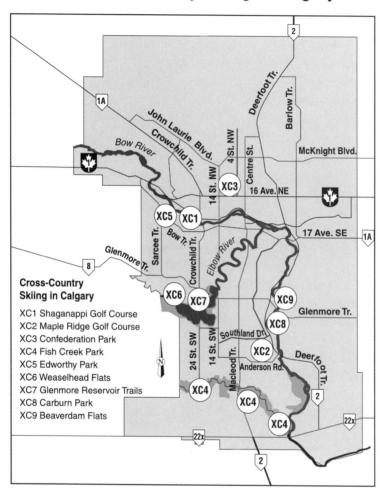

Cross-Country
Skiing in Calgary

XC1 Shaganappi Golf Course
XC2 Maple Ridge Golf Course
XC3 Confederation Park
XC4 Fish Creek Park
XC5 Edworthy Park
XC6 Weaselhead Flats
XC7 Glenmore Reservoir Trails
XC8 Carburn Park
XC9 Beaverdam Flats

◆ Shaganappi Point Golf Course at 1200 – 26 Street SW. 3 km (1.9 mi).
Regularly machine-tracked and groomed by volunteers.

◆ Maple Ridge Golf Course at 1240 Mapleglade Drive SW. 4.5 km (2.8
mi). Periodically machine-tracked and groomed by volunteers.

◆ Confederation Park Golf Course at 3204 Collingwood Drive NW. 2.2
km (1.4 mi). Regularly machine-tracked and groomed by volunteers.

◆ Fish Creek Provincial Park at the west end near Shannon Terrace Environmental Education Centre. Trail lengths vary. Skier trackset.

◆ Edworthy Natural Environment Park. From the north parking lot at 16 Avenue NW and Montgomery View, cross Harry Boothman pedestrian bridge over the Bow River. From the south, drive off Bow Trail to 45 Street SW and Spruce Drive. Trail lengths vary. Skiing beside pathway and on Douglas Fir Trail. Skier trackset.

◆ Weaselhead Flats Natural Environment Park. Southwest corner of Glenmore Reservoir. Parking lots at 37 Street SE or 66 Avenue SE. Trail lengths vary. Skier trackset.

◆ Glenmore Reservoir. To South Glenmore Park turn north at 24 Street from 90 Avenue SW. To North Glenmore Park exit south from Glenmore Trail on 37 Street SW or exit east from Crowchild Trail on 54 Avenue. To East Glenmore Park, exit west from 14 Street SW on Heritage Drive. Trail lengths vary. Skier trackset in North and South Glenmore parks.

◆ Carburn Natural Environment Park. East on Glenmore Trail, south on 18 Street, then follow signs to Riverview Drive SE. From Southland Drive, ski across the Eric Harvie Bridge spanning the Bow River. Trail lengths vary. Skier trackset.

◆ Beaverdam Flats Natural Environment Park. East on Glenmore Trail to 18 Street SE, then follow signs north for 1.5 km (.9 mi). Turn west on 66 Avenue, then right on Lynnview Road for .4 km (.2 mi) to parking lot. Trail lengths vary. Skier trackset.

IF YOU LIKE to cross-country ski, Calgary has a great selection of ski trails virtually in your own backyard. All you need is a good snowpack and motivation to take advantage of it. "We're very fortunate to have what we do here," says Alasdair Fergusson of the Calgary Ski Club. "The popularity of cross-country skiing in the city is rising." Calgary may not offer the same heart-revving thrills as roller-coaster mountain trails, but skiing in the city has a charm of its own.

Several factors make Calgary attractive to skiers. First, there's cost. It's free, except of course for some gasoline, which you'll burn getting there. Second, there's the crowds. You won't find any on Cal-

Peggy Maslen and son, Joey, cross-country skiing at Maple Ridge Golf Course in southeast Calgary.

gary's ski trails. Third, it's convenient. You're skiing within minutes, not hours, of leaving home. A post-work or post-school outing not only is possible, it's recommended as a great way to unwind. The setting provides a fine place to introduce kids or novices to the sport. The terrain is hilly enough to be entertaining, and, if you are inexperienced, it's flat enough to hone your technique without scaring you silly. With minimal travel and preparation time, you won't mind as much if your kids lobby to return home after a short time. It sure beats hearing pitiful calls for home 20 minutes after arriving in Kananaskis Country or Banff National Park. On the other hand skiing without your children along is easier than if you headed west. Hiring a baby-sitter, going for a ski and enjoying a steaming cappuccino afterward takes only a few hours. Lastly, don't forget about the scenery. Skier-trackset trails in Calgary's natural areas expose you to a winter wonderland of forests, wildlife and stunning views of the mountains.

There's only one cardinal rule when cross-country skiing: when snow conditions are right, take advantage of them sooner rather than later. Calgary's famous Chinook winds can be a blessing when they snap a three-week cold spell that causes the mercury to plunge to –35°c (–31°f). Unfortunately Chinooks are the bane of urban skinny boarders. When the wind howls from the west and temperatures climb to springlike levels, snow conditions can go from ideal to nonexistent in a few hours. Although it's dangerous to generalize, Calgary usually offers about one month of perfect cross-country ski conditions.

Many natural areas in Calgary are great for skinny-board skiing. Skiers who hit the trails after a couple of good snowfalls lay down good classic-style tracks for others to use. On the pathway system along the Bow and Elbow rivers, ski just off the main path to avoid conflicts with other users. Hikers walking in the area should walk beside twin tracks, not on them.

Keep in mind that snow in heavily treed, natural areas lasts longer and tracks remain in better condition than in areas exposed to more wind and sun. For example, conditions generally are better in the west end of Fish Creek Provincial Park than in the less protected eastern end. In natural areas along the Bow and Elbow river valleys, the best skiing usually can be found on the valley bottom rather than atop the escarpments.

In addition to the spots listed above, natural areas suitable for skiing include Bowness Park (8900 – 48 Avenue NW), Pearce Estate Park (1440 – 17A Street SE), River Park (Sandy Beach) (4500 – 14A Street SW) and Nose Hill Park (between 14 Street and Shaganappi Trail NW, north of John Laurie Boulevard). You can use the entire 330-km (205-mi) river pathway system.

If you prefer to ski on machine-tracked trails, you have your choice of three municipal golf courses. Avoid fenced-off areas, greens and locked gates, and respect all signs. Volunteers from local ski clubs maintain these trails when snow conditions and time permit. The Calgary Ski Club handles trail duties at Shaganappi Point and Maple Ridge golf courses. The Foothills Nordic Ski Club is responsible for Confederation Park Golf Course. Shaganappi is the site of the annual cross-country celebration called Ski Fest, organized each January by the Calgary Ski Club and City Parks and Recreation. The club is promoting development of a ski clubhouse and night lighting at Shaganappi to encourage more use by skiers.

Canada Olympic Park (88 Canada Olympic Road SW) has 1.8 km (1.1 mi) of machine-groomed and trackset trails. This is the only place in the city that charges a fee for cross-country skiing. It's $7 for adults, $6 for ages 13–17, $4 for juniors and senior citizens. One nice thing about Canada Olympic Park is snow making. Even if the snow cover has vanished everywhere else in Calgary, you can still practice your cross-country skiing on artificial white stuff.

Calgary has several cross-country skiing organizations, including the Foothills and Nordic ski clubs. Contact them through the Calgary Area Outdoor Council at 403 270-2262. Lessons can be arranged through clubs, the University of Calgary Outdoor Program Centre at 403 220-5038 and Outdoor/Nature Services at 403 268-1311. Many clubs cater to senior citizens.

Urban skiing requires many of the same preparations as those needed for heading out west. Plan for the weather and avoid overheating by dressing in layers. Every member of your ski party should have a day pack containing water and a snack. At least one member should carry wax and a first aid kit. Remember to bring a camera. Memories of skiing with friends and family within Calgary are just as precious as those experienced in the mountains.

Best Cheap Skating in Calgary

◆ Bowness Park lagoon at 8900 – 48 Avenue NW.

◆ Lake Sikome in Fish Creek Provincial Park off Bow Bottom Trail SE.

◆ Marlborough Park at 6021 Madigan Drive NE.

◆ Olympic Plaza at 228 – 8 Avenue SE.

◆ Prairie Winds Park at 223 Castleridge Boulevard NE.

◆ Stanley Park at 330 – 42 Avenue SW.

Contact: For city-managed rinks call 403 268-2300. For Sikome Lake call
403 297-5293.

THE SCENE IS MORE than a little incongruous on this midweek winter day at Olympic Plaza. Rising high above the streets are glass and concrete monuments to Big Business that teem with harried workers. The midweek atmosphere is tense, edged with anticipation of that next big deal, the next big oil find, the next big paycheck— or maybe even the last one. But wait a minute. Something's amiss.

Children are laughing in the middle of corporate Calgary. In the shadow of office towers, the skating rink at Olympic Plaza is abuzz with youthful enthusiasm, echoing with the joyful sound of kids having fun.

Each year an increasing number of Calgarians are discovering the benefits of recreational skating: it's good exercise, cheap family fun and a great way to make the most of winter. The plaza is one of the most popular of Calgary's free outdoor skating rinks (the all-time favorite remains the lagoon at Bowness Park). It's lit for night skating and features a bonfire area and picnic tables.

Calgary has dozens of outdoor and indoor rinks. Community associations manage many of the outdoor rinks, where you can skate for free. The city runs the indoor public rinks, where you can skate for a small fee. If you decide to head out to one be aware that Calgary's rinks post very few rules, if any, so common sense and courtesy should prevail. Hockey sticks are prohibited at city-run outdoor rinks, but they are tolerated at Fish Creek's Lake Sikome if users aren't disturbing recreational skaters. Any disruption invites an official boot.

School kids skating at Olympic Plaza in Calgary.

If you're heading west to skate, there is a good selection of scenic places, including Allen Bill Pond (in Kananaskis Country west of Bragg Creek), Sandy McNabb Recreation Area (in Kananaskis Country west of Turner Valley), Policeman's Creek (in Canmore), Banff Springs Hotel (in Banff townsite) and Lake Louise (beside the Chateau Lake Louise in Banff National Park).

Best Tobogganing in Calgary

◆ Confederation Park, east end, at 2807 – 10 Street NW.

◆ Deerfoot Athletic Park at 14 Avenue and 16A Street NE.

◆ Edgemont Joint Site at Edgemont Drive and John Laurie Boulevard NW.

◆ Edworthy Park at 5050 Spruce Drive SW.

◆ Fish Creek Escarpment on east side of Fish Creek Provincial Park, off Bow Bottom Trail SE.

◆ Monterey Park at California Boulevard and Catalina Boulevard NE.

◆ Pop Davis Athletic Park at Ogden Road and Millican Road SE.

◆ Prairie Winds Park at 233 Castleridge Boulevard NE.

◆ Richmond Park at 22 Avenue and 45 Street SW.

◆ River Park at 4500 – 14A Street SW.

◆ St. Andrew's Heights south of 16 Avenue at University Drive NW.

◆ Strathcona Park at Strathcona Drive and Strathcona Road SW.

Contact: For a complete listing call 403 268-3888.

Sledding Responsibly

◆ Keep control at all times.

◆ Avoid areas with trees, utility poles and fences.

◆ Ensure children under 12 are accompanied by an adult.

◆ Ensure youngsters wear helmets.

Best Winter Picnicking in Calgary and Area

◆ Beaverdam Flats Natural Environment Park. Lynnview Road between 61 and 66 Avenue SE.

◆ Carburn Park Natural Environment Park. East bank of Bow River south of Glenmore Trail. Travel east on Glenmore Trail, south on 18 Street SE, then follow signs to Riverview Drive SE.

◆ Edworthy Natural Environment Park. South bank of Bow River just east of Sarcee Trail SW. From the north, park at 16 Avenue NW and Montgomery View and cross Harry Boothman Bridge over the Bow River (pedestrians and cyclists only). From the south, exit Bow Trail to 45 Street SW and Spruce Drive.

◆ Fish Creek Provincial Park. Particularly in Bankside, Burnsmead, Hull's Wood and Bow Valley Ranch Visitor Centre, off Bow Valley Trail SE south of Canyon Meadows Drive.

◆ Kananaskis Country day-use areas and campground. West of Bragg Creek on Highway 22 40 km (25 mi) west of Calgary. West of Turner Valley on Highway 22 about 49 km (30 mi) southwest of Calgary. West of Longview on Highway 22 about 70 km (43.5 mi) southwest of Calgary.

◆ Sandy Beach Park. East of 14A Street off 50 Avenue SW.

WHEN A CHINOOK WIND blows through Calgary, it's hard not to think of spring, even in the middle of January. I've never subscribed to the theory that winter is the cocooning season, a time to huddle inside the house, read books and pine miserably for warmer weather. Like most outdoor enthusiasts in the Calgary region, I believe winter is just another opportunity to get outside and have fun. Picnicking is one way to do that.

A picnic in winter can be enjoyed in several different ways. It can be the main reason for the outing, which also may include some hiking or bird-watching. It can be a fine excuse for a relaxing drive. Or it can be part of a getaway to snowshoe, ski, skate or toboggan. The meal itself might range from wieners roasted over a bonfire (take your own firewood where allowed) to premade sandwiches to full-course meals prepared on a portable gas stove.

Usually the food is secondary to the novelty of the outing and the chance to enjoy a different kind of interaction with family and friends. But the ultimate objective is keeping winter picnics fun, which means planning carefully and choosing the right day to head out. Eating outside during the coldest season is more enjoyable if you go during a Chinook, when temperatures can reach well into double digits. Remember your camera. You'll want to send proof of your hardy (some would say foolhardy) adventure to cabin-bound friends and family members. Firewood is available at many venues, but it's a good idea to bring some dry wood from home.

Snowshoeing or skiing can provide the opportunity to picnic far from roads. You might find an old fallen log on which to sit or a remote picnic table. Or you may take a light waterproof tarp to place on top of the snow. A brightly checkered tarp really enhances the atmosphere.

For the first of what would become dozens of winter picnics, our family traveled to a pretty spot beside the Highwood River in Kananaskis Country. We sat at a picnic table beside a roaring fire, savoring lunch and the Christmas-cardlike setting. Our dog dried off from a chilly dip in the river. No phones rang. There were no unwanted distractions. On summer weekends, the area would have been hopping with people. On that January day, we basked in solitude. And swatted no bugs.

Chapter 3

Day-Trip Destinations

Great Escapes Within Forty-Five
Minutes of Calgary

I F YOU CRAVE an out-of-town trip, but don't have all day, read on. Featured here are the Magnificent Seven—seven of the best places to enjoy nature within a 45-minute drive of Calgary. All you have to do is pack a picnic lunch and binoculars, and head out. You'll be back home, refreshed and relaxed, a few hours later.

Big Hill Springs Provincial Park is a little-known natural nugget northeast of Cochrane. With one phone call, you can arrange a visit to the Ann and Sandy Cross Conservation Area, a ranching couple's generous gift to Albertans just outside Calgary's south city limits.

Birdwatchers can head southeast of the city to Frank Lake Conservation Area, an amazing story of wetlands resurrection. To the west, Ghost Lake offers a great place for a boat ride, picnic or fishing trip against a spectacular Rocky Mountain backdrop.

Heading into the foothills southwest of Calgary, the hidden Brown Lowery Provincial Park provides a scenic and peaceful respite.

To the east, the Bow River offers some of the world's best trout fishing, bird-watching and quiet canoeing. Boaters should plan for a longer outing because of the shortage of public take-out spots for water crafts.

And, finally, Wyndham–Carseland Provincial Park southeast of Calgary is a great place to fish, view American white pelicans and other birds or just enjoy a picnic.

Big Hill Springs Provincial Park

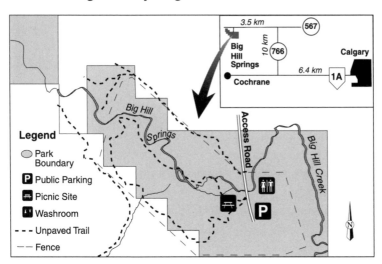

Access: West from Calgary on Highway 1A for 6.4 km (4 mi) to Secondary Highway 766, north for 10 km (6.2 mi) to Secondary Highway 567, then west for 3.5 km (2.2 mi) to the turnoff to the park.

Terrain: Rolling hills, rocky outcrops, trembling aspen and spruce woodlands, dogwood, willow, fescue grass on plateau uplands.

Activities: Hiking, picnicking (take your own firewood), wildlife watching.

Hours: Open 7:00 A.M. to 11:00 P.M.

Contact: 403 297-5293.

BIG HILL SPRINGS PROVINCIAL PARK is a hidden pocket of wilderness right in the middle of Canada's richest ranching country. Much of the surrounding land has been cut into country subdivisions. Houses verging on mansions perch on every hilltop. The mountain view costs extra. At 26 ha (64 acres), Big Hill Springs isn't a huge park. But what it provides is significant: a close peaceful respite to residents of country acreages, ranches, the town of Cochrane and the city of Calgary only 30 minutes away.

Signs along the interpretive trail tell the story of an area with a long history of human use. More than 12,000 years ago, torrents of glacial meltwater cut through the valley. An underground stream was exposed and became what is now known as Big Hill Springs Creek. Prehistoric natives used the site as a buffalo jump, stampeding the animals over a cliff to their deaths.

In 1881 the land became part of a massive grazing lease operated by area ranchers. Ten years later D.M. Radcliffe opened Alberta's first commercial dairy on the site. The creek powered the waterwheel that ran the churn. Its water cooled the butter and cream. A later owner known only as Mr. Brealey produced 23 kg (50 lb) of butter daily. The .5-kg (1-lb) blocks were wrapped in silk paper and sent by train to Vancouver. The site was known for several years as Brealey Springs.

The provincial government became involved in the area in the early 1950s. Drawn by the creek's trout-producing potential, the province built its first fish hatchery there. A dismal failure, the hatchery closed around 1956. Only its concrete foundations remain today. The land became Big Hill Springs Provincial Park in 1957.

Today the park provides important habitat for more than 60 bird species, including the slate-colored American dipper. Attentive hikers might spot this delightful wren-sized bird on the creek bank, head bobbing up and down before it slips into the water in search of tasty insects and small fish. The park also is home to mink, coyotes, Richardson's ground squirrels, pocket gophers, white-tailed and mule deer and nonpoisonous garter snakes. Stay alert if you hope to spot wildlife.

A total of 204 flowering plants have been reported here, including honeysuckle, creeping juniper, goldenrod and seven species of aster. A complete plant checklist for the park can be picked up at Fish Creek Provincial Park headquarters in Calgary. Big Hill Springs Park is particularly inviting in autumn, when aspens, dogwood and willows transform into a blaze of reds, yellows and browns.

The 1-km (.6-mi) interpretive trail follows the coulee and creek, which is braided in several locations. Its character ranges from short plunge pools to a trickle less than 1 m (3.3') wide. The trail rises gradually until it reaches a dead end at a four-strand barbed-wire fence.

The mud on either side of the fence is pocked with hoofprints of deer that have jumped the wire.

You will easily see where the trail veers to the left at a car-sized boulder that has been badly defaced with visitors' names and graffiti. After a few minutes, you reach a welcome bench on which to rest and take in the panoramic view to the northeast. From there, the trail winds past trembling aspen and cow parsnip as it drops gently back down to the parking lot.

Ann and Sandy Cross Conservation Area

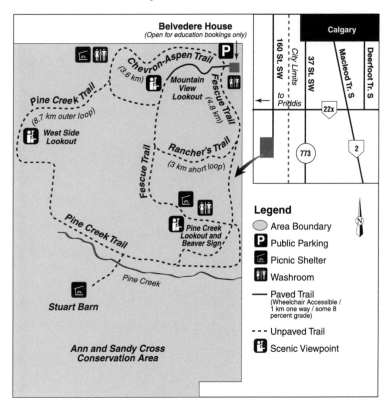

Access: West on Highway 22X. Pass Red Deer Lake School, then take first turn south at 160 Street SW after city limits sign.

Terrain: Rolling foothills, sandstone outcrops, aspen forest, native fescue grassland.

Activities: Hiking (one trail wheelchair accessible), wildlife watching, cross-country skiing (with permission), natural history educational programs.

Prohibited: Dogs, horses, bicycles, campfires, smoking, hunting, discharging firearms, picking flowers and plants.

Hours: Open 4:00 A.M. to 11:00 P.M.

Contact: 403 931-2042 at least one day in advance of planned visit.

SANDY CROSS simply calls it "the land." But when he gazes out across the rolling hills, fields of grass waving in the breeze and thick stands of forest, Cross's eyes speak of a love that goes far beyond soil and vegetation. The land is the rancher's life—and his legacy.

The legacy here is the Ann and Sandy Cross Conservation Area, encompassing 1,943 ha (4,800 acres) just five minutes from Calgary's southwest limits. The couple has given Albertans the property to use as a living classroom to help them learn about nature firsthand. They stipulated that the land be preserved in its natural state forever. Their generosity has resulted in a unique and exciting project.

"Here we have a story of vision and a great deal of generosity," says Mike Waites, former president of the Sandy Cross Conservation Foundation. "This is a truly great treasure."

Waites uttered those words at a ceremony in the fall of 1996 when Ann and Sandy Cross officially donated another 1,133 ha (2,800 acres) to the project. The couple initially gave 809 ha (2,000 acres) in 1987. Total market value of the contributed land approached $11 million. The Crosses also donated more than $1 million in cash. For rancher Cross, 72 years old when he made the initial gift in 1987, the project isn't about money. It's about the future.

A longtime bachelor before he married Ann in 1974, Sandy Cross has roots firmly planted in Alberta history books. He's the last survivor of seven children of Helen Rothney Macleod, eldest daughter of Colonel James Macleod, commissioner of the North-West Mounted Police, and A.E. Cross, rancher, brewer, legislator and one of the Big Four who bankrolled the first Calgary Stampede in 1912.

The idea for the conservation area sprouted when Sandy Cross worried about what would happen to his precious Rothney Farm property when he was gone. He'd started the farm in 1946 by buying two sections at $30 an acre ($19,200 per section). The property eventually grew to nine sections. In the 1970s and early 1980s Cross watched with alarm as much of the land around him was subdivided and sold as country residential properties. He was determined that wouldn't happen to Rothney Farm. But with the city of Calgary

Rancher Sandy Cross at the Ann and Sandy Cross Conservation Area.

encroaching more and more on the countryside, it seemed there would be no stopping it. From the property, you can view a 600-km (373-mi) span of the Rocky Mountains, then look to the northeast and see Calgary's downtown office towers and sprawling residential tentacles reaching far to the south.

Cross respects the wildlife—including elk, moose, deer, cougar, black bear, coyotes, beaver, porcupine, mountain bluebirds, red-tailed hawks and great horned owls—which live on the land. He wanted the property kept intact so wildlife would continue to thrive. Cross also wanted to leave the area untouched for future generations of Albertans, so they could study wildlife and ecology.

The solution came when the Nature Conservancy of Canada, a nonprofit land acquisition agency that specializes in relatively undisturbed habitat, agreed to manage the initial land gift. It was the largest donation of private land ever made in Canada. The conservancy also started an educational program and raised money to operate the facility. A $2 million operating endowment fund was created with donations by corporations and individuals. The conservancy ran the area for nine years. It turned over the reins in 1996 to the new conservation foundation when the additional land was donated. The Crosses retained only about 364 ha (900 acres) of the original nine sections.

Key to the project's operation are 20 km (12.4 mi) of interpretive hiking trails and Belvedere House, an educational center built by corporate donations. Called the Chevron Cross Conservation School, the educational program was underwritten by Calgary-based Chevron Canada Resources and the Crosses. More than 20,000 youths from Calgary and area have participated in ecology-based educational programs.

The user-friendly, compelling educational program starts inside Belvedere House, a low-level cedar building surrounded by wild flowers and other native vegetation. Kids get a crash course on plants, flowers, trees, birds and animals common to the area. They can study life-sized wooden cutouts of moose, elk and deer. Hands-on displays show how to identify them in the wild. Responsible use is the central theme.

Education continues outside by trained dedicated volunteers who lead visitors on hikes. Interpretive signs and hike leaders explain nature's delicate balancing act and the relationship between wildlife and habitat. Also offered is an extensive continuing education program for adults and families. Course subjects include animal tracks and signs, bird and wildflower identification and nature photography. Jacquie Gilson, area manager, says the conservation school uses hands-on experience and nature games to illustrate what wildlife and vegetation need to remain healthy. "You can't protect what you don't understand or appreciate," she says. Many city children raised on shopping malls and video games have never seen a hawk or hiked through a forest until they visit the conservation area. Inside Belvedere House, a wall is plastered with kids' letters of appreciation written in pencil, ink, crayon and colored marker.

Among Sandy Cross's original stipulations was the requirement that access to the property would be closely controlled to prevent damage from overuse and vandalism. You are asked to phone to book a visit at least one day in advance. Manager Gilson says having to arrange a visit helps people look at the area as unique and worth saving.

No problem there. It is unique. Even better, its future is secure.

Ghost Lake

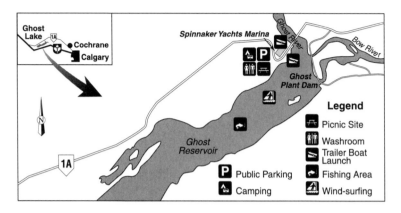

Access: West to Cochrane on Highway 1A or the Trans-Canada Highway, then west on Highway 1A for 18 km (11.1 mi).

Terrain: Mainly flat and exposed, poplars in campground. Ghost River flows into Ghost Lake, created by the dam on the Bow River.

Activities: Picnicking, camping, four-season fishing, water-skiing, canoeing, kayaking, wind-surfing, sailing, iceboating.

Hours: No set hours.

Contact: Spinnaker Yachts Ltd., operator of Ghost Lake Marine Park, at 403 932-6051.

To many Calgarians, Ghost Lake remains as mysterious as its name. Busy on weekends with boaters and anglers, the lake and recreation area are only lightly used on weekdays. Mike Weinert, co-manager of Spinnaker Yachts Ltd., calls Ghost Lake one of the best kept secrets around. Many people just don't know it's here. Many campers heading out on weekends don't even give the place a look as they pass by on their way to the mountains.

Weinert's family took over operation of the 20-ha (50-acre) recreation area in 1995 in a provincial government privatization program. It's resulted in a cleaner, better-managed area, complete with boat rentals and a store. With on-site managers policing and with help from the RCMP and Fish and Wildlife officers, the recreation area has been transformed from a popular party place into a great family destination.

Most of the shoreline outside the campground and recreation area is owned by the Stoney Indians. The reservoir, 14 km (8.7 mi) long and 2 km (1.2 mi) wide, is an impoundment of the Bow River. It was created in 1929 by Calgary Power Ltd. (since renamed TransAlta Utilities Corporation) to generate hydroelectric power. The Ghost River flows into the reservoir's northeast corner. The Ghost River was called Dead Man River as early as 1860. The name change recalls tales of a ghost prowling the valley, picking up skulls of Blackfoot Indians killed in battle by the Cree.

One of the largest modern-day mysteries surrounding the lake involves not ghosts, but fish. A popular fishing destination, Ghost Lake offers lake trout and other species that are elusive to many anglers, especially those who haven't fished it before. Calgary angler Darcy Thompson says Ghost Lake is hard to fish. Some days anglers will go home empty-handed. "But it's still my favorite spot to fish," says Thompson, who focuses his efforts on big lake and brown trout. He prefers trolling with diving Rapala-like plugs, preferably with an orange flank. Nothing else works as well, he says. Jim Stelfox, a provincial fisheries biologist, says Ghost Lake's lake trout grow fat on juvenile suckers. They're generally bigger than lakers caught at Spray Lakes Reservoir south of Canmore. Even the lake whitefish grow big at Ghost Lake. Whitefish weighing up to 4.5 kg (10 lb) were netted during a government test-netting project in 1988.

One February morning I was ice fishing at Ghost Lake when I spied a curious sight. Farther out on the lake, an ice fisher was sitting in a lawn chair, reading the latest edition of *Reader's Digest*. A fake fur-lined hood on his heavy parka shielded his face from the fierce wind. I slipped and skidded over the bare ice and met Al Crawford, then 63. He didn't care that the wind threatened to rip the dog-eared *Digest* from his mitten-encased hands or that there wasn't much activity at the three holes he'd bored in the thick ice. "This is the only way to fish," he grinned. "If you have a good book, you're set for the day—even if the fish don't bite."

Several years before, Crawford and his partners had a landmark day on the Ghost. They landed two 3.1-kg (7-lb) lake trout, another of 10.4 kg (23 lb) and a fourth one that weighed in at 11.3 kg (25 lb). Now Crawford considers himself lucky to catch one laker a day.

If the lake trout fishing is unpredictable, the wind certainly isn't. It's a rare day when the wind doesn't blast off the Rocky Mountains and sweep eastward across the reservoir. Crawford is used to the wind. He's learned a few tricks, such as anchoring his lawn chair to the ice with his ice auger. People who've had to chase a wind-pushed lawn chair down the ice for more than 1 km (.6 mi) tend to get a little innovative. Anglers willing to put up with a little wind, however, might just be rewarded with a lunker.

The lake's natural imitation of a wind tunnel may be a curse to anglers and boaters, but it's a blessing to wind surfers and sailors. On most weekends between spring and fall, the lake's surface is alive with dozens of brightly colored sails. And when the water freezes, it doesn't take long for iceboaters to move in, skidding over the smooth, clear ice at speeds that aren't for the weak of heart. Iceboaters should exercise caution. Raised bumps in the ice and runaway lawn chairs could prove hazardous.

Brown Lowery Provincial Park

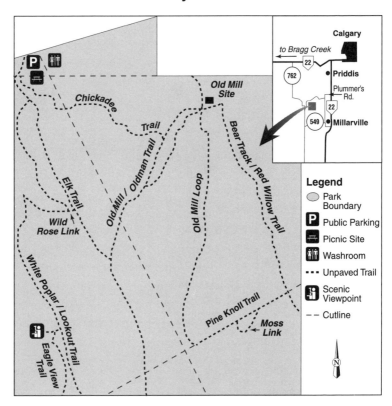

Access: From Highway 2 interchange south of Calgary west on Highway 22X for 16.8 km (10.4 mi), south on Highway 22 for 6.5 km (4 mi) to Plummer's Road, follow road west 3.2 km (2 mi) to T-intersection, then left for 8.4 km (5.2 mi). Parking on left side of road.

Terrain: Rolling hills, poplar, white spruce and lodge pine forest, cutlines, old sawmill buildings.

Activities: Hiking, picnicking, wildlife watching, horseback riding, cross-country skiing, snowshoeing.

Hours: No set hours.

Contact: 403 297-5293.

IT'S HARD TO BELIEVE this special place is just 25 km (15.5 mi) from Calgary's southwest limits. It's even harder to believe that this 281-ha (695-acre) provincial park is so difficult to find. "The area is kind of a hidden secret," says Wayne Meikle, whose chief park ranger duties at Fish Creek Provincial Park also take in Brown Lowery. Meikle doesn't jest. This park is so well hidden it would be impossible to find if you didn't know it was here.

Along the route west on Highway 22X from Calgary, then south on Highway 22, no road signs point to a provincial park anywhere in the area. Almost 12 km (7.5 mi) along Plummer's Road, the one and only location sign marks a parking lot with outhouses and garbage containers on the left side of the road. Inattentive drivers could miss the small sheet of plywood featuring a silly caricature of a great horned owl wearing a ranger's Stetson and blue uniform coat. The owl says, "Welcome to Brown Lowery Provincial Park."

Once you find this special place, however, you are in for a pleasant surprise. Designated a provincial park in 1992, it features 11 km (6.8 mi) of hiking trails winding through a forest of white spruce, poplar and lodgepole pine. Trails are lined with Indian paintbrush and other wild flowers, while ferns, mosses and mushrooms thrive in the undergrowth. Naturalists have counted more than 260 different plants in the area. Trail names reflect the area's natural highlights: Chickadee, Wildrose, Red Willow, Pine Hill and Crocus Loop. The Old Mill Loop is a reminder that the area was logged many decades ago. Today the old mill, for which the trail is named, is nothing more than a pile of weathered lumber. With numerous seismic lines bisecting the land, you should keep track of where you are to avoid getting lost.

The trails are natural single tracks. They are easy to follow for hikers of all ages, but protruding roots and blowdowns require your full attention if you do not wish to take a fall. Cloven-hoofed tracks in the mud tell of the year-round presence of white-tailed and mule deer, elk and moose. If you're lucky you might even spy the tracks of cougar, black bear, Canada lynx and coyotes. The park is home to smaller mammals, too, such as red squirrels, snowshoe hares, porcupines and striped skunks.

The trail system features several wooden bridges spanning low wet areas. Detailed maps are displayed at strategically located signposts. Most trails are easy strolls, suitable for all ages but not recommended for wheeled baby strollers. The only route that could be considered even moderately demanding also happens to offer the nicest view. The Lookout Trail, which requires some effort as it ascends a ridge, runs about 2.5 km (1.6 mi) to the two Eagleview viewpoints.

From the first bench you have a stunning view of heavily treed hills, luxurious acreage homes and downtown Calgary. A second bench located 50 m (164') to the south offers a spectacular panorama of classic Alberta ranching country set against a backdrop of foothills and jagged-edged Rocky Mountains. These viewpoints make excellent picnic stops and places to relax and forget the city, even though it's within spitting distance. Remember to pack out all garbage.

Although it wasn't designated a provincial park until 1992, the Brown Lowery area has been public land since 1969. That's when it was donated by Home Oil Company Limited in memory of founders Robert Brown Sr. and Major James Robert Lowery. Both men were pioneers in Alberta's energy industry and major players in early development of the Turner Valley oilfield. Brown, considered the father of the Alberta oil industry, logged numerous successful ventures in the Turner Valley oilfield dating back to 1914. He amalgamated his interests into Federated Petroleums in 1940. Lowery founded Home Oil in 1925 and completed his first successful well in 1928. The two companies merged in 1951. D.E. Powell, then Home Oil's president and chief executive officer, issued a press release when the area became a provincial park. He wrote, "Home Oil trusts that Brown Lowery Provincial Park will be enjoyed by all who tread these paths and serve as a reminder of the oilmen who helped build this province."

The park received another boost in 1992. Grades 7 and 8 students from C. Ian McLaren School in Black Diamond worked voluntarily with Fish Creek park staff for three months improving trails, measuring distances and repairing bridges that had fallen into disrepair. They also mapped out trails and developed field guides. "Many students have referred to it as their area," teacher Karen Hanna said at the time.

That sense of belonging also holds for many local residents who consider the park a personal preserve. It provides a convenient haven to escape to for a few minutes or several hours. Midweek, during the day, is the best time to visit. There's a good chance of having the entire area to yourself. Summer weekends can be busy, but on winter weekends only a few cross-country skiers and snowshoers use the area.

Yes, it's hard to find. Maybe that's part of this park's appeal. But there's no question this natural legacy is worth the search.

Frank Lake Conservation Area

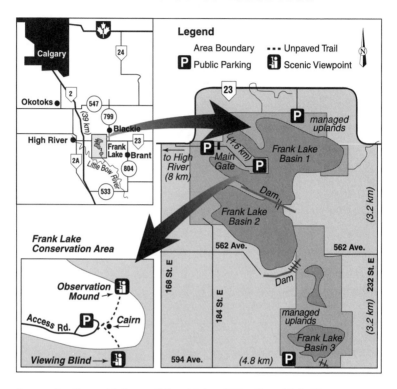

Access: South on Highway 2 for 40 km (25 mi) to High River, east on Highway 23 for 5 km (3.1 mi), then right on the access road for 1.3 km (.8 mi) to the main gate.

Terrain: Native prairie, wetlands, willows, cattails, bulrushes, seeded native grasslands.

Activities: Hiking, wildlife watching, hunting.

Hours: Main gate open during the summer 9:30 A.M. and 5:30 P.M. After hours, walk or cycle 2 km (1.2 mi) in from the main gate.

Contact: For general information, Ducks Unlimited Canada in Strathmore at 403 934-3102. For inquiries about guided tours, High River Chamber of Commerce at 403 652-3336.

FRANK LAKE CONSERVATION AREA is a 1,902-ha (4,700-acre) rejuvenated wetlands east of High River. It's become an increasingly popular outing for naturalists, students and families from Calgary and outlying towns. Hunters frequent the area in autumn as thousands of ducks and geese stop at the lake while migrating south. It's considered the most important wetlands in southwestern Alberta.

Amazingly, Frank Lake dried up between 1983 and 1989, after 50 years of fluctuating water levels. Then it was revived in a unique $9 million project managed in part by Ducks Unlimited Canada, which kicked in a cool $1 million. Starting in 1990, the lake has been kept full of water via a 12-km (8-mi) pipeline carrying treated sewage effluent from the town of High River and Cargill Foods Ltd. meatpacking plant, just north of High River. The water covers almost 1,255 ha (3,100 acres), surrounded by 688 ha (1,700 acres) of adjacent upland habitat.

Nutrients in the effluent promote growth of cattails, bulrushes, reeds and other aquatic plants, which help purify the water and provide needed cover and food for dozens of species of birds and animals. A total of 190 plant species, 2 amphibian species, 194 bird species and 16 mammal species—including white-tailed deer and coyotes—have been found in the area. Unusual birds include sharp-tailed sandpipers, curlew sandpipers, red-necked stilt, white-faced ibises and black-necked stilts. Frequent visits are made by piping plovers, burrowing owls, peregrine falcons, loggerhead shrikes, ferruginous hawks, bald eagles and white pelicans. Common ducks include mallards, ruddy ducks, and cinnamon and blue-winged teal.

Bird watchers frequent the viewing blind at the north end of the lake. A boardwalk extends out over the water. A viewing mound allows a closer look at birds in the main basin, but bring your binoculars, spotting scope and bird identification guide. Stay on trails, boardwalks and supplied viewing areas. Dogs should be kept on leash in springtime so they don't disturb nesting waterfowl along the water and in the adjoining uplands.

Part of Frank Lake's restoration project included providing homes or habitats for many kinds of wildlife. Nesting platforms were

George Freeman of Ducks Unlimited Canada talks to school kids at Frank Lake Conservation Area.

erected for hawks and Canada geese. Rock piles were set up for garter snakes. Mountain bluebird houses were installed on surrounding fence posts. A bat house is attached to the observation building provided by Cargill. Two gravel-lined pits for frogs, toads and salamanders are in front of the building.

As a living wetlands classroom, Frank Lake couldn't be better. Along the lake's reedy shores, students can catch and release freshwater shrimp, mayfly nymphs, dragonfly nymphs, water boatmen and other bugs which are a critical part of the birds' diet.

Bird watchers—especially those opposed to hunting—might choose to avoid Frank Lake Mondays through Saturdays during hunting season, which runs from early September to late December. Hunting isn't permitted on Sundays in Southern Alberta.

Despite some opposition, however, many outdoor enthusiasts would be more surprised if regulated hunting weren't permitted there. After all, hunting is a legal activity and an accepted wildlife management tool. Project manager Ducks Unlimited is a strong supporter of responsible hunting. With hunting allowed only three months annually, bird watchers can visit Frank Lake without being exposed to hunting for the other nine months. They also can go there on Sundays during autumn.

Wyndham–Carseland Provincial Park

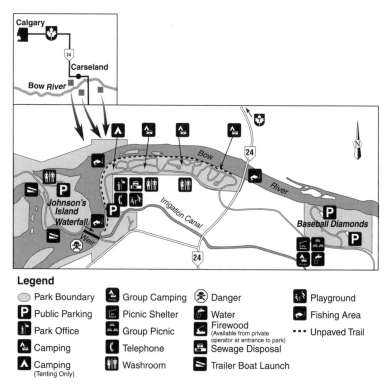

Legend

Park Boundary	Group Camping	Danger	Playground
Public Parking	Picnic Shelter	Water	Fishing Area
Park Office	Group Picnic	Firewood (Available from private operator at entrance to park)	Unpaved Trail
Camping	Telephone	Sewage Disposal	
Camping (Tenting Only)	Washroom	Trailer Boat Launch	

Access: East on Trans-Canada Highway for 30 km (18.6 mi), then south on Highway 24 for 32 km (20 mi).

Terrain: River valley, balsam poplars, cottonwoods, wolf willow, alder, buffalo berries, saskatoons.

Activities: Hiking, picnicking, camping, fishing, wildlife watching.

Hours: Day-use areas open 7:00 A.M. to 11:00 P.M. Quiet hours in campground from 11:00 P.M. to 7:00 A.M.

Contact: 403 934-3523.

WANT TO IMPRESS FRIENDS or relatives who've never seen an American white pelican? Take them to this scenic 180-ha (445-acre) park straddling the Bow River south of Carseland. It's paradise for pelicans and other fish-eating birds such as belted kingfishers and great blue herons.

The park is named after the closest town and a farmer named Wyndham, who at one time owned the land on which the park sits. In the 1920s, the campground became a popular local camping area. It was run by the local municipality and area residents before the Alberta government took it over as a park more than 50 years later, in 1975.

Year-round wildlife in the park includes mule and white-tailed deer, beavers and muskrats. More than 120 bird species have been reported here. Ferruginous, red-tailed and Swainson's hawks, and smaller prairie falcons regularly coast in the air space above the park. Bald and golden eagles are seen during spring and autumn migrations.

Visitor action picks up in the park in early spring and continues until Thanksgiving. Wyndham–Carseland's campground usually is dry and suitable for camping when the campgrounds west of Calgary are still snow-covered or very wet. Most years the park is busier in May (when campers are eager to go somewhere) than in July and August. It's also heavily used in autumn after snow and lower temperatures have chased most campers out of the mountains.

The busy season is explained, in part, by the park's 197 campsites. The best sites are tucked into the willows and poplars along the Bow River. Many Calgarians are drawn by the park's serenity and natural beauty. A ranger once told me some people like it because there's virtually no chance of seeing a bear.

Wyndham–Carseland's day-use area also is popular for family picnics. Bring your own firewood from home, or buy a bundle from the store at the park's main entrance. Two well-equipped playgrounds provide a welcome diversion for kids after a leisurely stroll along a scenic 2.5-km (1.6-mi) hiking trail flanking the terraced south side of the river. A reservations-only group camp and picnic area, plus baseball diamonds, are located on park property east of Highway 24. Vehicle access to the privately operated park is restricted during late fall and winter. However, visitors can still use the day-use sites during those times if they're prepared to walk more than 1 km (.6 mi) from the parking lot.

Located near the steeper north bank along the Bow River, Johnson's Island is home to birds, and mule and white-tailed deer. It's also a haven for bird watchers and for anglers eager to hook into the Bow River's world-famous brown and rainbow trout. It's one of several islands causing the river to braid into bayou-type side channels, which are perfect habitats for small wildlife and fish. The island has two public boat launches, but make sure you stay clear of the deadly weir spanning the river on the island's east side. The weir diverts water from the Bow into an irrigation canal flowing 32 km (20 mi) into Lake McGregor. Johnson's Island is accessible by vehicle year-round. Outhouses and picnic tables are provided.

Wyndham–Carseland is an ideal place to sneak away for a couple of hours or several days of rest and relaxation. If you arrive mid-week during fall or winter, there's a good chance you'll have it all to yourself. If you really want to be humbled, plan a trip during summer, when pelicans with 2.7-m (9') wingspans rule the river.

The Middle Bow River

Access: Foot access at Fish Creek Provincial Park, Policeman's Flats, McKinnon Flats, Highwood River confluence, Janzen's south of Highway 22X west of Carseland, upstream of Carseland Weir and in Wyndham–Carseland Provincial Park. Public boat launches at Fish Creek, Policeman's Flats, McKinnon Flats and Johnson's Island near Carseland.

Terrain: Steep river valley, cottonwoods, balsams, spruce, willow, grasslands.

Activities: Fishing, canoeing, kayaking, boating, wildlife watching.

Hours: No set hours.

Contact: Alberta Fish and Wildlife Division at 403 297-6423. Bow River Basin Water Council at 403 297-6476.

THE WORLD-RENOWNED Bow does something special to people. It doesn't make any difference if you've been there once or dozens of times. It's impossible to shake the feeling. Each year, more and more Calgarians are getting that feeling on the middle Bow River, a 55-km (34-mi) stretch between the city and the Carseland Weir. Many anglers drift in oar-powered, square-ended Jon boats or deep banana-shaped drift boats with raised seats from which to cast. Although anglers have frequented this scenic stretch for years— drawn by up to 2,000 rainbow and brown trout per 1.6 km (1 mi)— it's attracting a growing number of people who would just as soon watch birds or take pictures as fish. They float the river in canoes, kayaks and cartop aluminum boats.

This stretch of river has generated a busy outfitting industry. Guides charge up to $500 per day, including lunch, tackle and transportation. Some guides, are beginning to offer trips for people who just want to see the sights. Guides may be contacted through local fishing shops listed in Calgary's Yellow Pages.

The middle Bow River doesn't resemble the upper Bow River, which begins at Bow Lake in Banff National Park. The upper Bow tumbles eastward through the Rocky Mountains and rushes into

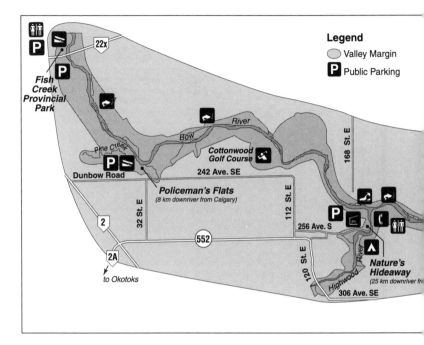

Calgary. A network of dams and weirs slows the river outside Calgary, transforming it into a more tranquil prairie river before it joins the Oldman River south of Brooks.

The generally gentle current during summer and fall (after runoff ends) makes the Bow highly user-friendly. Negotiating the river during low-flow periods is relatively simple if you're skilled with a paddle or oar. On the International Scale of River Difficulty this stretch is rated at the lowest (easiest) level. However, for several weeks during spring runoff, extra caution is required because the river flows fast, high and dirty. Hazards to watch for include bridge pillars, exposed rocks and trees that have fallen into side channels. The law requires the use of life jackets.

Hazards are not the only factors to consider when planning a trip down the middle Bow. There is, for example, a shortage of public access sites between Calgary and Carseland. It's dangerous to try to cover too much water in one day, so schedule some stops along the way. Keep in mind that land along the river, except at major takeout

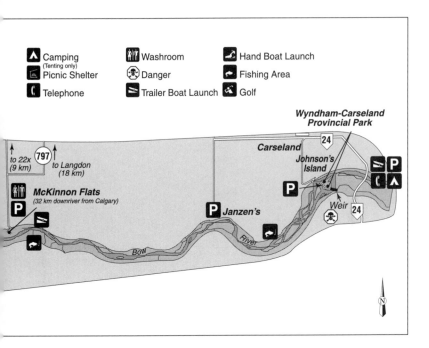

Camping (Tenting only)
Picnic Shelter
Telephone
Washroom
Danger
Trailer Boat Launch
Hand Boat Launch
Fishing Area
Golf

Wyndham-Carseland Provincial Park

Carseland

Johnson's Island

McKinnon Flats *(32 km downriver from Calgary)*

to 22x (9 km)   **797**   *to Langdon (18 km)*

Janzen's

Weir   24   24

Bow   *River*

N

points, is privately owned. You cannot set up camp, have a picnic or otherwise use shoreline property without permission. Stopping on islands generally avoids hassles, but privately owned islands should be avoided. You'll have to arrange for a friend, family member or shuttle company to have a vehicle waiting for you at the boat launch take-out spot. A handy Bow River map published by Trout Unlimited Canada is available for five dollars from local fishing shops. It shows the locations of all major boat launches and public access sites.

Local canoe clubs can help plan trips, too. Essentials include a dry change of clothes, a life jacket, a picnic lunch and lots of water. Taking a dunking or getting caught in a sudden severe rainstorm could lead to hypothermia if you aren't prepared, and the river water isn't safe to drink.

If you plan to fish, you should be aware of special fishing regulations before heading out. The daily limit is two trout smaller than 40 cm (15.5"). Bull trout must be released year-round, and all trout must be released in April and May. Bait is prohibited.

Fly-fishing for trout on the Bow River downstream of Calgary.

With public use increasing there's added potential for user conflicts. Jet boats used for fishing and sightseeing have infuriated other users in recent years. Some are so concerned about jet boats' noise and heavy wake that they've called for a ban similar to the powerboat prohibition on the Bow in Calgary. However, common courtesy can help minimize problems. Approaching boats should pass on the far side of the river rather than motor through shore-bound anglers' fishing areas or get too close to other boats.

Regardless of the purpose of your trip, don't forget a camera and binoculars. On an average day's float, you may see mule and white-tailed deer, beavers, waterfowl, mink, American white pelicans and bald eagles. Aside from the pleasure of these natural sights, you'll notice the noise or, more accurately, the absence of it. Except for the occasional buzzing jet boat or irrigation pump sucking water from the river, the most common sound is the gentle flow of the water punctuated by rapids rushing over rocks and the shriek of a red-tailed hawk circling overhead. It's a soundtrack made in heaven.

Chapter 4

Weekend Destinations

Great Escapes within
Three Hours of Calgary

WEEKDAYS ARE FOR DREAMING. Weekends and holidays are for making those dreams come true. The eight places featured in this chapter truly are the stuff of dreams. They are places that will make your heart quicken and your soul soar. They'll also threaten to put your film budget through the roof.

This diverse mix of destinations includes two parks anchoring opposing corners of Southern Alberta: Waterton Lakes National Park, which some people suggest is what Banff National Park was like before it was before it became developed and crowded, and Cypress Hills Provincial Park, Canada's highest point of land between the Rocky Mountains and Labrador, and an area steeped in history. Also featured is Head-Smashed-In Buffalo Jump, rich in aboriginal tradition and mysticism. Don't forget to pack your imagination for a visit here.

Writing-on-Stone Provincial Park is studded with sandstone hoodoos and boasts the largest concentration of native rock art on the North American Plains.

The best-known destination in the Drumheller badlands is the Royal Tyrrell Museum of Palaeontology. But you'll need more than a day to do justice to the museum and the circle tour—complete with a ferry ride over the Red Deer River—described here. The same goes for Dinosaur Provincial Park, where archaeologists are still unearthing the remains of prehistoric creatures. You shouldn't rush a visit to a place that took 75 million years to create.

Contrasting the arid starkness of the badlands are Kinbrook Island Provincial Park, a wildlife-rich oasis next to Alberta's largest man-made lake, and Chain Lakes Provincial Park, a trout-stocked irrigation reservoir nestled in the foothills of the Rockies.

Plan to spend a couple of days in any of these locations, maybe in a campground or local motel. The first day can be for traveling, getting settled and doing a quick reconnaissance of the area. The second day can be for really getting acquainted. Rest assured the trip will be well worth the effort.

Head-Smashed-In Buffalo Jump

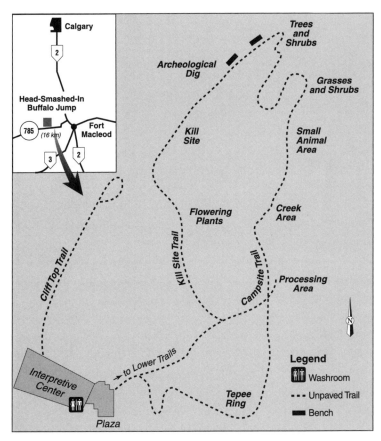

Access: South on Highway 2 for 145 km (90 mi), then follow signs west on Secondary Highway 785 for 16 km (10 mi).

Terrain: Prairie, sandstone cliffs, more than 80 species of trees, shrubs and flowers.

Activities: Hiking, wildlife watching, wheelchair accessible.

Hours: May 15 to Labor Day Monday open 9:00 A.M. to 7:00 P.M. Remainder of year open 9:00 A.M. to 5:00 P.M.

Cost: $6.50 for adults and seniors, $3.00 for ages 7–17, free for ages six and under, $15 family rate. Group rates available.

Contact: 403 553-2731.

IMAGINE HEARING the thunder of the hooves. Hundreds of stampeding bellowing buffalo are being driven by whooping and waving hunters dressed in animal skins. The shaggy horned beasts, nostrils flaring and thick tongues lolling, gallop in choking clouds of dust, herded along a deadly path lined with rock cairns. Too late they realize they're heading toward a cliff. But there's no turning back. One by one they plunge over, landing broken and bleeding on the rocks below. Hunters converge at the bottom of the cliff, throwing sticks, spears and arrows to finish off the beasts. Women and children arrive to skin the carcasses and cut the meat. The buffalo will feed the tribe and provide hides for clothing and tepees.

Today, during a visit to Head-Smashed-In Buffalo Jump, you can stand on a railed-off platform to view the panoramic prairie scene and 15-m (49') -high sandstone cliffs that brought death—and life—for 5,700 years. No buffalo can be seen unless you have a vivid imagination. A jet-black raven guards the cliffs. A cat-sized yellow-bellied marmot warily eyes visitors.

"That's an Indian gopher," quips interpretive guide Leo Bernard Pard. Pard is a full-blooded Blackfoot from the Peigan reserve at nearby Brockett. He was born in 1939 on a ranch along the Oldman River. Every day Pard sees his birthplace from the cliffs of the buffalo jump. As a child Pard used to sit spellbound for hours listening to elders tell how the buffalo jump sustained their ancestors until rifle-toting Europeans arrived and almost wiped out the herds with indiscriminate killing. Many stories came from Pard's paternal grandfather, Running Amongst the Buffalo. Now Pard is a Blackfoot elder who tells stories about the site to many of the 120,000 people who visit annually.

Head-Smashed-In Buffalo Jump was named 150 years ago when, according to legend, an unfortunate Indian youth decided to stand under the shelter of a ledge below the cliff as dead and injured buffalo piled up below him. The hunt was so successful that the mound of buffalo eventually reached the youth, pinned him to the rock face and crushed his head.

Interpretive guide Leo Bernard Pard on the cliff at Head-Smashed-In Buffalo Jump.

Representative of many jumps used by Plains Indians for more than 10,000 years in North America, Head-Smashed-In is one of the largest and best preserved. It's believed that about 150,000 buffalo died here. At least four major archaeological digs have been conducted. Dr. Junius Bird of the American Museum of Natural History oversaw the first excavation of the kill site in 1938. The site was heavily picked over by souvenir hunters before its designation as a provincial historic site in 1979 stopped unauthorized digging.

In 1981 the United Nations Educational, Scientific and Cultural Organization named it a World Heritage Site. The designation gave the site the same protected status as the Egyptian Pyramids and Arizona's Grand Canyon. The $2 million interpretive center, built by the Alberta government, opened in 1987. The five-level facility was built into a hill and blends in so well with the setting that you could easily miss it if road signs didn't mark its location.

About 90 minutes are needed to tour the center. The tour traces the area's rich history, including the fragile ecology of the northwestern plains, the lifestyle of prehistoric Plains Indians, the buffalo hunt itself, the decline of traditional buffalo hunting and the science of archaeology. The biggest event of the year happens annually on a mid-July weekend, when the center hosts Buffalo Days Pow Wow and Tepee Village. Visitors also can experience a taste of traditional aboriginal life by renting a tepee for $40 and spending the night in it.

A one-hour self-guided walking tour on the lower trail takes you through the kill site beneath the buffalo jump escarpment, where the meat was prepared and preserved after each hunt. Inside the center, the story of the jump is told by well-presented displays, short films and by local guides such as Leo Bernard Pard. A 10-minute film of a simulated hunt is so realistic that you may wonder if live buffalo were used to film it. In one scene a buffalo is seen flying over the cliff. The buffalo, however, was already dead. Its carcass was acquired from an Alberta buffalo ranch, then frozen for filming. A front-end loader dumped it over the cliff in a vivid scene that required several takes to get it right.

Just as the buffalo did hundreds of years ago, the site today helps sustain local natives. Most staff, numbering up to 40 in summer, are reserve residents. The center pumps about $2.5 million annually into the local economy.

The most common complaint heard here concerns the lack of

live buffalo. There are mounted, glass-eyed models inside the center, but no live animals to give you a real feel for their size and power. That may change. The Friends of the Head-Smashed-in Buffalo Jump Society plans to obtain a herd of 8 to 15 buffalo to house in a paddock near the base of the cliffs.

Chain Lakes Provincial Park

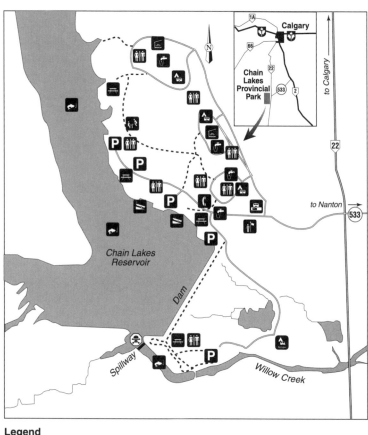

Legend

🅿 Public Parking		🏞 Picnic Site		Ⓧ Danger		👫 Playground
Park Office		Picnic Shelter		Water		Fishing Area
Camping		℄ Telephone		Sewage Disposal		▪ ▪ ▪ Unpaved Trail
Group Camping		Washroom		Trailer Boat Launch		

Access: Exit Highway 22X southwest of Calgary, south on Highway 22 for 100 km (62 mi). Or south on Highway 2 for 70 km (43 mi) to Nanton, west for 38 km (24 mi) on Secondary Highway 533.

Terrain: Rolling foothills, rocky outcrops, wooded ravines, bluffs, willow, native grasslands.

Activities: Hiking, picnicking, camping, year-round fishing, boating (speed limit 12 km/7.5 mi per hour), wildlife watching, playground, cross-country skiing, tobogganing.

Prohibited: Campfires

Hours: No set hours. Quiet hours in campground 11:00 P.M. to 7:00 A.M.

Contact: 403 646-5887.

MOST VISITORS to this 415-ha (1,025-acre) provincial park come for the fishing. The park is named for three spring-fed lakes flooded in 1967, when dams were built across the north and south ends. The reservoir, which supplies water to irrigators and the towns of Claresholm and Granum, is 12 km (7.5 mi) long. It is barely 500 m (1,640') across in most places, with a maximum depth of 10 m (33'). The province has stocked millions of rainbow trout in the reservoir since the late 1960s.

Most fish don't reach a large size for one basic reason: food. Fisheries biologist Jim Stelfox says fluctuating water levels limit production of the freshwater shrimp and aquatic insects upon which trout feed. White suckers, shown in one test netting to comprise 93 percent of the reservoir's fish population, compete heavily with trout for limited rations. Alberta's official fish, bull trout, could be a better species to stock in Chain Lakes because they thrive on suckers. However, bull trout are protected province-wide, so you would have to fish for fun, not food.

For now, at least, you have to settle for the plentiful, generally cooperative rainbows. High fish populations make this an ideal spot for youngsters to learn to fish, and kids don't seem to mind if the fish fighting at the end of the line is a sucker or a rainbow trout.

You can fish here from shore or a boat. From shore a consistently successful technique involves having a sinker several centimeters below a pair of No. 8 hooks baited with corn, cheese, salmon eggs or Berkley Power Bait. Using worms and maggots will guarantee suckers, but also will produce trout. When fly-fishing try small dry flies such as the Adams, Parachute Adams, Royal Wulff and ant patterns. When fishing from a boat, troll streamers and nymphs in dragonfly nymph and backswimmer patterns. Olive bead-head nymphs also work. Spin fishers can troll or cast small spinners, spoons, flatfish and spinner-worm combinations. The best fishing generally is in early morning, late afternoon and evening.

On winter weekends Chain Lakes is covered with anglers fishing for trout through the ice. The fresh air seems to blow here almost constantly, so it's a good idea to bundle up and batten down your gear to keep it from blowing all the way to Nanton. The bait used for summer fishing also works in winter. The key is to use the smallest bobber available, preferably a torpedo-shaped clear plastic one. This type is designed to register the least amount of resistance in the water when it's pulled by a nibbling fish below. Sometimes, a trout will hit a bait like a freight train (okay, a miniature freight train). Other times, a bobber will barely move in the water and the bait will be gone when checked.

When ice fishing with kids, it's a good idea to take their ice-skates, toboggan, comics or a good book. Then if they get bored trying to catch fish, they can read, skate or slide down the hills surrounding the lake.

The campground is often full, especially on summer weekends. Take note that fires are prohibited here year-round because park officials and neighboring ranchers are concerned about grass fires in the park and on adjacent land. A major grass fire in 1939 changed the main vegetation from prairie grasses to aspen and willow. The provincial park was created in 1969.

The park's popularity, according to park ranger Norma Campbell, leads to problems with littering, so remember not to drop food and bait containers, hook wrappings and old monofilament fishing line. Discarded along the shoreline, this refuse poses a danger to birds and other wildlife. Remember, too, that all suckers should be released or taken home, not left to become maggot-infested in garbage containers or on the shoreline.

Chain Lakes has much to offer if you simply want to savor flora and fauna. Here you can study more than 200 species of plants and use binoculars to scan for wildlife. A diverse variety of wildlife makes this park special. Moose, elk and both deer species live here year-round. Howling and yipping coyotes offer regular serenades. Cougars and black bears cruise the area occasionally. Great blue herons stalk the edge of the lake, hunting for frogs and other tasty morsels. Bald eagles and American white pelicans frequently drop in. If you're lucky, you'll hear the haunting calls of the common loon echoing around the lake. An interpretive trail tells the story of the area's deep ranching roots, extending back to the late 1800s.

Drumheller Badlands

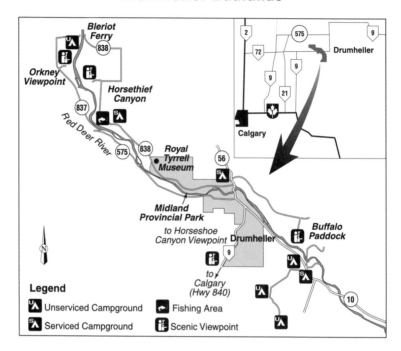

Access: North on Highway 2 for 20 km (12.4 mi) to Highway 9 turnoff, then east on Highway 9 for 80 km (49.7 mi). Alternate route, go east on Trans-Canada Highway for 40 km (24.9 mi), north on Highway 21 for 39 km (24.2 mi) to junction with Highway 9, then east on Highway 9 for 44 km (27.3 mi).

Terrain: River valley, badlands studded with hoodoos (sandstone towers), cottonwoods, cactus, wild flowers.

Activities: Hiking, cycling, picnicking, camping, fishing, swimming, ferry ride, museum tour, fossil hunting (to look at, not to keep).

Hours: Royal Tyrrell Museum open daily Victoria Day weekend through Labor Day weekend 9:00 A.M. to 9:00 P.M. Open in winter Tuesday through Sunday 10:00 A.M. to 5:00 P.M. Closed in winter on Mondays and holidays. Bleriot Ferry operates dawn to dusk, from the first weekend of May to the Thanksgiving weekend, depending on the weather. Midland Provincial Park is open year-round.

Contact: Drumheller and District Chamber of Commerce at 403 823-8100. Royal Tyrrell Museum of Palaeontology at 403 823-7707. Canadian Badlands Passion Play at 403 823-7750.

THE DRUMHELLER AREA is known throughout the world for its haunting badlands, mysterious hoodoos and abundant dinosaur bones. The Dinosaur Trail, a popular driving route, is just one of the region's many highlights. It will take you through some of the best scenery in the badlands. The trail is a 60-km (37-mi) loop that starts and ends in Drumheller. To do the trail justice, pack a picnic lunch, water and lots of film (make sure your battery is charged on the video camera). Plan to take it slow. You'll get more out of the circle tour if you don't rush through at breakneck speed. To really get a feel for the area, consider doing the circle on bicycle. But remember this isn't the Tour de France. Plan to be gone several leisurely hours. Start the trip with two or three water bottles. Refill them along the way if necessary. You can cool off at the start or finish with a dip at Newcastle Beach on the Red Deer River in west Drumheller.

The Dinosaur Trail starts at Drumheller. It proceeds northwest along Highway 838 on the north side of the river or on Highway 837 on the south side. If you start on the south route check out the Drumheller Valley Ski Area and the site of the annual Canadian Badlands Passion Play. The passion play, held in late June and early July, depicts the life of Christ in music and drama. Continuing on Highway 837, check out Orkney Hill Viewpoint. The viewpoint, used as a buffalo jump by early residents, provides a panoramic view of the valley and multilayered badlands.

If starting the tour at Drumheller on Highway 838 on the north side, make your first stop at Midland Provincial Park, an attractive picnic and hiking area beside the Red Deer River. The former site of the Midland Coal Mine, the park includes McMullen Island, which is a great spot for a shaded picnic. On hot summer days you'll quickly appreciate the value of shade in the valley. Midland Park features popular walking trails and interpretive hikes. An interpretive center is located in the old Midland Mine office, which operat-

The Bleriot Ferry crosses the Red Deer River near Drumheller.

ed between 1912 and 1959. The center is open daily between the May long weekend and Labor Day. It charges no admission.

Midland Provincial Park also is home to the Royal Tyrrell Museum of Palaeontology. One of the world's largest palaeontology museums, the Tyrrell features hundreds of exhibits depicting prehistoric beasts which lived on Earth for more than 150 million years. There's no question the Royal Tyrrell Museum of Palaeontology is the area's tourism showpiece. Its reputation has spread around the world since opening in 1985 to collect, research, conserve, display and interpret palaeontological history. About 400,000 people a year visit the museum. In the summer of 1997 the Tyrrell welcomed its five millionth visitor. You'll need at least three hours to do tour the museum, so plan a separate visit. Doing the museum and the circle tour in one day is too tiring for most people, especially young children.

The next stop of note on this stretch of the circle tour is Horsethief Canyon. It's just as spectacular, but less crowded than Horseshoe Canyon on Highway 9 southwest of Drumheller.

Horsethief Canyon is an inspiring mix of badlands and multilayered walls along the river. Formed when prairie was gouged out by pre-historic wind, water and ice, the area's geologic history dates back 70 million years, which makes it ideal for dinosaur fossil hunting, but nothing can be legally removed. Hazards to avoid during the circle tour include accidentally sitting on abundant prickly-pear or pin-cushion cacti, and stumbling into deep holes, down steep gullies or over loose rocks. So choose your steps carefully. Ensure youngsters are close to an adult at all times. Prairie rattlesnakes live in the area, but seldom are seen.

No matter what side of the river you start on, at the halfway point you can't help but notice that the highway pavement runs right into the Red Deer River. You've now reached the Bleriot Ferry crossing, where operators carry you across the Red Deer River on a steel-hulled ferry. There is no charge for the 200-m (656') ride, but that could change. The provincial government is considering introduc-ing a fee for privatizing this and the other six ferries it operates throughout Alberta.

The Bleriot Ferry, named after early settler Andrew Bleriot, start-ed operating in 1913. That year, it carried 1,230 vehicles, most of which were horse-drawn. Ferry use in the province reached its peak in 1919, when 77 ferries were operating. By 1992 the Bleriot Ferry was the province's busiest. Its annual usage was 27,684 vehicles carrying a total of 75,000 people. Today's operators can average 200 crossings in a nine-hour shift.

The original ferry was powered along its cable by boards set on an angle to the river current. The boards acted like sails and propelled the ferry across the Red Deer. In 1958 a motor and winch system was introduced and has been pulling the 17-m (56') craft across ever since.

Most tourists are wide-eyed when they see the ferry. Albertans and nonresidents alike often aren't aware the province has ferries. Their curiosity sparks dozens of questions, most of which the opera-tors have heard many times. The four-minute crossing often isn't long enough for the operator to answer them all. These are the four most common queries:

Q: How deep is the river here?

A: Up to 2.7 m (9') during spring runoff, generally about 1.2 m
     (4') in midsummer.

Q: Can I fish from the ferry?

A: Fishing in the Red Deer River can be very good. Walleye,
     northern pike and goldeye are found in good numbers.
     However, for safety reasons, nobody is allowed to fish from
     the ferry.

Q: Does the ferry run on underwater rails?

A: No. It's pulled by a winch powered by a 318 Dodge motor.
     Overhead cables keep the craft straight.

Q: Can I run the controls?

A: No.

Whew.

Dinosaur Provincial Park

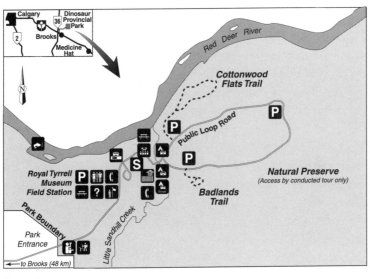

Legend

Park Boundary	Camping	Washroom	Unpaved Trail
Public Parking	Group Camping	Service Center (Showers, Laundromat, Concession)	Scenic Viewpoint
Information	Picnic Site		Historic Site
Park Office	Telephone	Sewage Disposal	Amphitheater
		Fishing Area	Interpretive Plaqu

Access: East on the Trans-Canada Highway for 185 km (115 mi) to Brooks, north on Highway 873, then follow signs 48 km (30 mi) to park.

Terrain: Badlands, hoodoos, gorges, cottonwoods, short and mixed grass prairie.

Activities: Hiking, picnicking, camping, fishing, canoeing, wildlife watching, guided tours, interpretive programs.

Hours: Open year-round. Day-use area open 7:00 A.M. to 11:00 P.M.

Contact: 403 378-4342.

THE LAND NORTHEAST of Brooks isn't much different from most of southeastern Alberta. Low brush, irrigation canals and weathered old farm buildings dot the prairie. But then just as you begin to fear that somehow you took a wrong turn, the sprawling badlands of Dinosaur Provincial Park appear suddenly as if out of nowhere. It's like entering a strange new world, a land that time forgot.

As far as the eye can see are hoodoos—brown and grey sandstone sentinels shaped by wind and water. Sparse green clumps of vegetation are scattered throughout a stark landscape of mesas, buttes and coulees. Peering through a pedestal-mounted viewing scope, you join the ranks of many who've stood in silent awe before this scene. Interpretive signs describe the area as one of the world's most important known deposits of fossilized dinosaur bones. Other signs warn against the park's more user-unfriendly inhabitants such as northern scorpions, black widow spiders and prairie rattlesnakes. The signs say these critters are rarely seen.

Dropping into the valley, you'll quickly feel the heat invade your vehicle, even in mid-September. But it could be worse. In summer, temperatures here have soared to an incredible 51°C (124°F).

The starkness of this hot, dry region can be overwhelming, but it wasn't always this way. A mere 75 million years ago, lush forests covered a coastal plain, rivers flowed into an inland sea and dinosaurs lived in warm swamps.

Today, dinosaurs are the area's main claim to fame, even though they haven't lived here for 63 million years. More than 150 complete skeletons have been found, representing almost 40 different species. Scientists have been drawn to the area for the last century. They come to track history, to trace the lives and times of beasts such as the *champossaur*, a crocodilelike reptile you wouldn't want to meet in a dark alley, or even an illuminated alley, for that matter.

One of the most spectacular modern finds was made in July 1995. Fossil hunters discovered the full skeleton of a 75-million-year-old ostrichlike carnivorous dinosaur *Ornithomimus*. Another giant meat eater, the *Albertasaurus*, was discovered in 1993 by a hiker in a public area. New fossils are uncovered every year as the ground and sandstone constantly erode. Hence a common description of the area: "Ever changing, but never changed."

The park's unique terrain was created by rivers whose deposits

Hoodoos at Dinosaur Provincial Park.

created the valley walls, hills and hoodoo formations. About 14,000 years ago, at the end of the Ice Age, glacial meltwater carved the Red Deer River Valley. The badlands continue to be sculpted by water, frost and wind.

Established in 1955, the 26-km^2 (10-mi^2) Dinosaur Provincial Park is a world heritage site, a status shared by Head-Smashed-In Buffalo

Jump near Fort Macleod and Egypt's pyramids. As early as 1898 the area was proclaimed as a significant dinosaur field by the Geological Survey of Canada. Although the park offers a variety of recreational activities, the main focus is on its natural and cultural history.

The field station of Drumheller's Royal Tyrrell Museum of Palaeontology is the cornerstone. Dinosaur Park is the museum's main source of fossils. The field station receives about 10 percent the number of visitors to the Tyrrell. Not as overwhelming, the smaller facility provides a more intimate hands-on experience than its mother ship. Using exhibits and films, it covers about 35 species of dinosaurs. It also provides a laboratory for palaeontologists to work on dinosaur bones.

About one-third of the park is a natural preserve, and you cannot enter without an official guide. From late spring to early fall guided bus tours are offered twice daily. They are so popular that tickets for the morning tour often are sold out two hours in advance. Bus tours are restricted to weekends between Labor Day and Thanksgiving.

If you're eager to guide yourself, you have a choice of three trails. The 3.2-km (2-mi) Quarry Trail, located within a looped road east of the campground and day-use area, takes you into the heart of the hoodoos. It features two sites (marked with brass plates) excavated in 1913 by Barnum Brown. A display case contains a near-complete dinosaur skeleton. The 1.6-km (1-mi) Badlands Trail is sandwiched between the restricted natural preserve and the driving loop road. Highlights are badlands and interpretive signs with information about the wildlife, vegetation and geology.

The 2.2-km (1.4-mi) Cottonwood Flats Trail is to the north, between the driving loop and the Red Deer River. This trail contrasts sharply with the other two because it passes through lush vegetation in the shade of huge cottonwood trees. In early morning and evening, mule deer can often be spotted. Before or after hiking the Cottonwood Flats Trail, you can fish for goldeye, northern pike, walleye and sauger in the murky slow-moving Red Deer River. Include in your fishing arsenal an assortment of small spinners, lead head jigs, worms, streamer flies and dry flies such as grasshopper imitations.

Other wildlife in the park include white-tailed deer, pronghorn antelope, white-tailed prairie hare (a.k.a. jack rabbit), cottontail rabbits, golden eagles and prairie falcons. In addition to venomous prairie rattlesnakes, the park also is home to nonpoisonous wandering garter snakes, western plains garter snakes and bull snakes.

About 70,000 people visit annually. The park is a big hit with people who live outside of this province and even outside of Canada. In recent years a growing number of Albertans are discovering this easily accessed palaeontological treasure trove. The best seasons to visit are spring and fall, when the crowds are few. Take two or three days to explore the park. Doing it all in one day is impossible. Any place that took 75 million years to create is worth at least a couple days of your time.

Kinbrook Island Provincial Park

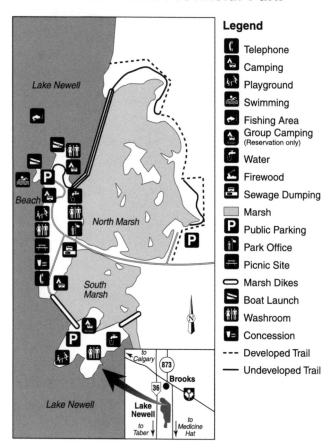

Legend

(	Telephone
🏕	Camping
🤸	Playground
🏊	Swimming
🎣	Fishing Area
🏕	Group Camping (Reservation only)
💧	Water
🔥	Firewood
🚽	Sewage Dumping
▓	Marsh
P	Public Parking
🧍	Park Office
🍽	Picnic Site
⬭	Marsh Dikes
◺	Boat Launch
🚻	Washroom
▮≡	Concession
- - -	Developed Trail
——	Undeveloped Trail

Access: East on the Trans-Canada Highway for 185 km (115 mi) to Brooks, then south on Secondary Highway 873 for 15 km (9.3 mi).

Terrain: Gently rolling prairie, wetlands, cottonwoods, willow, mixed grassland, sage.

Activities: Hiking, cycling, picnicking, camping, fishing, swimming, boating, wind-surfing, sailing, wildlife watching, playground.

Hours: Day-use areas and campground open 7:00 A.M. to 11:00 P.M.

Contact: 403 362-2962.

A LL THAT'S MISSING from this oasis is camels. And you may suspect that if you looked hard enough, you would find a dromedary or two resting in the trees. After driving long distances across sagebrush-covered prairie, you almost have to pinch yourself to make sure Kinbrook Island Provincial Park on Lake Newell's east shore isn't a monotony-induced mirage. Trust me—it isn't. This lush southeastern Alberta park, established in 1961, is a delightfully refreshing break from extended prairie flatness interrupted only by cows, oil wells and coulees. Coming unexpectedly upon Lake Newell, with its abundant trees and water birds, is like finding an oasis in the middle of a desert.

The lake was named after Frederick H. Newell, a United States Bureau of Reclamation Service director who worked as an adviser to the Canadian Pacific Railway (CPR). Newell oversaw the creation of the lake as an irrigation reservoir in 1914 as part of the CPR's plan to settle the prairie between Medicine Hat and Calgary. Irrigation water was diverted from the East Branch Canal off the Bow River to flood a naturally low area of prairie, which already held a small lake called Crooked Lake. To keep the water in the lake, eighteen dikes were built across coulees and natural water courses on the east side. It took three years for the lake to fill to its planned capacity. Water from Newell feeds the adjoining Rolling Hills irrigation reservoir in addition to providing irrigation to the immediate area.

Covering about 38 ha (93.8 acres), Kinbrook Island Provincial Park provides the easiest, most popular access to Lake Newell. The lake is one of the best spots in Southern Alberta for water-based recreation, including boating, swimming and fishing. At 115 km^2 (44.4 mi^2), Lake Newell is Alberta's largest man-made lake. Its maximum depth is approximately 20 m (65.5'), and the shallower water close to shore is clean and warm—ideal for swimming. The Eastern Irrigation District manages it as an irrigation reservoir.

The wide range of outdoor recreational activities available here also makes Lake Newell a perfect destination for a family vacation. The site offers a sprawling sandy beach (a rarity in Southern Alberta), developed and undeveloped hiking trails, almost 170 campsites, concession, day-use area, horseshoe pit, beach volleyball area and playground. A fish-cleaning stand is provided for anglers. Boating is allowed, but you are restricted to a maximum speed of 12 km (7.5 mi) per hour in some parts of the lake. In 1988 a small island at the southern end of the park was linked to Kinbrook Island by a causeway. The heavily treed piece of land has become a group day-use and camping area.

The lake is a favorite destination for bird watchers. More than 100 species of birds nest, live or migrate through the area. It boasts three bird sanctuaries: Pelican Island, Kinbrook Marsh and Sven Bayer Peninsula. Pelican Island, an important nesting site for endangered American white pelicans and double-crested cormorants, is off limits to people. Boats are prohibited within 1.6 km (1 mi) of the island, but you don't need to hang around just outside the restricted area to see pelicans and cormorants. These birds fly regularly over the beach, campground and lake.

The best bird-viewing areas are along the lake's eastern shore, where Kinbrook Park is connected to the mainland by a narrow strip of land. Kinbrook Marsh, just east of Kinbrook Island, is split north and south by the road leading to the park. The marsh is a haven for water birds, including ducks, geese, rails, coots, bitterns, grebes and great blue herons. It can be reached via an observation point crossing the lake just north of the park or by walking or driving back to the mainland on the main road. You are urged not to stray from paths or interfere with nests and birds. Make sure you pack a camera, binoculars or spotting scope, bird identification guides and a good supply of mosquito repellent. Mosquitoes outnumber the birds about ten to one. And there are plenty of birds.

If you carefully observe the prairie grasslands in and around the park, you may spot pronghorn antelope and burrowing owls. Coyotes and badgers also live in the area. Antelope are the speedsters of the prairies, reaching speeds of 65 km (40 mi) per hour, but they can be hard to spot because they blend extremely well with their terrain, especially when lying down. When looking for pronghorns, watch for white rump patches against the grass rather than scanning for entire animals. Burrowing owls aren't much bigger than Richardson's ground squirrels (more commonly known as gophers). In fact the tiny owls like to live in old dens left by gophers and badgers. The owls are often seen standing at the den entrance, head and tail bobbing erratically. Another resident of abandoned burrows in this area is the black widow spider, so be careful where you put your hands and bare feet.

Newell is extremely popular with anglers fishing for northern pike up to 13.6 kg (30 lb), walleye, lake whitefish, yellow perch, burbot and rainbow trout, which move in from the Bow River. The lake reportedly still contains some brook trout, remnants of a government stocking program in 1938. Cutthroat trout were stocked in 1953, but the species didn't survive. As is the case with most big bodies of water, the best fishing on Newell is enjoyed from a boat. With freedom during the day to search the lake for hot spots, you'll increase your chances of catching fish though some anglers do fish successfully from shore and the public docks on the east side.

Good pike techniques include casting near weed beds with large spoons and spinner-minnow combinations, and working the bottom with frozen smelts and minnows.

For walleye, try an assortment of lead head jigs with rubber bodies tipped with dead minnows, live night crawlers or leeches. Experiment with different colored jig bodies to find the one most appealing to walleye. Before fishing, study the government regulations to learn the latest rules. As part of a provincial program designed to boost flagging walleye populations across Alberta, all walleye caught in Lake Newell must be released.

Yellow perch can be caught using a tiny jig or wireworm tipped with small minnow, maggot, mealworm or earthworm. Rigging these baits on a No. 6 hook worked under a small slip bobber can be highly effective for perch.

Although most anglers focus on lake whitefish through the ice in winter, some like to catch them in open water. Slowly retrieving small weighted nymphs in freshwater shrimp patterns, casting tiny dry flies such as Parachute Adams and jigging with wireworms tipped with maggots are effective summer whitefish techniques.

Rainbow trout can be caught on worms, small spinners and spoons, Flatfish and Rapalas, weighted nymphs, streamers such as Woolly Buggers and an assortment of dry flies.

With fishing just one of many recreational attractions at Lake Newell, those of you accustomed to heading to the mountains for holidays have a great reason to turn east for Kinbrook Island Provincial Park. Camels aren't required or recommended.

Waterton Lakes National Park

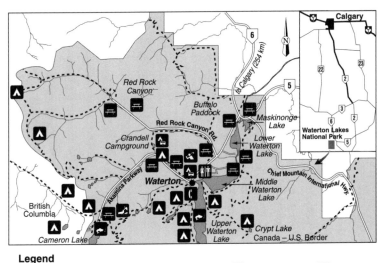

Legend

- ⬭ Park Boundary
- 🅰 Camping
- 🅰 Backcountry Camping
- 🔲 Picnic Site
- 🔲 Telephone
- 🔲 Hand Boat Launch
- 🔲 Washroom
- 🔲 Fishing Area
- ••• Unpaved Trail
- 🔲 Golfing

Access: South on Highway 2 for 150 km (93 mi) to Highway 3, west for 70 km (43 mi) to Highway 6 at Pincher Creek, then south for 48 km (30 mi).

Terrain: Rolling prairie to the east, mountains to the west, subalpine and montane forests, alpine fir, Douglas fir, lodgepole pine, white spruce, limber pine, white birch, black cottonwood, balsam poplar, alpine larch, whitebark pine, Engelmann spruce.

Activities: Hiking, golfing, picnicking, camping, fishing, scuba diving, boating, boat tours, wind-surfing, wildlife watching, horseback riding, cross-country skiing, snowshoeing, interpretive programs.

Prohibited: Lead fishing lures and sinkers, feeding wildlife.

Hours: No set hours.

Cost: $8 for family day-pass, $70 for annual pass (applicable for all national parks west of Manitoba), $6 per person per night for wilderness camping pass to maximum of $30 per person per trip.

Contact: Waterton Lakes National Park at 403 859-2224.

A NY PLACE where locals joke that their idea of urban gangs are cougars stalking supper in the streets is all right in my books. That's how it is in Waterton Lakes National Park. Alberta's smallest mountain park is hidden away in the province's southwest corner. Bighorn sheep and mule deer roam the townsite, chomping on gardens, bedding down on lawns, licking salt from parked vehicles and occasionally being pounced on by cougars, sometimes in a residential front yard.

The human population peaks at about 4,000 in summer. In winter, when most of the townsite is shut down for the season, wild animals far outnumber people. Solitude is what makes Waterton so appealing in winter. The crowds of summer are gone, downtown stores are boarded up and most houses are empty, their owners wintering in the city or south of the border. High on a hill overlooking Upper Waterton Lake, the regal Prince of Wales Hotel sits empty — unless you believe the tale of Sara, the ghost of a chambermaid that wanders its halls. Kilmorey Lodge (saskatoon pie is highly recommended), Crandell Mountain Lodge, the new Lodge at Waterton Lakes and a downtown convenience store are among the few commercial operations open in winter.

Despite initial appearances, winter offers plenty to do in the 525-km^2 (203-mi^2) park. Wildlife viewing opportunities abound. In addition to sheep and deer, the park's resident species include elk, moose, coyote, wolverine and cougar. An increasing number of people come each winter for snowshoeing, ice climbing, camping, picnicking and cross-country skiing.

There are hundreds of kilometers of cross-country ski trails, from trackset family-type runs to more challenging backcountry trails. A popular family ski destination is Cameron Lake at the end of the Akamina Parkway southwest of the townsite. Phone the park before leaving home in case snow or avalanche conditions have forced a temporary parkway closure. The winding 16-km (10-mi) parkway must be traveled carefully.

When snow conditions are good in Waterton, skiing can be fantastic. A few years ago our family skied into Cameron Lake with

Canoeist on Cameron Lake in Waterton Lakes National Park.

friends lucky enough to live in the park year-round. At the trailhead, we discovered about 25 parked vehicles. Within minutes our party of five kids and four adults was on the tracked and groomed trail leading to the lake. A glorious scene awaited at the frozen lake. Towering mountains were fringed with clouds, and the tops of trees which would be eye level in summer poked through the snow at our feet.

The lake is less than 1 km (.6 mi) east of the British Columbia border. Its south end dips into Montana. Sassy Canada and Stellar's jays may beg for handouts, but it's illegal to feed wildlife in the park. The 5-km (3.1-mi) round-trip is rated easy. The Dipper, a groomed trail rated moderate, covers 6.5 km (4 mi) from the Rowe Trailhead to Little Prairie and back.

If you prefer ski touring in uncrowded backcountry, you have several choices. Crandell Lake is rated easy to moderate while more difficult skiing is available on Rowe Trail, Akamina Pass, Summit Lake and Wall/Forum Lakes. These trails aren't marked and are subject to avalanches. Wardens urge everyone to register with the warden's office, carry emergency locator beacons, to know about avalanche condition evaluations and to be capable of rescuing yourself.

Winter visitors can rough it by camping for free at Pass Creek. The sheltered campground features a kitchen shelter, wood stove, firewood and chemical toilets. Water can be taken from the creek (wardens recommend boiling it before using) or from the village system at the firehall.

Although Waterton in winter is special, you should sample the park year-round to appreciate all her charms. The contrasting terrain grabs you early as you enter the park from the main north gate off Highway 6. Traveling 8 km (5 mi) along Highway 5, you will discover the origin of the park's slogan, "Where the mountains meet the prairies." The road starts on relatively flat terrain, moves into rolling foothills, then suddenly is in the Rocky Mountains.

The first stop should be at the public information center to learn about the park's natural history and varied recreational opportunities. This is a good time to check out the latest reports on problems with bears and other wildlife.

If it's your first visit, you may be overwhelmed by the number of potential activities to enjoy in the park, but there are some must-sees. They include Cameron Lake, which might be even more beautiful in summer than winter, if possible. Cameron offers picnicking, hiking and fishing for rainbow and brook trout. The use of lead lures, most lead sinkers and lead-weighted flies is prohibited in Canada's national parks. Rental boats are available. You have an excellent chance of seeing grizzly bears by using binoculars or a spotting scope to scan the snowslide areas of the mountain slopes across Cameron Lake. You also may stop on the way out of Cameron Lake at the Akamina Pass trailhead. The trail leads 6 km (3.8 mi) into British Columbia's Akamina-Kishinena Provincial Park.

The aptly named Red Rock Parkway through the Blakiston Valley is another must-see. Meandering for 15 km (9.3 mi) with a view of Mount Blakiston—Waterton's highest peak—the parkway ends at crimson-hued Red Rock Canyon. Watch closely for grizzly and black bears adjacent to the road. Crandell Campground is one of the nicest drive-in campgrounds in the park. Mule deer move casually among the well-treed sites. Other wildlife have been known to wander through.

In the townsite, popular stops include Cameron Falls, created by Cameron Creek dropping into Waterton Valley. Upper and Middle Waterton lakes offer picnicking and fishing for a variety of species, including lake, rainbow, brook and cutthroat trout, and mountain whitefish. Anglers use a variety of techniques, including trolling Rapalas, plugs and spoons, or jigging with nonleaded jigs. The lower lake and nearby Maskinonge Lake contain big northern pike. Upper Waterton, the largest lake, features boat tours to the Crypt Lake hiking trailhead and to Goat Haunt Visitor Centre in Montana's Glacier National Park. Crypt Lake is one of almost a dozen lakes in the park that offer tremendous hike-in fishing for trout. Trout fishing also is available in the Belly and Waterton rivers.

One of the nicest hikes in the park starts in the townsite. Bear's Hump is a moderately difficult hike leading from the visitor center to an impressive hawk's-eye view of the lakes, mountains and townsite. After reaching the top, take a rest, savor the view and carefully plan out the rest of your stay. This is also a good time to plan another visit. You'll discover your first time there that one trip to Waterton isn't enough. There's just too much to do and see.

Cypress Hills Provincial Park

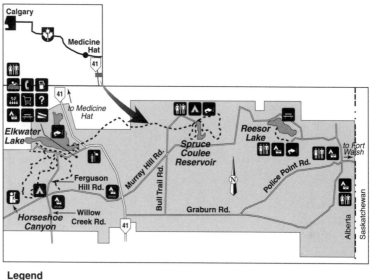

Legend

- ⬭ Park Boundary
- ? Information
- 🚹 Park Office
- ⛰ Camping (Tenting Only)

- 🏕 Camping
- 🏕 Group Camping
- 🎋 Picnic Site
- ☏ Telephone

- 🚻 Washroom
- ⊵ Trailer Boat Launch
- 🎣 Fishing Area
- ≋ Swimming

- • • • Unpaved Trail
- 🏞 Scenic Viewpoint
- 🎭 Amphitheater
- 🛒 Store
- ⛽ Gasoline

Access: East on the Trans-Canada Highway for 295 km (183 mi) to Medicine Hat, then drive on Highway 41 for 66 km (41 mi).

Terrain: Forested escarpment rising from Elkwater Lake's south shore to a flat-topped grassy plateau; boreal foothills forest with trembling aspen, balsam poplar, lodgepole pine, white spruce, aspen parkland, dry mixed grassland.

Activities: Hiking, cycling, picnicking, camping, fishing, swimming, water-skiing (on Elkwater Lake only), boating (electric motors only on Reesor Lake, nonmotorized boating on Spruce Coulee Reservoir), wildlife watching, horseback riding, limited hunting for elk, playgrounds, cross-country skiing, downhill skiing, snowshoeing, ice fishing, interpretive programs.

Hours: Day-use areas and campgrounds open 7:00 A.M. to 11:00 P.M.

Contact: 403 893-3777.

STRADDLING the Alberta–Saskatchewan border, this 200-km² (77-mi²) natural jewel is Alberta's second largest provincial park. It offers a wealth of recreational activities for day trips and extended holidays. Boredom is not an operative word here. There are more than 40 km (25 mi) of hiking trails ranging from an easy boardwalk stroll to an overnight backpacking trip atop the plateau overlooking Elkwater townsite and lake. Mountain bikes are allowed on all trails. Horseback riding is permitted on the plateau bench, but not on designated trails. There are 23 km (14 mi) of groomed cross-country trails to enjoy, and for downhill skiing there's the Mile High ski hill. Snowshoeing and tobogganing also are popular.

The park has nine campgrounds, including two walk-in tenting sites. You can fish for northern pike and yellow perch in the warm waters of Elkwater Lake, then try for brook and rainbow trout in Spruce Coulee Reservoir. Reesor Lake, in the park's south end 20 km (12 mi) from Elkwater Lake, is stocked with rainbow trout. Two attractive catch-and-release creeks that look like they belong in the Rockies are Graburn Creek, which has rainbows and brookies, and Battle Creek, which has rainbows, browns and brookies.

Cypress Hills is Alberta's only provincial park that allows hunting. Elk lived in the Cypress Hills in the 1800s but were hunted to extinction by 1909. Since elk were reintroduced in 1937, populations have thrived. The provincial government each autumn issues a limited number of elk hunting permits to hunters whose names are selected in a computer draw. Hunter harvest since 1978 averages 100 elk annually. An estimated 1,300 elk live in the park and surrounding area. The province wants to reduce the wintering elk population to 700. Four Tuesday-to-Thursday hunts between mid-October and mid-November are aimed at reducing damage to crops and haystacks on neighboring farms and ranches.

Elkwater Lake, located in Elkwater townsite at the base of Cypress Hills in the park's northwest corner, covers just over 2 km² (.8 mi²). The lake is used for swimming, fishing, sailing, boating, water-skiing and canoeing. An asphalt-covered, wheelchair-accessible lakeshore walking trail extends for 3 km (1.9 mi) on the south

On the beach at Elkwater Lake in Cypress Hills Provincial Park.

shore. Powerboating and water-skiing are limited to the north and west bays. Speed limits are in effect near the marina and public swimming area.

Arriving in the park from Highway 41 southeast of Medicine Hat, it's immediately obvious that the Cypress Hills region stands out, literally, from the rest of Southern Alberta. Encompassing an area 145 km (90 mi) long and up to 40 km (25 mi) wide, the hills are about 760 m (2,493') higher than the adjacent plains. It's Canada's highest point of land between the Rockies and Labrador. When lower grasslands are cooking in summer heat, the Cypress Hills are cool, green and lush. It's generally a few degrees cooler here than in Medicine Hat. These small temperature variations often mean the hills have great skiing even when Chinook winds have melted snow in Medicine Hat.

The Alberta park is connected to one in Saskatchewan. Between 1911 and 1930 the entire area was jointly managed as one federal forest reserve. In 1930 the feds handed over jurisdiction for natural resources to the provinces. Alberta continued managing its side of the Cypress Hills as a forest reserve until it became a provincial park in 1951. The Saskatchewan park was designated in 1931.

The Cypress Hills hold an important place in Canadian history books. Assiniboine, Sioux, Cree and Blackfoot Indians hunted bison and camped in the area. Their lives changed dramatically with the introduction of firearms and horses and with contact with Métis hunters and traders. Trading posts in the early 1870s were operated by traders who illegally swapped whiskey for furs. In 1873 a gang of wolf hunters looking for natives who had stolen their horses attacked an innocent band of Assiniboine. More than 20 natives were killed. The Cypress Hills Massacre contributed to the formation of the North-West Mounted Police. A contingent of mounted policemen rode west in 1874 to end the whiskey trade, introduce law and order and establish a strong legal presence. A large North-West Mounted Police post was built at Fort Walsh in 1875.

The park also has a rich natural history. Although grizzly bears and prairie wolves no longer roam the hills as they did in the late 1800s and early 1900s, wildlife is abundant. Mammals include white-tailed and mule deer, moose, elk, pronghorn antelope, coyotes, cougars, swift fox, red fox and bobcats. More than 200 bird species reside or migrate through the area, including wild Merriam's turkey (introduced in 1962), ruffed grouse, dark-eyed junco, yellow-rumped warbler, double-crested cormorant, white-winged scoter, saw-whet owl and red-breasted nuthatch. The park is the only Canadian nesting site of the pink-sided subspecies of the dark-eyed junco. It's Alberta's only home of the common poorwill.

Writing-On-Stone Provincial Park

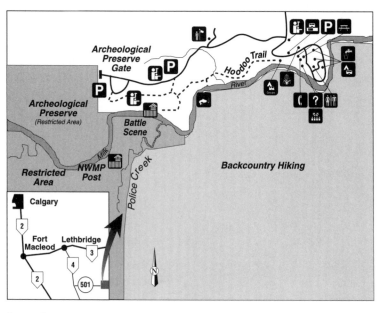

Legend

⬭ Park Boundary	🅰 Camping	🚻 Washroom	Fishing Area
🅿 Public Parking	Group Camping	Showers	• • • Unpaved Trail
❓ Information	Picnic Site	Water	Scenic Viewpoint
Park Office	Telephone	Sewage Disposal	Historic Site
			Amphitheater

Access: South on Highway 2 for 146 km (91 mi), east on Highway 3 for 50 km (31 mi) to Lethbridge, south on Highway 4 for 66 km (41 mi) to Milk River, east on Highway 501 for 32 km (20 mi), then south on Highway 500 for 10 km (6 mi).

Terrain: River valley, sandstone hoodoos and cliffs, coulees, cottonwoods, peach leaf willow, river birch, thorny buffaloberry, low junipers, saskatoon, choke cherry, dry and mixed grass prairie, prickly-pear and pincushion cactus, sagebrush.

Activities: Hiking, picnicking, camping, fishing, swimming, boating, wildlife watching, playground, cross-country skiing, snowshoeing, interpretive programs.

Hours: Day-use area and campground open 7:00 A.M. to 11:00 P.M.
Contact: 403 647-2364.

THIS 1,782-HA (4,400-ACRE) provincial park, located in Alberta's driest and warmest region, is classic prairie rattlesnake country. Dry, mixed grass prairie is dotted with prickly-pear cactus and prairie crocus flowers. Looming hoodoos topped with mushroomlike caps cast shadows on rocky outcrops, low shrubs and boulders that provide ideal cover for rattlesnakes and other creatures. This isn't to say there's a rattler under or atop every rock. Nothing could be further from the truth. Although the venomous snakes are seen in the park several times annually, most visitors never see one. Spotting a rattler on the prairie is akin to seeing a grizzly bear in the mountains — it's a thrill of a lifetime, one preferably experienced at a distance rather than at close range.

Probably the most significant reason for visiting Writing-On-Stone is the ancient artwork. The largest concentration of native rock art on the Great Plains of North America is found on about 50 sites on the valley's sandstone cliffs. Several centuries old, the rock art is composed of thousands of pictographs (rock paintings) and petroglyphs (rock carvings) representing figures, ritualistic symbols, spiritual images and actual events, such as successful hunts.

Although nobody is sure of the age of the oldest piece of rock art, archaeological evidence, including tepee rings and arrowheads, reveals that native people camped in the valley more than 3,000 years ago. It's believed that most rock art is between 100 and 500 years old. Archaeologists have been able to more accurately determine the age of some artwork because it features rough stick symbols of horses, which didn't arrive on the northern plains until about 1730. Rock art continued to be created through the 1700s and into the late 1800s. Members of the Blackfoot Nation likely created much of this art although other bands may have contributed. The Cree, Gros Ventre, Assiniboine, Crow, Kutenai and possibly the Shoshone Indians conducted hunting and raiding ventures into the area. Young Indian men undertook vision quests among the hoodoos, fast-

Looking at petroglyphs at Writing-On-Stone Provincial Park.

ing and seeking spiritual guidance for their life paths. Caves within the sandstone cliffs were used as tombs for chiefs and other high-ranking officials.

Before the advent of metal tools, early Indians used antlers or bones to scratch petroglyphs into the rocks. The pictographs were drawn with a lump of ironstone, or fingers and bone tools were dipped in red ochre pigment, a paste made of crushed iron ore, water and buffalo fat. Some of the rock art can be found along the main interpretive trail, but most sites can be seen only by taking a guided tour of the archaeological preserve, where access is restricted. Free guided hikes are conducted daily from mid-May to early September.

After surviving for centuries, rock art was threatened by early settlers and park visitors who defaced it by scratching their initials, names and drawings into the sandstone. Fortunately in 1977 the province closed off the archaeological preserve to all but interpreter-guided tours. The provincial Historical Resources Act threatens

$50,000 fines and yearlong jail terms for anyone altering, marking or damaging rock art.

At the park's main entrance you'll discover a natural montage of sandstone hoodoos, cliffs and ravines. These were carved by thousands of years of erosion by wind, water and freeze–thaw cycles. Mushroomlike sandstone cap rocks protect the hoodoos from the elements. The sandstone towers are doomed because they never stop eroding. Eventually they collapse. To the south the prominent Sweetgrass Hills in Montana contribute to the park's rich biological diversity. The United States border is just 4 km (2.5 mi) south of the park's southern boundary.

The first white man to visit was American Indian Agent James Doty, who dropped by in 1855. Blackfoot Indians gave up the land in 1877 by signing a treaty in exchange for reserves and government support. The North-West Mounted Police camped in the Sweetgrass Hills and a small number of them visited here in 1874, including Frederick Bagley, a 15-year-old trumpeter who wrote about it in his diary. Thirteen years later, the North-West Mounted Police set up a summer tent camp, later replaced with wooden buildings. Homesteaders flooded the area starting in 1910. Although the police post—the North-West Mounted Police's longest continuously staffed border post in Alberta—closed in 1918 and the buildings burned, replicas were built in the mid-1970s on the south side of the river.

The park is a popular destination for tourists, including families. It straddles the slow-flowing Milk River, which offers an unsupervised beach and perfect conditions for floating in canoes, rubber rafts and small rowboats. Boating is best in May and June before the water level drops. The river offers good fishing for northern pike. It's one of Alberta's top places to fish for sauger, a walleye lookalike. Hiking trails are user-friendly and marked with interpretive signs explaining the area's rich history. A word of advice: make sure every member of your hiking party has a full water bottle before heading out on the trails. The valley can become extremely hot and dry.

For wildlife and bird-watching buffs, Writing-On-Stone offers a virtual smorgasbord. More than 160 bird species have been reported, from American white pelicans and double-crested cormorants to threatened ferruginous hawks and pink-headed turkey vultures with 1.8-m (6') wingspans. Some species, including rufous-sided towhee and rock wren, are scarce in the rest of Alberta but common here. The park is home to mule and white-tailed deer, coyotes, seven species of bats, Nuttall's cottontails and white-tailed prairie hares, yellow-bellied marmots, badgers, porcupines, striped skunks and three types of shrew. Richardson's and thirteen-lined ground squirrels are found near the park but rarely in it. Muskrats, beavers, raccoons and mink wander the park's riverbanks. Bushy-tailed wood rats haunt sandstone caves and crevices. The occasional elk wanders into Writing-On-Stone from the Sweetgrass Hills.

In addition to prairie rattlers, the park's other snake species are the wandering garter and the bull, which lacks the triangular head and rattle of a rattlesnake.

Chapter 5

On the Rocks

The Beckoning Mountains

THE ROCKY MOUNTAINS stand proud and silent on the western horizon, seeming to beckon with a mystical and powerful siren song that can't be denied. The jagged mountains with ice-cream–cone peaks pervade the lives of Calgarians, distracting them from daily routines, teasing them with visions of trails waiting to be explored and peaceful rest spots beside pristine mountain lakes. City dwellers find themselves peering at the Rockies as if seeking a mental grounding, a soothing affirmation that even amidst the chaos of city life some things remain the same. It's a simple cause-and-effect process: mountains beckon and people respond with enthusiasm.

Every morning of the week, in every season, the Trans-Canada Highway becomes a paved, four-lane lifeline for people eager to make a personal connection with mountains in Kananaskis Country and Banff National Park. They go there to hike and ski, to fish and picnic, to climb and camp, but two major recreational pursuits draw the majority of people into the Rockies on day trips or extended visits: cross-country skiing and hiking. These are low-budget activities enjoyed by people of all ages, abilities and backgrounds. The stunningly beautiful setting offers perfect opportunities for introducing children to the outdoors, keeping fit and escaping the rigors of city living.

Approached as recreation, cross-country skiing and hiking produce no winners or losers, just satisfied participants. Banff and Kananaskis Country offer hundreds of kilometers of trails for hiking and skiing. Backcountry skiing opportunities for experienced skiers in both regions are virtually unlimited. With the exception of daily fees charged at the Canmore Nordic Centre and the usual gate admission at Banff National Park, no other user fees are charged to hike or skinny ski in Kananaskis Country and the national park. That may change in the future, however, at the government-run Kananaskis Country, where the user-pay concept seems to be favored by some politicians. Let's hope not.

Cross-Country Skiing

IN ADDITION to being a great family activity, cross-country skiing is one of the healthiest of winter sports. It's beneficial on two fronts: your overall physical fitness and peace of mind. Before the season starts it's a good idea to train by running, cycling, in-line skating, riding a stationary exercise bike, swimming, or by using a stair stepper, rowing or Nordic Track machine. Exercise three times weekly for at least 20 minutes a session. Climbing stairs instead of taking an elevator or escalator will help improve breathing and strengthen leg muscles. Poling action during skiing requires upper body strength, so alternate cardiovascular exercises with lifting weights to develop these muscles.

Local ski clubs and stores may be able to offer invaluable information about where to go. Groomed trails are generally rated easy to difficult. Make sure you pick the right trail for every member of your group. Good skiers can enjoy themselves on any trail, but novice skiers will scare themselves silly, possibly even get hurt, on a difficult trail. Banff National Park and Kananaskis Country both issue weekly ski trail and avalanche condition reports. The *Calgary Herald* offers free cross-country ski reports on the TELUS Talking Yellow Pages at 403 521-5222, extension 1286. Current cross-country ski and avalanche information can be obtained online at www.discoveralberta.com.

Getting into cross-country skiing is easy. After deciding to take the plunge, sign up for a course offered by local clubs (reach them through the Calgary Area Outdoor Council at 403 270-2262), ski stores (check the Yellow Pages), the University of Calgary (403 220-5038) and the city of Calgary Outdoor/Nature Services (403 268-1311).

Basic equipment—skis, boots and poles—can cost several hundred dollars. Adults should be able to get away with spending $250 to $350. Gear for children under 10 should be available for about $100. Technological advances in modern gear—as opposed to the stuff I learned on in the 1970s and still use today—help develop your skills faster. Boots have better bindings and more support; skis have increased glide and respond better in turns.

The best time to shop for equipment is after receiving basic education about what's right for you. Beware of classified ads or secondhand shops, unless you know what you're looking for. There's no point buying cheap but unsuitable equipment if it will have to be replaced next year.

For skiing on machine-groomed double tracks, veteran local skier Neil Glasser suggests a fiberglass, P-tex–based ski. Brands to consider include Karhu, Fischer, Atomic, Elana, Peleton, Rossignol and Morrotto. Waxless skis aren't recommended for this Chinook-prone region because they don't provide sufficient kicking traction on trails regularly melted and refrozen by widely varying temperatures. To determine proper length of ski, extend your arm at right angles. Your wrist should touch the end of the standing ski. The ski's stiffness, called camber, must be matched to your weight.

For bindings and boots, the three-pin system of old is rapidly going the way of the dodo bird. It's been replaced by the Salomon Profile System with single tracking and the Rottefella New Nordic Norm system. Both feature a horizontal bar on each boot that locks into the binding. Good boot makers include Salomon, Alpina, Rossignol, Karhu and Adidas. Boots range from $80 to $400 with bindings costing up to $60. Poles made of fiberglass or tapered shaft aluminum cost up to $50 a pair. Poles should fit just above the armpit, so your arm runs perpendicular to the ground when the pole is gripped in front of you. Recommended pole brand names include Swix and Exel.

On the trails wear several light layers of clothing, not the heavily insulated garb common in downhill skiing. Denim blue jeans are strictly *verboten* not only because they get cold, stiff and heavy when the snow melts and freezes on them, but because they increase your susceptibility to hypothermia. When dressing for a day of cross-country skiing, Glasser starts with a "high performance wicking layer" of midweight polyester underwear that takes sweat away from the body. He adds a zip turtleneck undershirt that can be opened to cool off or closed to block the wind and retain heat. Over that Glasser wears an expedition-weight top matched with stretch fleece pants. If the weather is really severe, he'll don wind pants and Gore-Tex or other breathable jacket.

Unless it's really cold, Glasser wears a single pair of socks made of polyester, wool and nylon. His toque is lightweight wool with fleece band. Heavier hats promote excessive sweating. Glasser wears synthetic, leather-gripped cross-country ski gloves because they allow a better grip on poles than wool mittens or gloves. His ensemble is completed with sunglasses and a day pack to carry first-aid kit, water, sunscreen, ski wax, matches, extra gloves and socks, and high-energy food.

Once he's geared up, all he has to do is pray for snow. Lots of it.

Hiking

TRUDGING UP the mud-slicked hill in a pounding rainstorm, Lena Daudey tightens the grip on her cane and smiles. "I wish I was 30 years younger," she muses. A few feet away, Peggy Kelley snaps off a lightning-quick retort. "A lot of people 30 years younger couldn't do this," the retired nurse proudly proclaims from under her drenched plastic poncho.

Kelley speaks from experience. Three decades earlier, she couldn't hike 14 km (8.7 mi) of steep mountain trails in a single day in any kind of weather. Now, at 82 years young, Kelley is hiking with the best of them each week in Kananaskis Country and Banff National Park.

Kelley and her hiking partner, Daudey, a mere 78, are among 260 members of the Calgary Seniors' Outdoor Club, one of at least 10 organizations catering to active older Calgarians. The Calgary Area Outdoor Council (403 270-2262) has a complete listing. Ranging from 45 to 960 members ages 55 to 90, the clubs organize weekly or twice-weekly outings to hike, cycle, camp, golf, skate, birdwatch, walk malls, snowshoe and ski both downhill and cross-country. Seniors regularly tackle outings many of their grandchildren

Rain-soaked senior hikers Peggy Kelly (left) and Lena Daudey.

would find impossible. For some members the end of a professional career marked the beginning of an exciting, active relationship with the outdoors.

Kelley, one of the original club members, started skiing and hiking with the group when she retired in 1979. For Daudey the club provided solace and exercise after her husband died 15 years earlier. "It feels good to be out here," says Daudey, beaming happily as rain pours off her canary yellow poncho. Retired RCMP officer Len Grant, the club's trail coordinator, revels in the exercise and fellowship of group hiking. "Being active is the only way to go," says Grant, 68.

Hiking is the perfect activity for Calgarians of all ages who want to be active. With their extreme changes in altitude, the mountains provide a great physical and mental workout along with a great opportunity for taking in spectacular scenery and wildlife. Hiking can become a tradition.

A 1989 study by the Calgary Chamber of Commerce revealed

almost 43 percent of local households contained at least one hiker. In Banff National Park the more popular trails attract upwards of 100,000 hikers each season. Calgary outdoor equipment stores do a brisk business with hikers seeking the latest in boots, backpacks and other gear. Membership rolls are bulging in local hiking groups.

Ellen Gasser, a Calgary wildlife biologist and outdoor educator, says getting into the sport can be a little intimidating for newcomers faced with so many places to go and store shelves full of equipment. Some first-time hikers expect to learn everything first time out. Hiking knowledge and ability, Gasser says, increases relative to the number of hikes you take and the amount you read. Gasser says many first-time hikers she's taken on outings avoided hiking because they were afraid of bears or didn't know where to go or what to do.

A good start is a hiking course offered by the Inglewood Bird Sanctuary (403 269-6688), Outdoor/Nature Services (403 268-1311) or the University of Calgary (403 220-5038). Courses range from easy hikes within the city to more challenging ventures in Kananaskis Country and Banff National Park. Instructors talk about how to stay safe from bears or other wildlife and avoid other natural hazards.

The main requirement for a successful hike is a good pair of hiking boots or shoes. Choosing the right footwear can make the difference between an enjoyable, trouble-free hike and an excruciatingly painful ordeal. Blisters or a sprained ankle mean big trouble if you're kilometers from the trailhead. "Your feet are your transportation, and you've got to take care of them," says veteran Calgary hiker Sonia Tyhonchuk. While working at the University of Calgary Outdoor Program Centre, she helped hundreds of city hikers to get off on the right foot, so to speak. You can rent boots from the university to help you determine what to buy.

Newcomers sometimes believe they have to mortgage the house to buy a good pair of boots. Not so. Tyhonchuk advises you to determine the type of boot you need based on the kind of hiking you're apt to do. Nobody needs Everest-style moonwalkers to stroll along a developed trail in the mountains. For that level of hiking, a sturdy pair of walking or athletic shoes will do.

If you get into more difficult terrain, or anywhere off the beaten path, you'll need more ankle support and should consider proper boots designed for light, medium or heavy duty hiking. The stiffness of the rubber soles should increase according to the difficulty of your regular outings: softer soles for less-challenging hikes and reinforced hard soles for scrambles or mountaineering. Softer rubber soles leave less of an imprint than a hard Vibram-type sole, so they are considered more environmentally friendly. Lightweight or mid-weight boots are often made of Cordura nylon and leather, either genuine or synthetic. Heavy boots, recommended for more serious mountaineering or scree-scrambling, generally are completely leather or even durable plastic.

Keep in mind that leather can be waterproofed with a commercial product such as Aqua Seal, while Cordura absorbs water. It also dries relatively quickly and is cooler than leather. Light to medium-weight boots cost $40 to more than $100. Recommended brands include Merrill, Scarpa, Nike and Hi-Tec. Heavier duty boots (Merrill, Scarpa and Basque are three of the best makes) can cost several hundred dollars. Tyhonchuk recommends that you ask about the store's return policy. Some retailers will allow you to try out new boots by wearing them inside the house for a week. Boots should fit snugly but not too tightly when you're wearing two pairs of socks— one thin synthetic pair under thicker wool ones. Your heel shouldn't lift inside the boot while walking.

No matter what you do, new boots must be properly broken in before taking off for a strenuous, all-day hike in the mountains. Wear them around the house or while walking the dog. Don them every chance you get to make sure your feet are used to them before doing a bigger trip. "If you have trouble with your feet, you'll have trouble getting back out again," Tyhonchuk notes. "That's no fun at all."

Ellen Gasser says the next most important piece of equipment is a day pack. It should be big enough to carry the essentials but not so big that you're tempted to pack more than you need. The checklist for a day hike should include sunglasses, bug spray, sunscreen, 1 l (3.8 gal) of water per person for an average day, rain gear, high-energy snack food such as a trail mix of raisins, nuts and chocolate, a healthy and hefty lunch (more than you'd eat at home) and a basic first-aid kit. Gasser suggests dressing in layers, so you can take off or add clothes according to the weather and amount of effort being exerted.

If you aren't in great shape, you shouldn't push yourself too hard. A rigorous hike several hours away from emergency aid is a poor time to try to beat yourself into shape. To avoid exhaustion, Gasser suggests a walking method popularized by Swiss mountain guides. When climbing a steep slope, don't walk on your toes. As you move your leg back, straighten it out completely before taking the next step. The weight is placed on your leg bones and your muscles do less work. Put the leading foot down flat, then bend the knee rather than the toes. Walk at a measured pace, stopping often to take in the scenery around you and to catch your breath. On extremely steep inclines you may need to sidestep for stability.

Gasser offers the gentle reminder that hiking is not an endurance test. A brisk pace from beginning to end may work every muscle in your body, but you may also miss the many sights, sounds and smells that comprise the total hiking experience. Take time to learn about birds, plants, animals and geology.

Outings with Children

I F YOU ENJOY an active lifestyle and have young children, you have to make a decision: do you stay home and mope with the kids, hire a baby-sitter and go without them or take them along?

The last option is not only viable but enjoyable. Sharing the outdoors with your children gives you a whole new perspective. It invokes a sense of freshness, an innocence that is difficult to match when exploring alone or with another adult. Granted, contemplating the logistics can be somewhat intimidating, especially for new parents. Lunches and enough clothing to stock a day care must be packed. After driving to the mountains the last thing many kids want to do is hike or ski, unless of course a McDonald's or water slide waits at the other end. After finally getting on the trail, kids sometimes immediately begin asking to go home. You may wonder if it's really worth all that effort.

Frankly, yes it is. Our two daughters, Chelsea and Sarah, started hiking and skiing early in their lives. Karen and I were eager to share elements of the outdoors that had become so important to our own lives. But it took an attitude adjustment. We had to accept that we couldn't do long, grueling trips like we used to in the era B.C. (Before Children). We also realized that the girls wouldn't get as much out of an outing if they were merely hoisted on our shoulders and carried for long distances. We wanted them to be participants, not passengers. With kids, a short hike that wouldn't even raise a sweat before parenthood turns into an entertaining all-day affair. Preparing to go can sometimes take longer than the actual outing.

But you can take steps to get the most out of a family outing. The University of Calgary (403 220-5038) and the city of Calgary Outdoor/Nature Services (403 268-1311) offer excellent programs on skiing and hiking with children. Several local ski clubs, which can be reached through the Calgary Area Outdoor Council, offer Jackrabbit learn-to-ski programs for kids. Many Calgary schools offer the Jackrabbit program as an extra-curricular activity. The program is named after Jackrabbit Johannsen, the patriarch of the sport in Canada, who brought cross-country skiing from his native Norway at the turn of the century.

When you're ready to head out, invite another family with kids of a similar age so your children can relate to others their own age. Outings should be planned according to the kids' sleeping and eating schedules and take into account their boredom and happiness thresholds. Get the kids their own day or fanny packs, even if they're only filled with a juice box and candy bar. Children carrying their own supplies feel like active, equal participants.

Loop trails should be selected to keep a children's interest. Bridges, lakes and waterfalls are great resting spots that provide distractions. Keep in mind that your desire to reach a particular destination in a certain amount of time might not jibe with your kids'

Hiking with children.

goals. Let the kids set the pace, and let yourself enjoy the scenery and their company.

Ardent skier John Janssen has taught the university course on cross-country skiing with kids. He and his wife, Eleanor Heinrichs, started skiing with their two kids when they were still in diapers. He suggests choosing destinations that include a nearby lodge or shelter with washrooms, running water, fireplace, interpretive displays and a trail system that never takes you far from the facility. Heading out on a slight uphill grade makes for an easier return on tired young legs. When your kids are just starting to ski, try out equipment and test their endurance on short outings such as a city golf course before heading to the mountains.

Carrying a child in a pack on your back is dangerous and must not be attempted. When skiing with babies or toddlers, Janssen recommends using some kind of sled. These can range from a basic wooden sleigh rigged with rigid tow bars (instead of the usual pull rope, which isn't as stable or safe) to a specially designed fiberglass unit called a pulk. A less expensive jerry-rigged version can be made with a molded plastic sled rigged with tow bars made of split lengths of PVC plumbing pipe. Some manufactured pulks come with tinted windscreens and nylon covers to protect children from the sun, snow and ice. Kids can be securely tucked in with seat belts, blankets and sleeping bags.

Pulling a sled or pulk is more challenging, so Janssen urges you to ski only on familiar comfortable terrain. Trails with steep hills leading into sharp turns should only be attempted if you are a proficient skier. Kids should be encouraged to graduate from the pulk to skis as soon as they are able, possibly as early as two or three years of age.

Janssen warns against skiing with kids when it's colder than –10°C (14°F). Cold little fingers, toes and faces make for a miserable outing for both child and parent. Make it easier on your skiing child by taking a nylon webbing rope 4–5 m (13–16') long. Tie it around your waist and pull your children up hills or even along flat stretches when they becomes tired. It also can be used to slow their descent on a steep hill. Join yourselves with the rope and have the child go down first.

Whether hiking or skiing, it's important to keep children fed and watered on the trail. Carry juice, water or hot chocolate in plastic bicycle bottles, which are easy to drink from. Pack plenty of snacks: granola bars, fruit roll-ups, cookies, fruit bars, carrot sticks, crackers, cheese slices, apple wedges and trail mix containing raisins, candy-coated chocolate, Cheerios and granola.

When you hit the trail, make the experience fun. Remember, this isn't an endurance or speed test. Take flora and fauna guides so you can answer those tough questions. Sing songs, play games and take lots of breaks. Help your young partners identify animal tracks, watch for birds' nests and squirrels and offer rewards—a snack, drink or special game—for each stretch of trail completed. Once you reach that small goal, take time to make snow angels or a castle of sticks.

For many kids cross-country skiing and hiking are their introduction to the outdoors. It's a good time to sow the seeds of environmental responsibility, teaching them not to litter and to pack out all garbage, even if it's not theirs. It's also an opportunity to teach them not to collect fossilized rocks, flowers or anything else. Taking time to calmly explain about bears and other wildlife will teach them respect rather than fear.

"The trick is to keep it light and keep it fun," says Kendy Bentley, who teaches hiking with kids courses through Outdoor/Nature Services. Bentley, who has hiked with her two daughters since they were toddlers, is an enthusiastic proponent of hiking birthday parties. Her blueprint for success? A short, interesting but relatively easy route and party bags featuring trail mix, pencils, cheap plastic whistles and colorful water bottles. Kids should bring their own backpacks. You may want to add a nature scavenger hunt, including items such as animal tracks, green leaves and birds, or a wiener roast at a nearby day-use area.

The rules for a birthday party hike are simple. Children must stay together on the trail, always in sight of an adult, and shout or sing to announce their presence to wildlife. They should be encouraged to ask questions about animal tracks and other important topics. An hour on the trail is sufficient for younger children, several hours for older ones. After the hike, the party can move indoors for cake and hot chocolate.

Lake Hikes

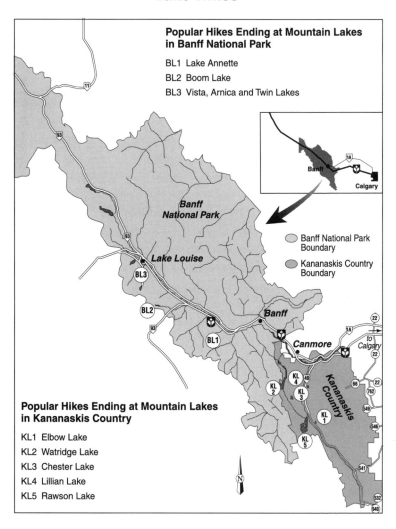

Popular Hikes Ending at Mountain Lakes in Banff National Park

BL1 Lake Annette
BL2 Boom Lake
BL3 Vista, Arnica and Twin Lakes

Banff National Park Boundary

Kananaskis Country Boundary

Banff National Park

Lake Louise

Banff

Canmore

Kananaskis Country

Popular Hikes Ending at Mountain Lakes in Kananaskis Country

KL1 Elbow Lake
KL2 Watridge Lake
KL3 Chester Lake
KL4 Lillian Lake
KL5 Rawson Lake

"A LAKE IS THE LANDSCAPE's most beautiful and expressive feature. It is the earth's eye; looking into which the beholder measures the depth of his own nature," wrote Henry David Thoreau in *Walden.* Whether it's a scenic lake or glacier-carved cirque tucked away in a mountain valley, water attracts hikers like bees to flowers.

Perry Davis, a human use researcher in Banff National Park, says people like to have a destination when they hike, and lakes are perfect.

The shores of mountain lakes in Banff National Park and Kananaskis Country are great places to sit, rest and enjoy a snack while recuperating for the return hike. With some exceptions you can expect a tough lung-testing climb on the way in and an easier march on the way back. Many lakes also offer backcountry campgrounds, an added bonus if you enjoy backpacking. If you like to fish as well as hike, you have a special thrill waiting for you at scenic lakes near the end of hiking trails. Dozens of mirror-surfaced lakes have populations of brook, rainbow and cutthroat trout just waiting to be offered an artificial fly, small spinner or spoon. Fishing regulations vary, so it's a good idea to check out the rules with Kananaskis Country or Banff park offices before casting a line.

Jim Stelfox is the Calgary-based Alberta Fish and Wildlife Services fisheries biologist responsible for Kananaskis Country. The 40-plus high mountain lakes within the region are recreational fisheries rather than spots where people can catch a load of trout for the freezer, he says. Some lakes allow a two-trout daily limit; others are strictly catch-and-release. That's just fine with Calgary construction workers Dave Thoresen and Patrick Moy. On opening morning each summer, the fishing partners hike into Rawson Lake, a 16-ha (40-acre) emerald-hued jewel nestled in a basin at the foot of Mount Sarrail. Getting there means a 3.9-km (2.4-mi), mainly uphill hike south of Upper Kananaskis Lake.

For Thoresen and Moy the hike is worth it. They caught dozens of scrappy cutthroat trout by late morning on opening day a few seasons ago. Some were hooked on artificial flies, but most were fooled by small Panther Martin spinners. All were caught as the anglers drifted around in donut-shaped inflatable float tubes and used flipper-clad feet to propel themselves. All the trout were released. Even before no-bait and catch-and-release rules came into effect at Rawson and three other Kananaskis Country high mountain lakes in 1996, many anglers voluntarily released all trout. "This lake is a

Landing a nice cutthroat trout from a float tube at Rawson Lake in Kananaskis Country.

keepsake," says Calgary angler Stuart Davidson, making his first trip into Rawson on a bright summer day. "The fun's not really in keeping the fish anyway."

If you hike as a family, your kids will enjoy a chance to skip stones (please, not near anglers!) and explore the shoreline. Turning over rocks and logs on the edge of the water can reveal a fascinating assortment of bugs and other tiny critters that can keep kids amused. Wildlife watching can be very productive at mountain lakes. Like people, animals such as deer, mountain goats, bighorn sheep, moose and bears are attracted to lakes and surrounding habitat.

One of our family's strangest wildlife encounters occurred at a mountain lake. It was early evening and my oldest daughter, Chelsea, and I were fishing for brook trout. We were walking along the trail to the other end of the lake when suddenly we stopped in our tracks. Three moose, two bulls and a cow, stood frozen in gangly legged midstep on the narrow, rock-lined trail just 75 m (246') away. With huge snouts and ears that seemed too small for their massive heads, they fixed us with looks only a moose can make. Their perplexed expressions seemed to ask, "What are you doing on my trail, and what do I do now?" The moose seemed to be weighing their options: walk past us on the trail, turn around and go back the way they came or detour across a steep loose scree slope. Instead, before we had a chance to reverse our course to let the moose pass, the single-minded creatures took a fourth option. They went swimming. Speechless, we stared as the moose stepped off the rocks and began dog-paddling toward the far shore a few hundred meters away.

The cow was in the lead, followed by the smaller paddle-horned bull and the larger bull grunting behind. The moose almost reached the distant shore when they changed their minds. The trio veered right and headed toward the other end of the lake, swimming within 50 m (164') of wading fly-fishers. Standing chest-deep in the frigid water, the anglers stopped casting to watch in wide-eyed astonishment as the moose swam by.

Tiring of this roundabout detour, the larger bull split for the lake's west side. He emerged onto the rocky shoreline, shook like a wet dog and vanished in the trees. His buddies hit the shallows at the lake's far end. They, too, were swallowed up by the forest. The fly-fishers looked like they were going to cheer. After all, it's not every day that moose mingle with fly-fishers at a Rocky Mountain lake.

The ten spots shown on the accompanying map are among the best lake destinations in Kananaskis Country and Banff National Park. However, they are a highly subjective and select sampling, representing only a fraction of the lakes which make great hikes in those two regions. Visitor information centers can provide a more complete roster of lakes waiting at the end of invigorating hikes.

In Banff one of the most popular lakes is Boom, off the Banff–Windermere Highway. The hike is about 5 km (3.1 mi) one way, but you'll be rewarded by the scenic lake at the foot of Boom Mountain. Washrooms and a picnic area can be found at the trailhead. Within 2 km (1.2 mi) past Boom Lake, hardy and energetic hikers can visit Vista, Arnica and both Twin Lakes. You'll first descend 1.6 km (1 mi) into Vista at the base of Mount Storm before climbing to Arnica and Twin.

Another popular mountain lake hike is Elbow Lake on the eastern edge of Peter Lougheed Provincial Park. It features a 20-site camping area complete with a raised horizontal pole so you can hang food well out of reach of bears. The hike to Elbow is only 1.3 km (.8 mi), much of it uphill. Hikers of all ages and physical conditioning can easily make it, especially with a couple of stops to enjoy the view (otherwise known as catching your breath).

Chester Lake is a 4.5-km (2.8-mi) hike off the Smith–Dorrien Highway. Nestled in the shadow of Mount Chester, the lake's setting is distinctly Canadian. The French Alps pale in comparison. On a blue-sky day, golden larch trees surrounding the lake can blaze brilliantly in the warm sunlight.

Autumn's Gold Rush

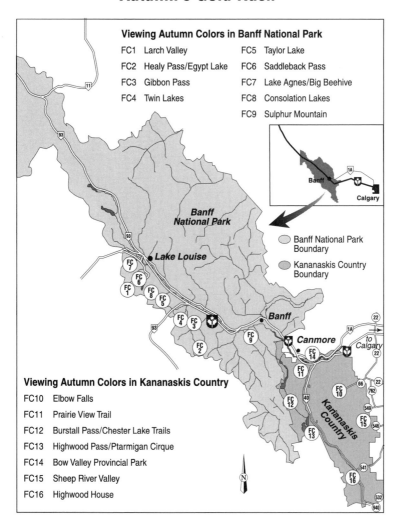

Viewing Autumn Colors in Banff National Park

FC1	Larch Valley	FC5	Taylor Lake
FC2	Healy Pass/Egypt Lake	FC6	Saddleback Pass
FC3	Gibbon Pass	FC7	Lake Agnes/Big Beehive
FC4	Twin Lakes	FC8	Consolation Lakes
		FC9	Sulphur Mountain

Banff National Park Boundary

Kananaskis Country Boundary

Banff National Park

Lake Louise

Banff

Canmore

to Calgary

Kananaskis Country

Viewing Autumn Colors in Kananaskis Country

FC10 Elbow Falls
FC11 Prairie View Trail
FC12 Burstall Pass/Chester Lake Trails
FC13 Highwood Pass/Ptarmigan Cirque
FC14 Bow Valley Provincial Park
FC15 Sheep River Valley
FC16 Highwood House

F SEASONS WERE PEOPLE, autumn would be the wildly eccentric relative you love to visit. There's nothing subdued or boring about fall. Going strictly on looks, the other three seasons are relatively lackluster. Autumn's colors are vivid and varied, bursting from nature's palette in a remarkable celebration of contrasts. It's simultaneously kaleidoscopic, psychedelic and magical. "It's the nicest time of year to be outdoors," says Mairi Babey, ranger-naturalist at the Inglewood Bird Sanctuary. For her the exciting process of trees and bushes changing from green to yellow, orange and red is "like a little spurt of energy to help get us through the winter."

In late September and early October, Calgarians head out to the mountains in droves to witness the annual changing of nature's color guard. Poplars and aspens turn bright yellow with tinges of scarlet. Dogwood, Rocky Mountain maples and other shrubs turn brilliant yellow, orange and rust. Without question, the most popular attraction is the subalpine larch tree, the only conifer that drops its needles each fall and grows new ones in spring. Before the needles fall, larches undergo a stunning transformation from green to yellow to orange and finally blazing gold. Eastern Canada may have its bright red maple leaves, but Calgarians take great pride in their golden larches.

Larch Valley in Banff National Park traditionally has been Mecca for larch lovers, but the huge crowds the area draws have caused environmental damage that will take years to reverse. The crowds also may be a turnoff if you understandably don't like to line up to experience nature. Fortunately larch are found in many other parts of Banff and Kananaskis Country. The attached map shows 16 of the best places to see larches and other autumn displays of color. Visitor centers in Banff and Kananaskis Country can provide information on other spots where you can take in the colorful scenery. If you don't want to leave Calgary, you can view spectacular autumn shows at Fish Creek Provincial Park, Carburn Park, Sandy Beach and Lawery Gardens.

The window of opportunity for larch viewing is relatively narrow, lasting two to four weeks. In the Rockies, larches and other trees generally start to change color in mid- to late-September and retain their autumn hues until mid- to late-October. The weather plays a major role in how long larches remain golden. Extremely low temperatures, heavy snow and high winds can knock off needles earlier than usual. An unseasonably early snowpack also reduces hiking access into the backcountry.

If hiking in the mountains isn't an option, you can view the changing colors of autumn from your vehicle on scenic drives through Banff and Kananaskis Country. Pack a picnic lunch to munch at roadside recreation areas. Plan to make a day of it. An autumn colors tour shouldn't be rushed. Don't forget binoculars and a camera.

Hiking and mountain biking in autumn means packing warm clothing. Weather conditions in the mountains in autumn can change quickly and drastically. Be prepared for snow at higher elevations even if there is none in the parking lot. Pack gaiters to keep your boots and pant legs dry just in case. City naturalist John McFaul, who has led hiking trips to the mountains since 1986, cringes in fall when he sees hikers unloading extra clothes from day packs before leaving the parking lot. This usually happens after they carefully study the sky and find the weather warm and sunny with nary a cloud to be seen. But blizzards can blow in within minutes. If weather turns bad while you're on the trail, McFaul advises you turn back immediately.

During pre-hike stops at visitor centers, ask for updates on bear sightings. Grizzlies and black bears are extremely active in fall, when they gorge themselves on berries, roots and anything else they can find to put on fat before tucking in for winter's big sleep. Finding out where bears have been spotted will help you plan your outing to avoid close encounters of the ursine kind. Trouble usually can be avoided by making lots of noise, especially near flowing waters and blind corners on trails. Leave your dog at home or keep it leashed. Children should remain close to parents and not allowed to run ahead on the trail and out of sight. Bull elk also should be avoided in their fall breeding season. Rutting bulls can be aggressive and unpredictable. (See Chapter 7, "Playing it Safe in the Rocky Mountains.")

Autumn also is a prime time to spot other wildlife as waterfowl, warblers, eagles and other birds of prey migrate over the mountains. The crowds of autumn are smaller, except on weekends in extremely popular areas, and solitude is virtually guaranteed on a midweek outing. Black flies and mosquitoes are all but gone, and rivers and creeks generally are much lower. New areas that might not have been accessible in spring and summer now can be reached with easy, albeit chilly, fords. Bear in mind, however, that the days are getting shorter and an extended outing could bring you back to the parking lot in the cold, after dark.

Be aware, too, that in autumn you share the land with hunters seeking big game animals such as deer, moose, elk and upland birds including ruffed, spruce and blue grouse. Hunting isn't allowed on Sundays, or in national parks, provincial parks and day-use recreation areas, but it is permitted in other parts of Kananaskis Country, excluding the Sheep River Wildlife Sanctuary. In Kananaskis Country, hunting is prohibited within 385 m (1,263') of Highway 40 between the southern boundary of Peter Lougheed Provincial Park and Secondary Highway 940, and along Secondary Highway 541 between Highway 40 and the eastern boundary of the Rocky Mountain Forest Reserve.

Wear bright clothing when traveling the backcountry in areas open to hunting. Hunters prefer to frequent areas not used by hikers, and vice versa, but sometimes paths cross. Keep in mind that hiking and hunting both are legal activities. Hunters have just as much right as anybody else to be in the woods in autumn.

Best Cross-Country Skiing

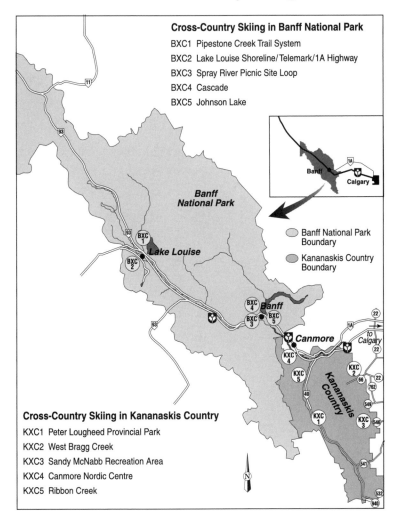

Cross-Country Skiing in Banff National Park

BXC1 Pipestone Creek Trail System
BXC2 Lake Louise Shoreline/Telemark/1A Highway
BXC3 Spray River Picnic Site Loop
BXC4 Cascade
BXC5 Johnson Lake

Banff National Park Boundary
Kananaskis Country Boundary

Banff National Park

Lake Louise

Banff

Canmore

Kananaskis Country

to Calgary

Cross-Country Skiing in Kananaskis Country

KXC1 Peter Lougheed Provincial Park
KXC2 West Bragg Creek
KXC3 Sandy McNabb Recreation Area
KXC4 Canmore Nordic Centre
KXC5 Ribbon Creek

COMMUTERS CURSE IT, but cross-country skiers can't get enough of it. The snow that blankets the Rocky Mountains starting in late fall is roundly cheered by anyone who loves strapping on skinny skis for an invigorating slide-and-glide outing. Every good dump of snow is regarded as a gift straight from heaven. The snow cover you see from the window of your house in Calgary might not look sufficient for cross-country skiing, but it can be super in parts of Kananaskis Country and Banff National Park. Great conditions may exist anywhere from 30 to 90 minutes from city limits.

The trick isn't in finding a place to go but in narrowing down the selection to a single destination. Even if you skied every day of the winter for the next 10 years, you couldn't hit every trail in Banff and Kananaskis Country. There are different spots for every taste and skill level. Some like jump-starting their hearts with grinding uphills, fast downs and tight turns; others prefer gently rolling terrain with few surprises. And some like a happy combination of the two. So where do you go, especially if you're new to the sport or the region?

The following is my personal list of the ten best places to cross-country ski in Kananaskis Country and Banff. My selections are based on suitability for family groups and novices, scenery, facilities and type of terrain. The recommendations focus on places with groomed and trackset double tracks suitable for classic-style skiing, though some of the areas also have wide freestyle—skate skiing—lanes. The list doesn't cover backcountry skiing. More technically and physically demanding than track skiing, venturing onto untracked virgin snow in rugged backcountry terrain is more suited to highly experienced skiers with considerable ski, survival and snow-evaluation skills.

Banff National Park

Access: West on the Trans-Canada Highway for about 100 km (62 mi) to the Banff townsite, then another 50 km (31 mi) west to Lake Louise.
Contact: Banff Visitor Centre at 403 762-1550; Lake Louise Visitor Center at 403 522-3833.

Pipestone Creek

Access: Off Slate Road on the north side of the Trans-Canada Highway, 1 km (.6 mi) west of the Lake Louise turnoff.

Cross-country skiing the Pipestone Trail system in Banff National Park.

This is one of the park's most underrated, overlooked and nicest ski systems. A national park official once told me it's a hidden secret compared to some of the more popular trails in the Lake Louise area. Offering 21 km (13 mi) of groomed trails, it's sandwiched between Mount Hector and Mount Whitehorn, the downhill skiing Mecca for many Calgarians. Trails rated easy to moderate pass through rolling hills, towering spruces, benchlands, frozen lakes and open clearings with spectacular views of surrounding mountain peaks.

Lake Louise Shoreline/Telemark/1A Highway

Access: Southwest from Lake Louise turn off the Trans-Canada Highway along Lake Louise Drive toward the stately Chateau Lake Louise, where both the Shoreline and Telemark trails begin. On the right-hand side is the parking lot for the 1A Highway Trail.

Alasdair Fergusson of the Calgary Ski Club likes this area for two reasons: dependable snow cover early and late in the season, and Chateau Lake Louise. "The chateau makes a great base," he says. "You've got indoor heated washrooms, wine and hot chocolate at your fingertips." And excellent skiing to boot. The Shoreline Trail, rated easy, is 3 km (1.8 mi) one way and follows a pony trail through the trees around the lake's west shore. Keep off the lake, especially early and late in the season. The Telemark Trail, rated moderate, is a 9.3-km (5.8-mi) loop running north over the Bow Valley Parkway and following a short section of the 1A Highway Trail, which is 7.5 km (4.6 mi) one way and rated easy.

Spray River Picnic Site Loop

Access: South on Banff Avenue and Glen Avenue toward the Banff Springs Hotel. On the left-hand side is the parking lot for the Bow Falls viewpoint.

Rated moderate but suitable for novices, this 11-km (7-mi) hairpin-shaped trail follows the lodgepole-lined Spray River south from the Bow Falls viewpoint. You can start either at the golf course trailhead by parking at the falls viewpoint or at the Banff Springs Hotel trailhead after parking on Spray Avenue. Walk past the hotel to the wooden gate across the Spray River fire road. Beginning from the golf course, the trail starts halfway down the first fairway. At the halfway mark, a wooden bridge crosses the river. There's a picnic spot here, so rest and enjoy lunch beside a warming fire. Skiing isn't recommended on the Spray River. After finishing the route, treat yourself to a soak in the nearby Sulphur Mountain Upper Hot Springs.

Cascade

Access: From the Trans-Canada Highway interchange outside the Banff townsite, drive north 3.5 km (2 mi) on the Lake Minnewanka and

Two Jack Lake Road to the Upper Bankhead picnic area parking lot. From the parking lot, ski north to the far corner of the meadow and follow the roadway through a spruce forest. When the trail branches, take either route leading to the trail.

This is an easy, extremely popular trail running for 13 km (8 mi) return along the old Cascade fire road near Lake Minnewanka. Past the gravel pit on the right, you'll encounter two fairly challenging uphill grinds. The hills are followed by several kilometers of flat terrain, swamps and meadows before winding down to the Cascade River. Cross the bridge to rest at a picnic spot on the north side of the river. The hills encountered on the way in are a blessing on the return trip.

Johnson Lake

Access: From the Trans-Canada Highway interchange outside the Banff townsite, drive north 6 km (3.7 mi) on the Lake Minnewanka and Two Jack Lake Road to the trailhead at the west end of Johnson Lake.

Diversity is the name of the game here. Rated easy to moderate, the trails feature thrilling downhills, flatland, straight and winding sections, and challenging climbs. Ski loops can be mixed and matched according to the skills of your group. The main trail, running 8.2 km (5 mi), loops around Johnson Lake, passing through gently rolling hills of aspen poplar. Make sure you point out to kids in your group signs of beaver activity in the poplar stands. After completing the route around the lake, continue south through more hilly terrain in the shadow of Mount Peechee. To avoid this, two short trails heading west connect with the main trail, which heads north back to the parking lot.

Kananaskis Country

Peter Lougheed Provincial Park

Access: West on Trans-Canada Highway for 80 km (50 mi), south on Highway 40 for 50 km (31 mi), then turn right onto Kananaskis Lakes Trail.

Contact: Peter Lougheed Provincial Park Visitor Center at 403 591-6322

This area has it all for all levels of skiers. It offers almost 100 km (62 mi) of groomed and trackset trails in the Kananaskis Lakes region and dozens more skiable backcountry kilometers in the north end of the park. The area features Kananaskis Country's earliest and latest snow conditions; in a good year, skiing at higher elevations can last from early November to May. Some diehard skiers end the season by hiking up snow-free trails, then strapping on skis when they hit the Tyrwhitt or upper Elk Pass trails. Trails range from easy to difficult. Additional bonuses include the Peter Lougheed Visitor Centre and Pocaterra Hut, which provide information, washrooms and a place to enjoy a bag lunch in front of a fire. The main visitor center is a good starting point to determine current snow conditions and trails best suited to your skill level. Catch a post-ski hot chocolate and muffin in the Boulton Creek Trading Post (403 591-7678), which is open on winter weekends.

West Bragg Creek

Access: Take either Highway 8 or 22 west to Bragg Creek. Cross Elbow River Bridge, turn left onto West Bragg Creek Road and follow for 1 km (.6 mi) to parking lot inside Kananaskis Country boundary. The location also can be reached from the Elbow Trail off Secondary Road 66 at Allen Bill Pond parking lot.

Contact: Elbow Valley Visitor Centre at 403 949-4261

Though frequent Chinooks can make skiing iffy here, this area is hard to beat when snow conditions are right and crews are kept hopping, trying to maintain grooming and tracksetting on as much as 100 cm (39") of fresh snow in a single week. Just 40 minutes west of Calgary, West Bragg Creek has 51 km (32 mi) of trails, many suitable for family groups and novice skiers. Take advantage of conditions here when you can. The area's proximity to Calgary and great trails make this one of Kananaskis Country's most popular destinations on a nice weekend.

Sandy McNabb Recreation Area

Access: South on Highway 22 to Turner Valley, then west on Secondary Highway 546 to Sandy McNabb Recreation Area. (The highway is closed for the winter just past the main entrance to Sandy McNabb.)
Contact: Elbow Valley Visitors' Center at 403 949-4261. Highwood Visitors' Center at 403 558-2151.

Chinooks also can play havoc on this 37-km (23-mi) trail network west of Turner Valley. But a well-timed visit will treat you to great skiing in a beautiful river valley setting. Bring your own firewood and enjoy a picnic at the summer group campground at the end of the road leading down to the river. Don't forget to pack toboggans and skates. The closed road beyond the group campground and the nearby hills make for great sledding. Parks people flood a nifty little skating rink and trail leading to it from the parking lot across the road from the group campground. Skiers can travel through poplars in the valley overlooking the Sheep River or challenge tougher ridge terrain to the north.

Ribbon Creek

Access: West on the Trans-Canada Highway for 80 km (50 mi), south on Highway 40 for 23 km (14 mi), then take Kananaskis Village turnoff to west.
Contact: Barrier Lake Visitors' Center at 403 673-3985.

This area is a triple winner with its accessibility, great scenery and 54 km (36 mi) of well-marked trails compatible to all skill levels. Backcountry skiing is available for more experienced skiers. When Calgary is locked in a double-digit deep freeze, temperatures here can be balmy. The area can get a bad rap because lower trails are susceptible to Chinooks, but trails such as Kovach and Aspen are more sheltered and usually retain a skiable snowpack even after several days of Chinooks. Enjoy a picnic at Kovach Pond or Ribbon Creek parking lot. To ski, take Hidden Trail north of the parking lot and enjoy a rest at the Nakiska ski area day lodge. Then take the Kovach Trail and treat yourself to lunch in Kananaskis Village. Ribbon Creek can be extremely busy on weekends, especially when the weather's nice in Calgary.

Canmore Nordic Centre

Access: West on the Trans-Canada Highway for 100 km (62 mi) to Canmore. Follow signs along Main Street to the nordic center.
Contact: 403 678-2400.

This is the only place in Kananaskis Country (so far at least) where you pay to cross-country ski. But it's worth the price of admission, which ranges from $3 for kids ages 6 to 11 to $5 for adults for a day's skiing. Built for the 1988 Winter Olympics Nordic events, it has an extensive 70-km (43-mi) well-maintained trail system, which includes some truly expert runs that you shouldn't tackle on a dare if you're inexperienced. Streamlined skiers in form-hugging Lycra suits race against stopwatches on tougher trails, while young families trundle along more user-friendly routes such as the Banff Trail. The day lodge features fireplace, washrooms, showers, public lounging area and cafeteria. The center, which is open for mountain biking and hiking in summer, provides great winter entertainment. Major winter events include sled dog races, fun loppets for skiers and more serious biathlon and cross-country ski competition at provincial, national and world levels.

Cross-country skiing at Canmore Nordic Centre.

Banff's Triple Crown

BANFF NATIONAL PARK offers enough trails for a lifetime of enjoyment, but three venues stand out for their ease of access, stunning scenery, varied activities and suitability for family outings. If you're looking for something else, your best bet is to stop at the visitor information centers in Banff (403 762-1550) and Lake Louise (403 522-3833), where staff can suggest an outing that suits your style. The guide books listed at the back of this book are excellent references. Keep in mind when making your plans that it costs to enter Banff National Park. You must pay $10 for a day pass for a carful of up to 10 people or purchase a $70 annual pass.

Johnston Canyon

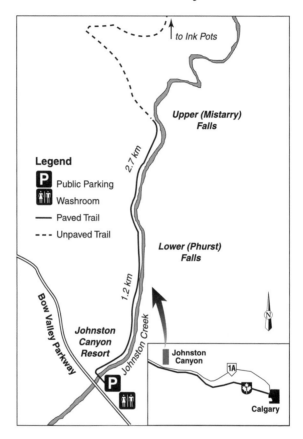

Access: West on the Trans-Canada Highway for 100 km (62 mi) to Banff National Park, west 20 km (12.4 mi) to Bow Valley Parkway, then north 17 km (10.5 mi).

Activities: Hiking, picnicking, camping, wildlife watching, cross-country skiing.

Terrain: Sheer rock walls, lodgepole pines, white spruce, mosses and ferns.

Hours: No set hours.

Contact: Lake Louise Visitor Centre at 403 522-3833.

There's something almost mystical about Johnston Canyon. Frothing rapids tumble into deep-blue pools several feet beneath suspended steel catwalks. The raw power of the water erodes the rock streambed by about 2 mm (1/16") a year. Rock canyon walls tower over the trail. In places where catwalks are fixed to and shrouded by the walls, you feel more a part of the canyon than merely a visitor to it. The canyon's sheer beauty and accessibility makes this one of Banff's most popular hikes for people of all ages.

Signs at the trailhead warn that snow and ice can make the route hazardous. Appropriate footwear, preferably rubber- or Vibram-soled, is recommended. Signs also urge you to hold on to catwalk railings. After viewing the perilously steep drop to the raging water below, few people need the added encouragement. Keep a firm grip on children's hands while on the catwalks.

There is a cave at the lower falls, 1.2 km (.7 mi) from the trailhead. You have to stoop to avoid the cave's low ceiling, but it's worth it. Exiting the other end, you're greeted by the cool spray of a spectacular waterfall plunging into a deep pool. The spray refreshes on a hot day. A second more impressive set of falls dropping 30 m (98') is about 1.5 km (.9 mi) beyond the lower falls. Although the hike to the lower and upper falls isn't strenuous, several wooden benches have been strategically located to ease tired legs. If you're feeling really energetic, keep going into a high meadow, where you'll find the Inkpots located 5.9 km (3.7 mi) from the trailhead. The Inkpots are clear green-tinted pools formed by artesian springs. Water temperature remains at a constant 1°C (34°F).

If you're a cross-country skier, you'll bypass the canyon while skiing on a trail to the west. However, you can view part of the canyon from the summit. The trail is rated moderate for the first 2.2 km (1.4 mi) and difficult for the next 3.7 km (2.3 mi). Heading uphill, you should be alert for returning skiers, who hopefully will be under control on the downhill run.

If you hike, you'll feel dwarfed by Johnston Canyon's limestone walls. Banded in various hues created by 25 different kinds of algae, the canyon is dark and damp. It's lined with mosses and ferns, over-

Hikers on catwalk along Johnston Canyon Trail in Banff National Park.

shadowed by giant lodgepole pine and white spruce trees. The trail features several informative interpretive signs. Wildlife to watch for along the route includes golden-mantled ground squirrels, which look like animated Disney characters as they beg for food that tourists regularly break the law by providing. There's also a good chance of seeing rare black swifts, which nest in dark corners of the canyon, and soot-colored birds called American dippers bobbing in the water, searching for aquatic meals.

Lake Minnewanka

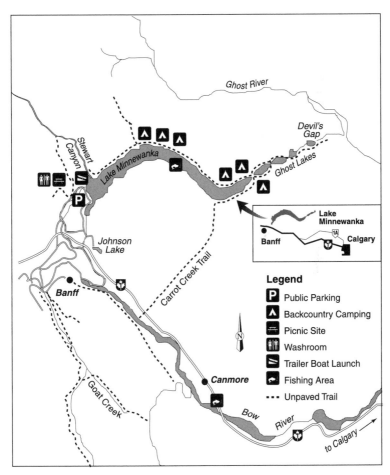

Access: West on the Trans-Canada Highway for 110 km (68 mi), then follow the signs north for 5.6 km (3.5 mi).

Terrain: Mountains, white spruce, dry creek beds.

Activities: Hiking, backpacking into backcountry campgrounds (special permits required), picnicking, fishing, scuba diving, boating (this is the only lake in in Banff National Park to allow motorboats), cruise-boat tours, wildlife watching, cross-country skiing.

Prohibited: Lead fishing lures and sinkers, fishing with bait.

Hours: Boat tours from mid-May to early October, with several scheduled trips daily.

Contact: Banff National Park Visitor Centre at 403 762-1550. Lake Minnewanka Boat Tours at 403 762-3473.

The 30-km (18.7-mi) trail around Lake Minnewanka is a good destination in spring, summer and autumn. The trail is especially popular in late May and fall, when it's generally one of the park's few snow-free hiking routes.

Tourists and locals flock to Minnewanka, Banff National Park's largest lake. They come to hike, mountain bike, camp in the backcountry, fish for lake trout in the lake's azure-tinted, 110-m (360') depths and enjoy a scenic 34-km (21-mi) return guided cruise to Devil's Gap at the far end of the lake. "The lake is famous for fishing, but we get our fair share of people just wanting to take the trip up the lake," says Alita McKinley, supervisor of Lake Minnewanka Boat Tours. It's easy to see why. The Assiniboine Indians, who named the lake, which means "Water of the Spirits," clearly knew what they were talking about.

On the trail along the lake's north shore, bighorn sheep share the single track with hikers, heavily laden backpackers and iron-legged mountain bikers. Mountain goats, mule deer, Columbian ground squirrels, black bears and grizzly bears sometimes can be seen. Although the trail has a net elevation gain of only 85 m (279'), parts are so steep and scree-covered that some bikers are forced to dismount and walk up, their legs having lost some of their iron. The massive wooden-truss bridge over the Cascade River at Stewart Canyon, just 1.5 km (.9 mi) from the parking area, is a favorite destination, especially for families with small children.

A pretty trail can be followed up the Cascade River. Or you can keep on the main Lake Minnewanka trail as it switches back uphill

Backpacker Byron Hagan on Lake Minnewanka Trail in Banff National Park.

through the forest before breaking out into more open areas from which you can watch toylike boats plying the waters far below.

If you're feeling ambitious, veer off on the trail to Aylmer Lookout. From the lookout, you are treated to a spectacular view of Minnewanka and the surrounding mountains, including Aylmer, Inglismaldie and Girouard. At 12 km (7.5 mi), it's a long trail, taking six or seven hours round-trip. The trail includes some steep stretches, but most of it is relatively easy.

Heavy use of the Minnewanka area has brought it under the official microscope in recent years. The Banff–Bow Valley management study in 1996 recommended that only 100 people per month be allowed on the trail though no justification was provided for that number.

Fishing is allowed, but the rules, it seems, change annually. The changes that went into effect in spring 1997 set a two-fish daily catch maximum and prohibit the use of lead weights and lures weighing less than 50 g (1.8 oz). Outlawed are lead split shot, bell weights, some spinners, lead-weighted nymphs and streamers, lead-head jigs and lures made of lead. These include standard-sized Buzz Bombs, once the lake's most popular lure. Larger lead lures and downrigger lead balls weighing more than 50 g (1.8 oz) are permitted. Charlie Pacas, the park's aquatic biologist, says the lead ban is based on Ontario studies, including one indicating that the deaths of up to one third of adult loons were related to ingesting small lead sinkers and lures left by anglers.

The use of bait and scent-impregnated lures also is prohibited, and all bull trout and cutthroat trout must be released. A $13 annual or $6 weekly permit is required to fish in the park. The fishing season at Minnewanka runs from Victoria Day weekend to Labor Day. With lead banned, you have to expand your bag of tricks to include trolling Rapalas, Rat-L-Traps and spoons. Jigging can be effective.

Some anglers suspect that the ever-changing rules are an attempt by Ottawa to discourage or perhaps even stop fishing in the park. The Banff–Bow Valley management study of 1996 recommended that fishing eventually be eliminated within Banff. Pacas says the recommendation was a broad 50-year objective. Although several lakes containing native trout might someday be closed to fishing, he says the sport will never be totally banned in Banff. "The intent within mountain parks is to allow fishing to keep on going," he says. That's good news if you want to fish at Minnewanka, where you can try your luck at catching lake trout up to 14 kg (30 lb).

Plain of Six Glaciers Trail

Access: West on the Trans-Canada Highway for 184 km (114 mi) to the Lake Louise trailhead at the front of Chateau Lake Louise.

Terrain: Scrub alpine fir, alpine meadows.

Activities: Hiking, rock climbing, picnicking, wildlife watching.

Costs: Guided hikes $12 for adults, $6 for children. Phone 403 522-3833 for updated departure times.

Hours: From mid-June to late September, Plain of Six Glaciers and Lake

Agnes teahouses both open daily 10:00 A.M. to 6:00 P.M. depending on snow conditions.

Contact: Lake Louise Visitor Centre at 403 522-3833.

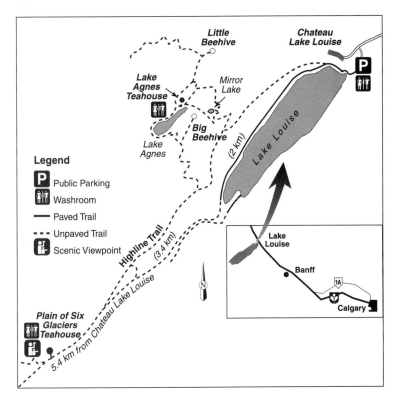

The rustic teahouse on the Plain of Six Glaciers Trail isn't designed for post-meal chatter. Depending on the time of your visit, you can probably forget about gabbing over two or three post-meal cups of coffee. You might even think twice about getting up to visit the outhouse. That's because your seat at the table may be grabbed by another hungry hiker who's been perched vulturelike nearby, just waiting for an opening.

The two-story log teahouse, featuring a handful of tables on the open-air verandah upstairs, is a popular destination for hikers making the 5.5-km (3.4-mi) trek from Lake Louise. It often serves hun-

Hiker on Plain of Six Glaciers Trail with Lake Louise in background.

dreds of people per day. It's especially busy on weekends and between 11:00 A.M. and 4:00 P.M. on sunny summer days.

The possibility of encountering a crowd shouldn't deter you from hiking the Plain of Six Glaciers Trail. The teahouse is a delightful spot to quench your thirst, grab a bite and rest after the 90-minute to two-hour hike from Chateau Lake Louise. After a total climb of 370 m (1,214'), you will be rewarded with a spectacular view of surrounding mountain peaks and, yes, at least six glaciers. The view probably hasn't changed much since 1924, when the building was erected by Swiss guides working for the Canadian Pacific Railway. Originally built as an overnight shelter for climbers bound for Abbot Pass, the teahouse has been operated since 1961 by Joy Smith.

Being fed and watered at the teahouse is far from cheap, an economic reality acknowledged by posted signs noting that all supplies are hauled in on horseback. The food, including cakes, scones and breads, is all baked on site. A hiker we passed on the way up had told us the cake itself was worth the trip. She was right. But that's definitely not the only reason to go there.

Scenery and wildlife top the list. Take time to observe and you'll spot hoary marmots, Columbian and golden mantled ground squirrels, pikas, Clark's nutcrackers, golden eagles and mountain goats. You'll also have a panoramic look at the luxurious chateau and the emerald-hued waters of Lake Louise far below. If you're feeling ambitious, follow the trail another 1.3 km (.8 mi) beyond the teahouse to a viewpoint of Abbot Pass and the Death Trap, a glacier-filled gorge between Mounts Lefroy and Victoria.

The trail to the teahouse starts at Chateau Lake Louise. Follow the Shoreline Trail to the end of the lake. For some free entertainment and to prepare yourself for the hike ahead, stop to watch rock climbers fearlessly scaling the vertical rock walls of the Big Beehive to your right. The trail starts climbing steadily just after the end of the lake. However, it remains relatively open, providing plenty of opportunities to stop to take photographs and glass for mountain goats and other wildlife. While you're at it, take a breather.

Although the hike isn't particularly challenging, you'll enjoy it more with a sturdy pair of hiking shoes or boots. Be prepared to encounter snow high up on the trail as late as early July. A quick check at the Lake Louise Visitor Centre will reveal whether you'll need gaiters on your boots to keep dry. Packing water with you in a day pack or fanny pack is highly recommended. You can refill them from a spring at the teahouse.

If you don't like returning on the same route, turn left on the way down to follow the Highline Trail. Follow it to the marked turnoff to the larger Lake Agnes Teahouse or past the aptly named Mirror Lake before dropping back down to Lake Louise. If you're still feeling peckish, check out the Lake Agnes Teahouse. This route adds 2.3 km (1.4 mi) and gains some elevation, but it provides an impressive goat's eye view of Lake Louise—and a chance to work off that chocolate cake.

Chapter 6

Kananaskis Country

The Natural Playground
at Calgary's Doorstep

KANANASKIS COUNTRY is Calgary's closest and most accessible mountain playground. Since this 4,156-km^2 (1605-mi^2) provincially operated recreation area was officially dedicated in 1978, Calgarians have adopted it as their own. Of the estimated 2.4 million annual visitors, about 1.5 million come from Calgary and area. No matter where you live in the city, it's possible to access Kananaskis Country in an hour or less by heading west of Bragg Creek on Highway 66 or south of the Trans-Canada Highway on Highway 68 into the Sibbald Flats area. Other access points are south of the Trans-Canada on Highway 40 and south of Canmore to the west. You can also get there off Highway 22 west of Millarville, Turner Valley, Longview and just northwest of Chain Lakes Provincial Park.

A multitude of recreational opportunities, many ideally suited to families, are available in this special region. You camp, fish, hike, backpack, picnic, ride horses, mountain bike and bicycle tour, hunt (outside provincial parks only), golf, climb, canoe, kayak, raft, cross-country ski, downhill ski, watch wildlife, snowmobile, snowshoe, dogsled and drive off-road vehicles (in designated areas only).

The Alberta government is establishing a new recreational development policy for this special area after a public consultation process conducted. For years Albertans have told the province to leave K-Country alone, to preserve its ecological integrity and not permit major developments. Most people like the area the way it is. It will be interesting to see if this time the government listens.

This chapter highlights several selected regions of Kananaskis Country and what to do when you get there. It is by no means a complete guide to outdoor recreation in the area. It will, however, point you in the right direction so you can experience varied activities in the region's most scenic terrain. If you're planning to camp or picnic in Kananaskis Country and wish to have a fire, take wood from home or be prepared to pay dearly for a small bundle. You should also check with Kananaskis Country visitor centers and ranger stations to learn more about available opportunities and current regulations and conditions. To avoid long distance charges, dial through the provincial government RITE line by first calling 403 310-0000.

Peter Lougheed Provincial Park

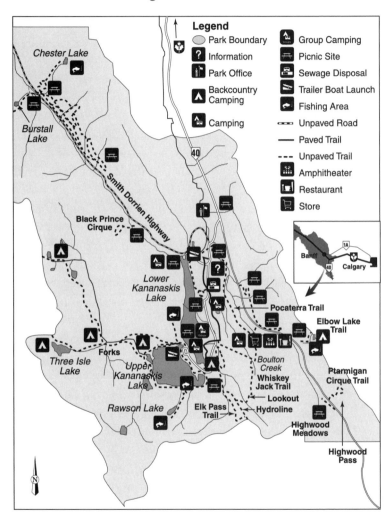

Access: West on Trans-Canada Highway for 80 km (50 mi), south on Highway 40 for 50 km (31 mi), then turn right on to Kananaskis Lakes Trail.

Terrain: Mountains, alpine lakes, evergreen-lined river valleys, glacial streams, alpine larch, fir.

Activities: Hiking, cycling, picnicking, camping, fishing, boating, wind-surfing, wildlife watching, playground, cross-country skiing, snow-shoeing. Swimming and water-skiing are not recommended at Upper and Lower Kananaskis lakes.

Hours: Day-use areas and campgrounds open 7:00 A.M. to 11:00 P.M.

Contact: Peter Lougheed Provincial Park Visitor Centre at 403 591-6344. William Watson Lodge at 403 591-7227. Boulton Creek Trading Post at 403 591-7678.

TORONTONIAN CHARLIE DEE and his wife, Mary, have made the trip to Kananaskis Country every summer for 30 years, even before it became known as K-Country. On this recent summer day, he is sitting on a wooden bench on the west shore of Elbow Lake, on the eastern edge of Peter Lougheed Provincial Park. The couple has hiked the 1.3-km (.8-mi) trail to Elbow Lake from the parking lot beside Highway 40. Within view are hikers, anglers fishing for brook trout and backpackers retrieving rope-suspended food bags from a bear pole at a backcountry campground on the lake's southwest shore. Two mountain bikers bounce along the rock-strewn trail, dodging lumps of equine-processed hay. The bench Charlie and I share with my youngest daughter, Sarah, was installed in spring 1995. It features a bronze plaque inscribed in memory of Gene Cottrell.

The Calgarian died two winters previously not far from here on Blueberry Hill, a stunning viewpoint overlooking Upper and Lower Kananaskis lakes. Cottrell was just 54 when he suffered a massive heart attack while cross-country skiing with members of Calgary's Norseman Ski Club. A few minutes before he died, Cottrell remarked to friends on the "fantastic" day he was enjoying. Toron-tonian Charlie Dee never knew Gene Cottrell. But he knows one thing about him. "That man was lucky to live so close to all this splendor. You all are. You should count your blessings. This is God's world."

Charlie's reverence is common among visitors to Peter Lougheed Provincial Park and, indeed, all of Kananaskis Country.

Canoe on Upper Kananaskis Lake.

Originally called Kananaskis Provincial Park, the park was renamed in 1986 (amid great controversy) in honor of the premier whose government created Kananaskis Country. At 500 km² (193 mi²), Peter Lougheed Park is Alberta's largest provincial park.

Elbow Lake, headwaters of the Elbow River, Calgary's main water source, is one of the park's special jewels. It's a perfect family destination and jumping-off point to longer hikes or mountain bike rides into the Sheep and Elbow river watersheds. The trail is the only one in Peter Lougheed park where horseback riding is allowed. The lake's feisty brook trout make this a great spot to take kids fishing. Recommended fishing techniques include small spinners, worms used below tiny casting bubbles, or flies (weighted nymphs, black Woolly Bugger streamers and dry Adams, Parachute Adams and Royal Wulffs sized 14 to 18).

Elbow Lake is virtually inaccessible in winter unless you're willing to cross-country ski several kilometers. Highway 40 is closed to vehicle traffic from December 1 to June 15 between the turnoff for Upper and Lower Kananaskis Lakes and Highwood House, 56 km (35 mi) to the south. The closure is designed to protect wintering herds of elk.

However, the rest of Peter Lougheed park is highly accessible year-round. That includes the Upper and Lower Kananaskis lakes. Think of these scenic lakes as a giant wet hub. Ringed by mountains, they are the focal point for a myriad of four-season recreational activities. Accessibility and beauty combine to make them among the most popular attractions in Alberta's Rocky Mountains.

Upper Kananaskis Lake was dammed in 1932 by TransAlta Utilities to store water for hydroelectric power generation. The lower lake was dammed in 1955. The upper lake, the more popular of the two with anglers and boaters, is clear and deep, plunging to a maximum depth of 108 m (354'). The water rarely gets warmer than 14°C (57°F) so swimming isn't recommended in either lake. The water is so cold that cramps or hypothermia can set in rapidly. In addition, the steep drop-off and dangerous undercurrents near the dams make swimming extremely risky. There are no sandy beaches or lifeguards.

Even without swimming, however, recreational activities aren't lacking. On any day from ice-out to late fall, visitors ply the lakes in canoes, kayaks, rowboats and motor-propelled crafts. Some boaters fish for trout—rainbows in the upper lake, cutthroats, rainbows and bull trout in the lower. Other boaters go out to exercise or enjoy the view, or both. A 12-km (7.5-mi) per hour speed limit is posted on parts of both lakes. Although the lakes are calm most days, they can get rough quickly if bad weather rolls in from the mountains. Head for shore at the first sign of building waves. Another danger to boaters is posed by stumps and other deadheads scattered around the lake. With fluctuating water levels caused by power draw-downs, deadheads often poke out of the water. Others lie hidden just under the surface.

For Benny Cheung, a Calgary construction company owner, Upper Kananaskis Lake is a favorite ice fishing hot spot. One recent winter morning he was perched on a stool on a midweek afternoon, watching hopefully for a tiny lime-green bobber to signal the bite of a fat rainbow trout down below. Although most trout average about .5 kg (1 lb), rainbows of several kilograms are caught every year. Frozen shrimp and worms are the most consistently producing baits. On the ice beside Cheung lay a pan-sized rainbow he'd caught earlier. "This is just mainly an escape from the city," he says. "I come here for the scenery, not for the one or two fish I might catch."

Upper Kananaskis Lake is ringed by a 16-km (10-mi) gentle hiking trail providing impressive views of the lake and mountains. A highlight is a wooden bridge crossing Sarrail Creek, where spray from a plunging waterfall cools hikers, who should use the handrails since the bridge can be a little slippery. If you're feeling energetic, detour off the trail to Rawson Lake, a 2.7-km (1.7-mi) mainly uphill hike. The trek to the lake is worth it. So's the fishing for cutthroat trout.

Most of the park's campgrounds are located near Upper Kananaskis Lake. They range from drive-ins to walk-ins. Day-use areas provide great picnic spots. A paved 13-km (8-mi) trail runs from the Mount Sarrail campground to the park's interpretive center. Hikers share this path with cyclists and in-line skaters. The park also features William Watson Lodge, a provincially operated facility providing inexpensive overnight accommodation for people with physical, mental and sensory limitations. Lodge buildings and nearby interpretive trails are wheelchair accessible.

Peter Lougheed Provincial Park offers some of Kananaskis

Country's best hiking and cross-country ski trails (See Chapter 5 "Best Cross-Country Skiing" for best destinations.) Great hikes away from the busy hub surrounding the Kananaskis Lakes include Black Prince Cirque, Chester Lake and Burstall Pass off the Smith–Dorrien Highway. A particularly scenic and popular hiking trail is Ptarmigan Cirque Trail, leaving from the trailhead just off Highway 40 at Highwood Pass in the park's south end. Sixty meters (197') below tree line at an elevation of 2,206 m (7,238'), Highwood Pass is Canada's highest driveable mountain pass. The moderately difficult Ptarmigan Cirque Trail covers about 5 km (3.1 mi). It's a world of 350-year-old alpine larch and fir trees, Columbian ground squirrels and hoary marmots, wild flowers, rare alpine grasses and white-tailed ptarmigan, a mottled grouselike bird. On a part of highway included in the winter closure, Highwood Pass is inaccessible by vehicle in winter.

Anywhere in the park, there's an excellent chance of seeing moose, mule or white-tailed deer, elk or grizzly and black bears.

The Big Spawn—A Very Bullish Hike

THE PLACE-MAT–SIZED photograph in interpretive guide Melissa Mauro's hand spoke volumes. It showed a weak trickle of water flanked by barren mudflats studded with dead tree stumps. Photographed in early spring, the desolate depiction of the northwest bay of Lower Kananaskis Lake bore little resemblance to the deep, healthy-looking bay now showing in late summer. The contrasting scenes dramatically illustrated how a sharply fluctuating water level caused by the TransAlta Utilities dam challenges long-term recovery of threatened bull trout—Alberta's official fish—and cutthroat trout in Lower Kananaskis Lake. The lake was one of Alberta's top cutthroat fisheries before the dam was built in 1955.

A draw-down of up to 13 m (43') each winter to generate electricity prevents formation of a stable littoral zone around the lake edges. Trout need this shallow area of vegetation, insects and baitfish to thrive. Mauro says the lake now is like an aquatic desert.

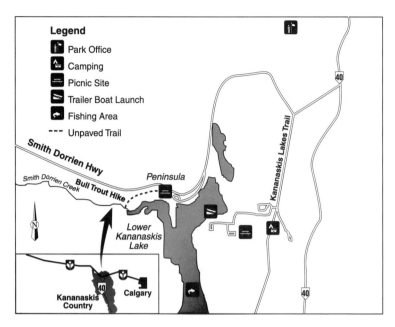

So what, an inquisitive tourist **asked during** the interpretive hike led by Mauro, is the alternative? **The answer:** TransAlta Utilities could stabilize the level of the lake **to promote** development of a life-giving littoral zone. And what **would a healthy** ecosystem cost consumers? Less than a nickel **on a $100 electricity** bill.

The somber message is **included in an** informative free guided hike offered on weekends **from August** to October in Peter Lougheed Provincial Park. School and other groups can book midweek tours by calling 403 591-6322. Visitors get an up-close look at bull trout of several kilograms spawning in Smith–Dorrien Creek, a shallow, clear creek that you could jump over in places. The 90-minute interpretive hike traces the troubled history of bull trout (which, it should be noted, is a native char, not a trout). The hike leaves from the Peninsula day-use area at the north end of Lower Kananaskis Lake off the Smith–Dorrien Highway. It covers less than 1 km (.6 mi) of relatively flat terrain.

This could be the best place in Alberta to see bull trout, especially **big bulls** of almost 5 kg (11 lb). It's Kananaskis Country's

Fisheries researcher Craig Mushens with big female bull trout from Smith–Dorrien Creek in Kananaskis Country.

answer to the sockeye salmon spawning runs of the Adams River in eastern British Columbia. Bull trout start moving up Smith–Dorrien Creek in early August and return during September and October. Big bulls can be seen digging nests in the streambed with their tails and aggressively defending them from other fish. On days when the interpretive hike isn't on, visitors can take a self-guided tour. Walk carefully along the bank and don't throw rocks or otherwise disturb the spawning bull trout. Polarized sunglasses help spot big fish holding in the current. The University of Calgary has operated a research station along Smith–Dorrien Creek to study the spawning bull trout.

Making use of songs and games, the highly interactive guided tour traces the bull trout's checkered history from the early days, when the species was considered vermin, through an era when populations plummeted due to overfishing and habitat loss. Bull trout, like grizzly bears, are considered symbols of wilderness. The province is trying to restore their numbers and raise awareness among anglers and others. All bull trout in Alberta must be released by anglers.

The park tour promotes proper identification of bull trout. The main identification key is the lack of black spots or dark markings on the dorsal fin or anywhere else on the body. The common slogan of conservation-minded anglers is "No black, put it back."

To further protect the Lower Kananaskis Lake population, fishing is prohibited year-round in the northwest bay and in Smith–Dorrien Creek. Use of bait also is prohibited in the lake. In 1992, the first year of restrictive fishing rules in Lower Kananaskis Lake, just 60 adult spawning bull trout were counted. A year later researchers spotted 155 spawning adults. About 650 mature spawning bull trout were tallied in 1996. Fisheries biologist Jim Stelfox says 1,280 adult bull trout were counted in the autumn of 1998. He considers this proof that bull trout populations can rebound—as long as anglers can properly identify them and don't kill them in error.

While the population of mature fish is increasing, there's ongoing concern that the poor littoral zone impedes survival of small cutthroat, rainbow and bull trout. Adult trout prey on small fish, including the lake's healthy population of suckers, but younger trout feed on aquatic insects, freshwater shrimp and smaller baitfish, which in turn need a littoral zone in which to live.

Elbow River Valley

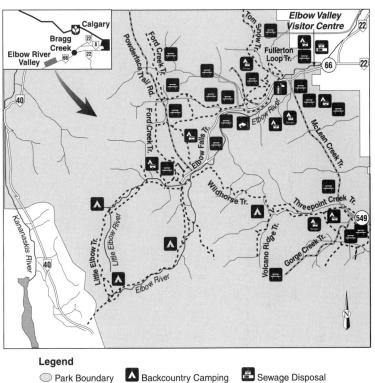

Legend

◯ Park Boundary	🅰 Backcountry Camping	🅰 Sewage Disposal
🚹 Park Office	🅰 Camping	🎣 Fishing Area
🪑 Picnic Site	🅰 Group Camping	--- Unpaved Trail

Access: West on Highway 8 then Highway 22 for 49 km (30.4 mi) to Bragg Creek. Or, from south Calgary, west on Highway 22x then Highway 22 for 37 km (23 mi) to Bragg Creek turnoff, then Highway 66 for 12 km (7.5 mi).

Terrain: Mountains, alpine meadows, river valley, subalpine forest, aspen parkland, grasslands.

Activities: Hiking, cycling, off-road driving (in designated area only), camping, fishing, canoeing, kayaking, wildlife watching, horseback riding, hunting, cross-country skiing, skating.

Hours: Day-use areas and campgrounds open 7:00 A.M. to 11:00 P.M.

Contact: Elbow Valley Ranger Station at 403 949-3754. Elbow Valley Visitor Center at 403 949-4261. Elbow Valley Campgrounds and Store at 403 949-3132.

THE ELBOW RIVER VALLEY region is one of Kananaskis Country's most popular destinations. About 40 minutes from city limits, it's flush with picnic and camping sites and trails for hiking and cross-country skiing. Many Calgarians are introduced to—and get hooked on—Kananaskis Country by visiting this user-friendly region.

I've visited the Elbow River Valley dozens of times, yet would have to spend dozens more before claiming even moderate familiarity. I've hiked Fullerton Loop, a 5-km (3.1-mi) trail that follows the Elbow River before climbing Ranger Ridge and providing a sweeping view of the valley. I hiked it for the first time in 1989 with John Ryan, a Bragg Creek outfitter who used the outing to showcase his new string of pack goats. That's right. Domestic farm-type goats, complete with colorful little packs to carry gear. I've also hiked Fullerton Loop by myself, with my family and with friends we don't see nearly enough.

In winter, we've skated and roasted wieners at a pretty little picnic spot called Allen Bill Pond. It's named after the *Calgary Herald's* former editor and outdoor columnist. I never met Allen Bill, who died in 1970, but I've read enough of his columns to know that he would like this place, even if the rainbow trout are stocked, not wild. I've hiked all over the ridge at the end of the Moose Mountain Road, where at night you can see the eerie glow of Calgary's lights. I've fished for rainbow trout in the Elbow River, where the fishing improves in relation to the distance from your vehicle. I've cast flies for the scrappy brookies, cutthroats and bull trout of Quirk Creek, which cuts through a pretty valley savaged by many years of overgrazing by cattle. Several times we've been awed by Elbow Falls, a spectacular rush of water where handrails are provided to keep you and your children from falling in. I've never seen the Harlequin ducks that swim at the base of the falls, but it seems everybody else I know has.

Playing hockey at Allen Bill Pond in the Elbow district of K-Country.

I've hunted mule deer in the McLean Creek off-highway vehicle area, the only place in Kananaskis Country that allows off-roading. I've heard the area once was pristine. Now it's chewed up by four-wheel-drive weekend warriors who seem to take it as a personal challenge to make it up the highest ridge or through the deepest mud-hole without spinning out. On a November afternoon I'd rather forget, I joined the ranks of the warriors. The quad assigned to me tipped over backward on a hill, briefly trapping me underneath and permanently curing me of any desire to do it again. Now whenever I'm lucky enough to get drawn to hunt this region, I rely solely on shank's mare, sticking to trails that have never seen a truck, motorized trike or bike.

I've hiked Nahahi Ridge with the Tuesday Hikers women's out-door group, who invited me to be only the third man to accompany them in the first 20 years they'd been together. On that fall day we didn't see the grizzly bear that regularly causes the trail to be closed. But I saw some incredibly stunning terrain. I also witnessed strong friendships that have outlasted marriage breakdowns, sickness, deaths and loss of jobs. Later we shared a celebratory cake back at the Little Elbow Recreation Area. I felt honored to be the token male on that trip and didn't feel bad when the women invited *Herald* colleague Susan Scott to accompany them on their 25th anniversary.

Like I said, there's still much to do in the Elbow Valley. There are the foul-smelling Sulphur Pools, a 1-km (.6-mi) hike from Ing's Mine parking lot. There are at least four backcountry campgrounds—Wildhorse, Mount Romulus, Big Elbow and Tombstone—where someday I'd like to pitch a tent. And although I've biked (in a blizzard, I might add, but that's another story) from Elbow Lake southeast to Bluerock campground in the Sheep River Valley, I still want to pedal the northeast route from Elbow Lake to the Little Elbow Recreation Area.

I've driven the Powderface Trail Road from the Elbow Falls Trail north to the Sibbald area, but I've never hiked the scenic Powderface Creek and Powderface Ridge trails. I've also never kayaked or canoed the Elbow River, which provides some great white water for thrill seekers. Frankly I don't even want to kayak or canoe the river. Nothing personal, mind you. It's just that I prefer to fish in water, not be fished out of it.

Guido Panara moved to Calgary from Montreal in 1982, five years after Kananaskis Country was created. In 1984 he and his wife, Gabriella, opened Da Guido Ristorante in north Calgary. After moving to Calgary, Guido developed a passion for Kananaskis Country. He'd sneak away every chance he could to camp, fish and hunt. "This is the best land I've ever seen in my life," says Panara, who includes the Swiss Alps in his assessment. That's why he didn't hesitate when the province decided in 1995 to privatize campground operations in Kananaskis Country. Panara's company, Elbow Valley Campgrounds Ltd., received a 10-year contract to operate 12 government-built and owned campgrounds in the Elbow, Sheep and Highwood river valleys. In 1996 the company built a camping service center at McLean Creek in the Elbow region. Panara says he loves traveling into Kananaskis Country to check on his business and indulge himself in personal recreation. "It's so relaxing after being in the city," he says.

I found it particularly relaxing on a recent outing when the intoxicating smell of spring hung heavy in the air. The aroma is like no other, sweet with the freshness of budding vegetation, yet musty from ground wet with newly melted snow. I breathed deeply while my winter-weary legs strained to pedal up the long hill to my parked vehicle. I longed for a lower gear but knew there wasn't one. The top of the hill seemed kilometers away.

Despite the grind it was the kind of day that makes a person grateful to be alive. I was cycling solo back to the Elbow Falls parking lot, where my car was parked. Five hours earlier I'd jumped on my 21-speed hybrid bike and headed west on the paved highway to Forget-Me-Not Pond. The road, which had been closed to vehicles since December 1, was scheduled to reopen in a few weeks, on May 15. After reaching my destination I'd inhaled a sandwich, chugged a juice box and set off to explore the Big Elbow Trail for several kilometers to the south. I never saw another person after leaving the car.

While cycling on the rolling trail with tree root speed bumps, I stopped several times to examine fresh deer and moose tracks in the mud. Although I carefully scanned adjacent trees and brush, I couldn't spot any animals. When I suddenly spied the moist track of a heavy black bear walking in the direction I was headed. I checked my watch. What a coincidence, I thought. Time to head home.

Now, on the last big incline before the parking lot, I hogged the road by zigzagging up the steep hill, quietly cheering myself on every meter of the way. The next few minutes spent straining up the hill gave me ample time to reflect on the day—and on the wide variety of recreational opportunities in the Elbow River Valley.

Sibbald Recreation Area

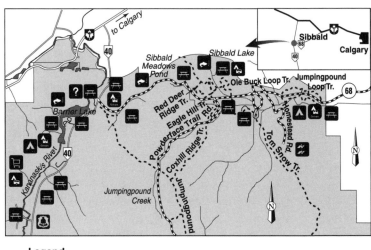

Legend

- ⬤ Park Boundary
- ❓ Information
- 🅰 Camping
- 🅰 Group Camping
- 🍽 Picnic Site
- 🚹🚺 Washroom
- 🎣 Fishing Area
- Unpaved Road
- --- Unpaved Trail
- 🔷 Emergency Services Center
- 🔫 Gun Range
- 🛒 Store

Access: West on the Trans-Canada Highway for 30 km (18.6 mi), then south and west on Highway 68 for 21 km (13 mi).

Terrain: Rolling foothills, ridges, forested valleys, open meadows, lodgepole pines, beaver ponds.

Activities: Hiking, cycling, picnicking, camping, fishing, wildlife watching, horseback riding, interpretive driving tour through Jumpingpound Demonstration Forest, snowmobiling (in Sibbald snow vehicle forest land-use zone only), target shooting (at designated range only), hunting.

Hours: Day-use areas and campgrounds open 7:00 A.M. to 11:00 P.M.

Contact: 403 673-3663.

Ed Soltys found this hidden jewel almost by accident. For years the ardent angler had entered Kananaskis Country via Highway 40 off the Trans-Canada Highway. But one summer day Soltys was westbound when, on a whim, he turned onto Highway 68, just 30 km (18.6 mi) from Calgary's western city limits. As he drove south and then west along a road that went from paved to gravel, Soltys discovered Sibbald Flats, a scenic under-rated recreation area less than an hour from Calgary. "This is a terrific place," Soltys observed while casting a fly to a rising trout in Sibbald Meadows Pond.

Hundreds of feeding brook and rainbow trout dimpled the surface of the clear pond. The fish spurned every fly Soltys served up to them. But he didn't mind. He was just happy to be enjoying a day out of the city in a part of Kananaskis Country many Calgarians don't even know is here.

The Sibbald region offers a wealth of outdoor activities from camping and horseback riding to hiking and hunting. Common wildlife in the area includes elk, moose, mule and white-tailed deer, and black bear. Target shooting is permitted at the public Homestead Gun Range, operated by the Alberta Provincial Rifle Association. It's a popular place, especially in summer and fall, when hunters are sighting in their firearms for the hunting season. Hunting for most big game species is restricted to hunters holding a special license drawn by computer. Hunting isn't allowed in recreation areas surrounding campgrounds and day-use sites.

Centered at Sibbald Lake, just 21 km (13 mi) off the Trans-Canada Highway, the recreation area features a well laid-out campground complete with outhouses, playground and amphitheater. The lake has been stocked over the years with brook and rainbow trout. The best fishing in the area is considered to be either in Sibbald Creek, where many of its stump-fringed beaver ponds have been stocked with trout, or in tranquil Sibbald Meadows Pond, just 8 km (5 mi) west of Sibbald Lake. Sibbald Meadows Pond offers day-use facilities, including picnic tables, fire pits and outhouses.

Angling techniques in Sibbald Lake and Sibbald Meadows Pond include bottom fishing with worms or marshmallows and casting small spinners. Fly-fishers should try weighted streamers and nymphs and dry flies in Adams, mosquito and caddis patterns. The best fishing action in summer is in early morning and evening. The fish aren't big—a 25-cm (10″) trout is considered a whopper—but they're fun to catch. Shoreside chatter with other anglers hint at the presence of trout of several pounds. But as friend George Harper likes to say of such unconfirmed reports, "I'm from Missouri." In other words, he'll believe it when he sees it.

Bait isn't allowed in Sibbald Creek or any of its beaver ponds. Minimum size limits are in effect for trout. Check the regulations. No such restrictions apply in Sibbald Lake and Sibbald Meadows Pond. To ensure future fishing opportunities, limit your take by releasing most or all of your catch. There's also a designated snowmobiling area, but because the terrain is relatively open, snow conditions generally aren't as good here for snow machines as in the Cataract region in south Kananaskis Country.

Hikers and horse riders also should take a gander at this area. The terrain is a mix of foothills, valleys, ridgetops and mountains. Hiking, horseback and mountain biking trails range in difficulty and length. You can enjoy an outing of a few hours or an entire day. Many hiking trails originate at Sibbald Lake, including Eagle Hill, Deer Ridge, Sibbald Flat Interpretive, Reforestation, Sibbald Creek Trail and Ole Buck Loop.

Highway 68 is a scenic alternate route to Highway 40 from or back to Calgary. It runs 36 km (22 mi) from the Trans-Canada Highway southwest to Highway 40, about 1 km (.6 mi) south of the Barrier Lake Visitor Centre. The portion of the road within Kananaskis Country is gravel and well-suited to most vehicles during spring, summer and autumn. The route is dotted with several picnic areas.

On a late July day several years ago, I visited the area with Wally Buono, head coach–general manager of the Calgary Stampeders, and his son, Michael, then five. The outing launched a tradition of Wally and I sharing a fishing trip at least once a year. On our first outing together in 1992, the Stampeders were set for a homestand that evening against the Toronto Argonauts. It was their first meeting

Wally Buono and son, Michael, release small trout at Sibbald Meadows Pond in K-Country.

since the Stamps lost the Grey Cup to Toronto the previous November. While other coaches might have spent the day in the office fussing over pre-game business and fighting nerves, Buono opted to continue his tradition of going fishing before every home game.

"It helps me to relax," he says. "Fishing's really something I enjoy doing. It doesn't matter if I catch fish or not." It also gives him a chance to share rare time off with Michael and his three older sisters. While Buono insists he's not an environmentalist, he appreciates the "beauty of nature . . . Nature helps put a perspective on life."

That was why, five hours before the scheduled kickoff at McMahon Stadium, Buono was still standing on the shoreline at Sibbald Meadows Pond, casting a fly to an uncooperative trout, teasingly rising well within casting range. "Just one more cast, just one more," Buono told Michael, who sat patiently on a nearby stump. A few hours earlier Buono had caught the only fish of the day, a scrappy rainbow fooled by a silver-bladed spinner. He released it, explaining that if he wanted to eat fish, "I'd go to Safeway. The fun is in the catching."

During a stop for homemade salami and ham sandwiches, it was apparent that a CFL head coach has a tough time completely escaping both the game. Invited by his dad to say Grace before eating, Michael asked God to "help my dad win his game tonight." A few minutes later an angler and his teenaged daughter approached and asked," Well coach, are we going to win tonight?" Buono's instant reply? "Did you catch any fish?" Incidentally, the Stamps won the game.

Eagle Fever: The Migration

EXPERTS BELIEVE that up to 10,000 golden eagles wing through Kananaskis Country and the Canmore region each spring and autumn in the world's largest golden eagle migration. In spring they fly 4,000 to 5,000 km (2,486 to 3,107 mi) from wintering areas in Wyoming, southern Montana and eastern Colorado to their summer range in Alaska, Yukon and possibly Siberia. They return each fall. "It is a magnificent force that is way beyond us," says Delores Janzen, who teaches science at Canmore Collegiate High School.

Canmore holds an annual family oriented celebration in mid-October to commemorate this major natural phenomenon. It includes guided hikes, speakers and displays. Call the Canmore Special Events Bureau at 403 678-1878 for information.

To view the eagles you'll need binoculars or a spotting scope to search off Highway 40 in Kananaskis Country, especially around Mounts Kidd, Lorette, Allan, Bogart and McDougall. Other prime eagle watching spots include the Nakiska Lookout, Barrier Lake, Hay Meadow Trail near Ribbon Creek, Mount Lorette Ponds pulloff and Highwood Pass area west of Longview. Others include the Canmore area above the craggy rocks of Mount Lady MacDonald, Grotto Mountain, Gap Lake and Cougar Creek. The west end of Lake Minnewanka in Banff National Park and above the lakes in Waterton Lakes National Park are prime eagle watching spots.

The best viewing times are from mid to late afternoon from early March to early May, with the peak period being between March 19 and 24. The return migration runs through September to the end of October.

You'll know when you've truly caught eagle fever. It starts with a stiff neck from hours of peering high into the mountains. Soon, eagle fever moves into the eyes, which become tired and strained. Then it starts playing games with your mind. When that happens you might for an instant glimpse an eagle far overhead, then lose it in a blink, leaving you wondering if it was only a figment of your imagination. Then the fever starts affecting the arms, which become

Researcher Peter Sherrington spots for golden eagles in Kananaskis Country.

tired from holding up binoculars and spotting scopes for extended periods of time. In almost all cases eagle fever eventually spreads to the heart. "Once it's in your heart, it's incurable," says Bruce Bembridge, a Canmore resident who's been happily stricken with eagle fever for several years. He even helped organize Canmore's annual celebration of the fever.

Although the eagle migration was known to native people centuries ago (they called it "a river of big dark birds") it wasn't generally recognized as a major natural phenomenon until 1992. That's when Peter Sherrington, an ardent birder from Cochrane, visited Kananaskis Country on a spring bird-watching trip. He stopped to focus his binoculars on a pine grosbeak singing in a tree. A golden eagle flying overhead entered the picture well beyond the grosbeak. By the end of the day Sherrington and his partner had spotted 102 golden eagles soaring northward, more than most people see in 10 lifetimes. Sherrington knew it wasn't a random event. He launched

Golden eagle.

a monitoring system that has grown to include birders manning 16 viewpoints each spring and fall along the Rockies from Waterton Lakes to Jasper. About 6,000 golden eagles are recorded each year, but Sherrington believes the migration involves up to 10,000 birds.

One March day I accompanied Sherrington on an eagle watching trip to Kananaskis Country. For six months of the year, this is the former oilpatch geologist's office. He works here in late winter, spring and fall, laboring independently, on nobody's payroll. Sherrington is motivated only by his passionate interest in the intricate, still mysterious migration of golden eagles. He records sightings of every bird species he sees, from redpolls and tundra swans to eagles. He believes the huge raptors have migrated through this region for 11,000 years.

Sherrington and friend Jack Steeves, a retired dentist, set up spotting scopes in a meadow with a sweeping view of surrounding mountains. All was quiet for the first several minutes. Then Steeves suddenly went on full alert. He tightened the grip on his binoculars and shouted excitedly, "There's a bird!" Several feet away Sherrington raced to his own tripod-mounted scope and trained it in the same direction. "Our first of the day," he proclaimed proudly. "A three to four-year-old golden eagle."

Untrained eyes easily could have missed the feathered speck whizzing by 2.5 km (1.6 mi) away at a speed of 130 km (81 mi) per hour. But Sherrington and Steeves, who will spot 120 golden and six bald eagles before this day is done, seem to have the same sharp eyesight as their quarry. From a distance it's difficult for most viewers to pick out a golden eagle's features. Up close, however, it's hard not to be impressed. With wingspans of more than 2 m (6.6') golden eagles stand up to 100 cm (39") and can be as heavy as 5.5 kg (12 lb). They're dark brown, with gold tinge on the back of the neck and slightly lighter at the base of a broad tail. Immature goldens show a white flash on the underside of the wings and on the tail.

Sherrington, founder of the Rocky Mountain Eagle Research Foundation, personally has recorded nearly 50,000 sightings. Every eagle he sees is greeted with the same enthusiasm as that first one in 1992. Each one evokes a fresh feeling of awe. "It's tremendously exciting," he says. "This is not a random event. These birds aren't just tooling around." Although the discovery has earned Sherrington worldwide fame among birders, his feet remain firmly on the ground. His enthusiasm is contagious.

Calgary naturalist Lynn Vogt, who learned about the migration when a "very dynamic" Sherrington described it in a speech in 1993, takes her two young sons on eagle watching trips to Kananaskis Country each spring and fall. She once led her older son's elementary school class on a field trip to spot eagles. The kids still talk about it. "We use the eagles as a real outdoor experience," Vogt says. "It's a real learning experience."

Sheep River Valley

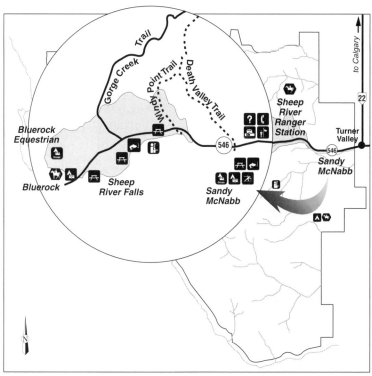

Legend

◯ Wildlife Sanctuary	⬛ Camping	⬛ Sewage Disposal	••• Unpaved Trail
⬛ Information	⬛ Group Camping	⬛ Fishing Area	⬛ Scenic Viewpoint
⬛ Ranger Station	⬛ Picnic Site	⬛ Cross-Country Skiing	
⬛ Camping (Tenting Only)	⬛ Telephone	⬛ Equestrian	

Access: West on Highway 22X for 17 km (10.6 mi), south on Highway 22 for 27 km (16.8 mi) to four-way stop in Turner Valley, right to Secondary Highway 546 for 15 km (9.3 mi) to Kananaskis Country boundary. Special attractions are spaced along the next 24 km (15 mi) of paved road.

Terrain: Mountains, gorges, rocky outcrops, windy ridges, valleys, meadows, lodgepole pine, poplars.

Activities: Hiking, cycling, picnicking, camping, fishing, wildlife watching, horseback riding, hunting.

Hours: Campgrounds open 7:00 A.M. to 11:00 P.M.

Contact: July and August only at 403 933-7172. Elbow Valley Visitor Information Centre weekends only at 403 949-4261. Elbow Ranger Station weekdays only at 403 949-3754.

IT'S DIFFICULT TO IMAGINE a more ideal spot for a family outdoor experience. Tucked away in eastern Kananaskis Country, this area has it all: classic mountain scenery, wildlife, paved access less than an hour from Calgary, picnic spots, campgrounds and fishing for trout and mountain whitefish in the clear, tumbling waters of the Sheep River.

It's easy to start getting caught in this area's spell on the drive west of Turner Valley. Highway 546 runs through sprawling ranch country as it flanks the Sheep River. From the minute you leave Turner Valley, keep a close eye out for coyotes, elk, moose, mule and white-tailed deer. Upon entering Kananaskis Country, there's a good chance of seeing bighorn sheep and black bear. The best wildlife viewing times are early morning and late afternoon or evening.

Your first stop should be the government information center. Check out the large map outside the building or grab a pamphlet highlighting the area's trails and other features. Hiking and cross-country skiing are popular activities here. A few kilometers past the information station, you'll hit the Sandy McNabb Recreation Area, one of the area's most popular four-season destinations. Visitors lucky enough to get away midweek will beat the crowds. Cross-country skiing here can be wonderful when snow conditions are right. (See Chapter 5 "Best Cross-Country Skiing" for top places to cross-country ski in Kananaskis Country.) The road is closed beyond the Sandy McNabb turnoff from December 1 to May 15 to allow wildlife to winter with minimal disturbance.

After driving past Sandy McNabb, you enter the Sheep River Wildlife Sanctuary. This 54-km^2 (21-mi^2) area was set aside as a no-hunting zone in 1973, primarily to protect wintering bighorn sheep. Dave Hanna, a provincial park ranger who worked in this region for several years, says visitors should give the bighorns lots of room to avoid stressing them. Use binoculars or spotting scope to bring them closer. Stay on the road, don't chase the sheep into the hills or approach too close to them. Pets should be kept in the vehicle. For a relaxing look at grazing sheep, park at the Bighorn viewing area, then walk a few hundred meters to a wooden platform. Complete with interpretive signs and benches, the viewing area overlooks a sprawling grass meadow used by the sheep.

Beyond the Bighorn viewing area, stop at the Sheep Falls day-use area. A short trail leads to a spectacular waterfall. The paved highway ends at the Junction Creek day-use area, another popular picnic area and trailhead for a network of hiking and equestrian trails. The nearby Bluerock campground is one of Kananaskis Country's nicest.

The region also is popular with horse riders. Several years ago I encountered Calgary real estate agent Marge Harasymuk riding her purebred Arabian gelding, Cozon, just outside the wildlife sanctuary. "This is the most relaxing, enjoyable thing I can do," she told me. "It's a tonic from a very busy work schedule."

Conflicts sometimes arise between horseback riders and mountain bikers. Some bikers wonder why horse manure isn't cleaned off the trails, and others question why horses are allowed at all. Some horse people don't like mountain bikers because they tend to spook their mounts. Such disputes can be resolved with mutual respect and cooperation. Hikers and bikers are wise to make lots of noise on trails to avoid surprising horses. Bikers should dismount and wait for a horse to pass. If the trail is on a hill bikers should wait on the lower slope because horses are more easily spooked from above. Bikers wishing to pass horses from behind should shout their intentions at a distance and leave plenty of room. "To have access to all this beautiful country is fantastic," Harasymuk says. "There are lots of trails for everyone."

The Sheep River region also is popular with hunters in early spring, when black bears can be hunted, and in autumn. The provincial government limits the number of hunters in fall by issuing a designated number of tags for moose, elk, white-tailed and mule deer and nontrophy bighorn sheep. Hunting is prohibited in the wildlife sanctuary, recreation areas and on Sundays. Bighorn sheep hunting also is prohibited within 1.6 km (1 mi) of the Sheep River between Kananaskis Country's east boundary and Dyson Creek. The regulation prevents the unethical practice of shooting record-book rams as they move along the river a short distance from the road.

Not all hunters in this area have two legs. The region has a healthy population of wolves and cougars. The Sheep River area was the focus of North America's most intensive cougar study, launched in 1982 under the tutelage of provincial biologist Orval Pall. After Pall's tragic death in a plane crash in 1986, the study was taken over by colleagues Martin Jalkotzy and Ian Ross. Ross and Jalkotzy used sophisticated telemetry equipment to track radio-collared cougars. Their findings formed the backbone of Alberta's first cougar management plan.

Focusing on a 780-km² area (301-mi²), the biologists identified more than 70 different cougars during almost 200 captures and releases. They estimated 40 different cats lived in the study area. The study also revealed that while moose, elk and deer comprise the bulk of cougars' winter diet, they also eat coyote, rabbit, beaver, porcupine and mice. During a four-month period one winter, a female cougar with two juvenile kittens made 11 major kills—10 deer and an elk calf. One day in early April I accompanied Ross while he was hot on the trail of a female cougar and her kitten. Fresh snow covered the foot of a ridge where Ross had last traced the cats. When he held up the antenna the receiver emitted a faint chirping signal, indicating the cougars were nearby. The day before Ross had followed the signal into a beaver pond area, where the adult cougar had killed two beavers in five days. A slight movement caught his eye. Ross watched the two cats furtively cross the beaver dam just 100 m (328') away.

While still several hundred meters from the pond, Ross stopped often to monitor the strengthening radio signal. As we crept through the trees he paused once to point out a big pile of fresh cougar dung on the snow. Then Ross spotted two fresh sets of round tracks, one larger than the other and all distinguished by four distended toes. Where the tracks vanished in dense vegetation, the signal grew louder. Ross whispered that we were within 200 yards of the cougars.

Not wishing to disturb them we retreated to check on the location of another cat. I wasn't disappointed that I didn't get to see the mother cougar and her kitten. Knowing we were so close, albeit briefly, was ample reward.

Highwood–Cataract Region

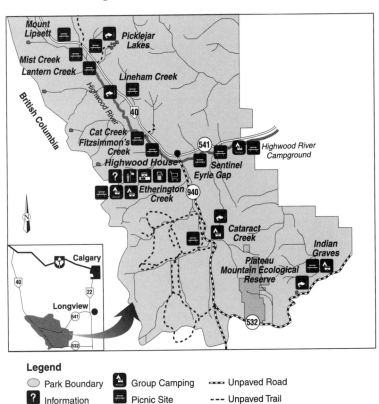

Legend

- ◯ Park Boundary
- ❓ Information
- 🏕 Park Office
- ⛺ Camping
- Group Camping
- Picnic Site
- Sewage Disposal
- Fishing Area
- ▰▰▰ Unpaved Road
- - - - Unpaved Trail
- Gasoline
- Store

Access: West on Highway 22X for 17 km (10.6 mi), south on Highway 22 for 45 km (28 mi) to Longview, then west on Secondary Highway 541 for 35 km (21.7 mi) to Kananaskis Country boundary.

Terrain: Mountains, high alpine lakes, creeks, alpine meadows, spruce and lodgepole pine forests.

Activities: Hiking, cycling, picnicking, camping, fishing, canoeing, kayaking, wildlife watching, horseback riding, hunting (most big game permits issued by draw), snowmobiling.

Hours: Campgrounds open 7:00 A.M. to 11:00 P.M. Highwood House store open May 15 – October 15.

Contact: Ranger stations and information centers at 403 558-2151 and 403 933-7172. Highwood House store at 403 558-2144 (open May 15 to October 15).

COMPARED TO OTHER PARTS of Kananaskis Country, this region appears to be relatively undiscovered. While many people come here because of its low level of regional development, that factor also helps keep the crowds down. And that's just dandy for people who consider this region their own little secret. Hiking trails and campgrounds tend to be not as crowded as those in Peter Lougheed Provincial Park, Bow Valley Provincial Park, Barrier Lake–Ribbon Creek, Sheep River Valley and the Elbow River Valley areas.

The region boasts excellent trout fishing in the Highwood River and its tributaries, in stocked beaver ponds and in high mountain lakes such as Picklejar, Carnarvon, Lake of the Horns and Loomis. Small spinners and flies—especially a bushy Royal Wulff or Tom Thumb—are most productive. In the southeast corner of the region, just north of Secondary Highway 532, both Bear Pond and Big Iron Lake were restocked with Arctic grayling in 1997 after suffering successive winter kills. First stocked in 1985, the catch-and-release grayling fisheries proved so popular with anglers that Alberta Fish and Wildlife introduced the species in two other Kananaskis Country locations: Wedge Pond and Quarry Lake. Fishing rules for this region are complex, so study the provincial fishing regulations before wetting a line.

In the region's southwest corner, snowmobilers have more than 100 km (62 mi) of groomed trails from which to choose. Although there are no groomed cross-country ski trails in this region, excellent skiing can be had by skinny boarders willing to lay down their own tracks on hiking trails. Developed hiking trails also are at a minimum with most located in the south part of the region. The Plateau Mountain Ecological Area is at the south end. North of the junction of Highways 40 and 541 are the Cat Creek and Mist Creek trails, both of which are dandy hikes. Cat Creek is an ideal family interpretive hike of 4 km (2.5 mi) round-trip. It passes through an old coal mining site and ends at a pretty waterfall. Dozens of other unsigned

Hikers near Sundance ceremony lodge on Zephyr Creek Trail in Highwood district of Kananaskis Country.

hikes in this region are detailed in Gillean Daffern's excellent Kananaskis Country trail guides.

The Highwood–Cataract region is a great place to watch wildlife. Motorists and hikers frequently see elk, deer, moose, coyotes, and black and grizzly bears. At night, eerie distant howling reminds visitors this also is wolf country. From early May to Labor Day, birders are attracted to the Highwood House Visitor Centre, where entertainment is provided by rufous and calliope hummingbirds flitting between nearby trees and hanging feeders. While there, check out store operator Laurie Powell's homemade rhubarb muffins. My daughter, Sarah, and I stumbled into the store early one morning after being rained out of a backcountry camping trip. The muffins had just come out of the oven. Sarah and I thought we were in heaven.

Much of this region is closed to vehicle traffic for more than half the year. A 56-km (34.8-mi) stretch of Highway 40 from Highwood House north to the Kananaskis Lakes Trail is closed December 1 to

June 15 to protect wintering wildlife, especially elk, from poaching and legal hunting by treaty Indians.

The vehicle closure is a bonus for cyclists. When the snow starts melting in spring, Highway 40 becomes what a park ranger once called "one of the most spectacular bike rides around." The return ride from Highwood House to Highwood Pass is 78 km (48.5 mi); on the north route through Peter Lougheed Provincial Park, the return ride is 34 km (21.1 mi). With a growing number of cyclists discovering the joys of cycling the Highwood Pass, problems with wildlife have developed.

Former ranger Ken Powell, who's married to the muffin-meister of Highwood House, says many cyclists don't show proper respect to wildlife, including bears. One spring, cyclists repeatedly rode within 15 m (49') of a grizzly sow digging roots in the ditch. Other cyclists have gleefully reporting patting a newborn elk calf. Either incident could have led to injury or death.

Other cyclists put themselves at risk by not treating the trip as a wilderness experience. They don't pack extra clothes, food, a first-aid kit or even basic bicycle repair supplies. Some take cellular phones for emergencies without realizing most are useless in the mountains. Cyclists have been hurt after losing control, getting a flat tire or sustaining other mechanical breakdowns on steep downhills. The highway is littered with loose stones, large rocks and fresh animal droppings that can cause high-speed wipeouts.

Since the highway isn't regularly patrolled by rangers, it can take several hours to reach an injured cyclist. Ranger Dave Hanna worries about overuse by cyclists. He urges them to "do all they can to restrict their impact on the area." The message is clear: use it properly or risk losing this unique, automobile-free spring cycling destination.

Kananaskis Country has a rich First Nations heritage. The name *Kananaskis*, believed to mean "meeting of the waters," traces back to an Indian of the same name. For our family on a late summer day several years ago, a simple hike linked modern-day native tradition with drawings etched in stone 300 years ago that had near-mystical overtones. When we reached the meadow in the shadow of the north face of Mount Burke, it was obvious this was a special place.

Two rickety wood structures stood alone, festooned with hundreds of brightly colored cloths, flapping in the warm west wind. The open-framed towers rested in lush grass, dotted with late wild flowers and clumps of willow.

Clearly this creation had special meaning. We suspected it had native roots and were encouraged, since we were searching for centuries-old Indian rock drawings called pictographs. This was a good omen. The structure, it turned out, was a Sun Dance lodge erected by the Stoney Indians of Eden Valley for a special spiritual ceremony a few years before. The cloths represented prayers, and the four center poles signified the Earth's four corners. Other standing poles symbolized significant Indian virtues.

After viewing the lodge we continued our 4.5-km (2.8-mi) pictograph quest up Zephyr Creek. A few minutes earlier, we had waded the chilly Highwood River from the Sentinel day-use area. It was late August; crossings are impossible in spring or early summer when the water flows higher and stronger. With no signs marking the way, we followed a trail skirting a meadow to the left of the Sun Dance lodge, then hit a gradual uphill trail cutting through the forest. The first sound of something big crashing through the trees had us thinking bear. Wrong. White-faced Hereford cows on the trail ahead occasionally lumbered off into the trees to watch us walk past.

Just as we started to think we'd gone too far and missed the turnoff to the pictographs, we came across a creek flowing from the east. Beside it ran a slightly worn trail along Painted Canyon. About 15 minutes and several easy creek crossings later, we were wondering if we'd ever find the pictographs. Suddenly, there they were. Two red-hued pictographs were at eye level on a rock wall to the north. The images were smaller than we'd expected, but that didn't reduce their impact. One was a stick figure of a man apparently being chased by a strange long-tailed animal. The other was a feathered bird.

As we sat peacefully for a few minutes eating lunch, our group tried to envision the scene back then. How many artists were there? How old? What events had inspired the paintings? Our imaginations ran wild.

Kananaskis Country Circle Driving Tour

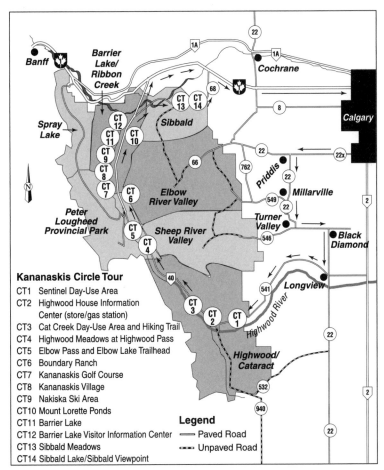

Kananaskis Circle Tour

CT1 Sentinel Day-Use Area
CT2 Highwood House Information
Center (store/gas station)
CT3 Cat Creek Day-Use Area and Hiking Trail
CT4 Highwood Meadows at Highwood Pass
CT5 Elbow Pass and Elbow Lake Trailhead
CT6 Boundary Ranch
CT7 Kananaskis Golf Course
CT8 Kananaskis Village
CT9 Nakiska Ski Area
CT10 Mount Lorette Ponds
CT11 Barrier Lake
CT12 Barrier Lake Visitor Information Center
CT13 Sibbald Meadows
CT14 Sibbald Lake/Sibbald Viewpoint

Legend

— Paved Road
╍╍╍ Unpaved Road

Route: Calgary to Longview via Highway 22X for 17 km (10.6 mi) and Highway 22 for 53 km (32.9 mi), west on Secondary Highway 541 for 35 km (21.7 mi) to Kananaskis Country boundary, west on Highway 541 for 12 km (7.5 mi) to Highway 40 junction at Highwood House, north to the Trans-Canada Highway for 110 km (68.4 mi), then east on Trans-Canada Highway for 80 km (49.7 mi) to Calgary.

Alternate Route: Right off Highway 40 just south of Barrier Lake Visitor Centre to Highway 68, drive 37 km (23 mi) on mainly gravel road to the Trans-Canada, then east 30 km (18.6 mi) to Calgary.

Trip Time: Total distance is about 307 km (190.8 mi), but you shouldn't rush it. Take your time and allow about 6 hours.

Contact: Barrier Lake Information Centre at 403 673-3985.

I**F YOU TAKE ONLY ONE** scenic family drive this year, make it this one. Featuring the most spectacular foothills and mountain scenery in Canada, this tour can be done only between June 15 and the end of November, when the entire length of Highway 40 is open to vehicles. The best period is September and early October, when holiday traffic is down, there's less chance of snow or ice, and autumn colors are at their most glorious.

This is an ideal trip for seniors, families with young kids or anyone else seeking a scenic easy getaway from the city. And since it is vehicle-based, you can take the trip at your leisure. You can get out and enjoy a picnic at one of the many well-equipped day-use areas. Stop to take photographs. Enjoy a short stroll or a vigorous hike if you feel like it. If not, stay in the vehicle the entire way.

From Calgary, it's best to start the trip in early morning before the sun obscures your vision while you head south toward Longview. Chances of spotting wildlife improve the earlier you leave the city. By the same token you'll see more wild creatures on your way home in late afternoon and evening. By starting early and doing the route in the direction described, you'll keep the sun behind you after turning west from Longview.

Heading south on Highway 22 past Millarville, Turner Valley and Black Diamond, you'll travel through classic cattle country. Rolling hills are punctuated by thick expanses of poplar and pine. At Longview, head west along Highway 541 in the Highwood River Valley. Herefords graze in lush green fields while hawks perch on fence posts and circle in the clouds above. You'll pass ranches steeped in Western heritage: The O.H. (owned by Daryl "Doc" Seaman, Calgary businessman and Calgary Flames part-owner), Y Cross, Stampede and Buffalo Head. If you're traveling in late spring or summer, watch fence posts and wires for mountain bluebirds flitting around tiny wooden houses placed there by Bluebird Trail supporters.

Cyclist dwarfed by mountains on Highway 40 in K-Country.

Upon entering Kananaskis Country you'll notice this is still cattle country. Keep your foot near the brake to avoid hitting bovines standing in the middle of the highway. Slow down for cows in the ditch, which have a habit of suddenly wandering out in front of a moving vehicle. If you encounter a cowboy or cowgirl on horseback herding cattle along the road, pull over to the shoulder and stop until they pass. Don't honk the horn or try to thread your vehicle through the herd. That can spook the cattle, possibly causing them to stampede. If that happens, the cattle would have to be rounded up again and you'd probably receive some dirty looks.

When you're not watching for cattle, you might just get lucky and spot some wildlife. Stay alert. One hot summer day, a grizzly bolted across the highway in front of me at 3:00 P.M. Not all wildlife is seen early and late in the day. Slow down or stop for all critters, especially deer, elk, coyote, bear, bighorn sheep and moose. They can dart suddenly out onto the road. If you spot wildlife, don't leave your vehicle. Stop only briefly, then resume your trip. This way animals won't become accustomed to people, possibly becoming a hazard later. People who stop for long periods of time to view wildlife also run the risk of causing tragic traffic pile-ups. (See Chapter 7 "Playing it Safe in the Rocky Mountains.") On the drive also watch carefully for hikers, cyclists or people walking dogs off-leash.

Just inside Kananaskis Country's east boundary on Secondary Highway 541, you'll come to the first picnic spot, the Highwood River site. It's one of many along this stretch that offer picnic tables, water and outhouses. You'll have to bring your own firewood or buy it along the way. At the intersection of Highways 40 and 541, stop at Highwood House for information, gas and a snack. Check out the hummingbirds in summer. Then head north on Highway 40, resting at day-use sites at Fitzsimmons Creek, Cat Creek, Lineham Creek, Lantern Creek, Picklejar, Mist Creek and Mount Lipsett. If you're feeling energetic, take a hike from any of these sites.

After entering Peter Lougheed Provincial Park, you'll soon climb to the Highwood Pass. Stop for an easy stroll along the interpretive trail at Highwood Meadows or tackle the more demanding Ptarmigan Cirque Trail. This is a good place to glass the adjacent slopes for grizzly bears and elk. A few kilometers farther north is the Elbow Pass day-use site. It's also the trailhead for an initially steep but relatively easy hour-long hike to scenic Elbow Lake, source of the Elbow River.

Continuing north on Highway 40, you'll come to several other picnic spots. After leaving Peter Lougheed Provincial Park, you can gas up or grab a snack at the Fortress Junction service station and store. A few minutes later, prepare to stop for a picnic at Wedge Pond, which has been stocked with Arctic grayling. If you miss this spot, pull over a few minutes later at Evan-Thomas day-use area. Shortly after, you'll hit the turnoff for Boundary Ranch (403 591-7171), operated by Denise and Rick Guinn. Get a bite to eat, view the horses, visit the gift shop and ask about trail rides.

Shortly after leaving the ranch, you have the option of making a short detour to the west to check out Kananaskis Village, comprised of three resort hotels, store and service center. This is a good chance to stretch your legs, have a full-course meal or stock up on snacks if you're running low.

About 4 km (2.5 mi) farther north on Highway 40, check out Mount Lorette Ponds, a beautiful picnic and fishing spot. Facilities and trails are accessible to wheelchairs. It's one of the few spots in Kananaskis Country designed for anglers with disabilities. Unfortunately many able-bodied anglers also fish for Lorette's stocked trout, despite having the pick of dozens of other spots not so easily accessed by disabled people. Continuing north you'll pass the University of Calgary Kananaskis Field Station. It's across the highway from the azure-blue waters of Barrier Lake, a photographer's dream.

Just past the lake you can turn right onto Highway 68 for a 36-km (22-mi) trip through the Sibbald Flat recreation area to the Trans-Canada Highway. This route goves you a choice of several nice picnic areas. And you can drive through the 10-km (6.2-mi) self-guided interpretive auto tour of the Jumpingpound Demonstration Forest.

If you opt instead to continue heading north on Highway 40, stop at the Barrier Lake Visitor Centre for pamphlets and a final pit stop before hitting the Trans-Canada en route home to Calgary. Say hello to Ruth Oltmann, a longtime Kananaskis Country visitor services employee and author of two Kananaskis Country history books. Oltmann's also been immortalized by having a short section of cross-country ski trail, Ruthie's, named after her in the Ribbon Creek area.

No matter what route you take back to Calgary, you will be left longing for the day when this spectacular trip can be repeated.

Chapter 7

Playing it Safe in the Rocky Mountains

246

A FRIEND OF MINE, a father of young children, once told me he won't take his kids into the mountains because he feels incapable of protecting them there. He recognizes that this fatalistic attitude can rob children of valuable life experiences and exposure to the natural world that is a key part of life in this part of Alberta. It's true that within those scenic peaks, valleys and foothills lie potential hazards that well-traveled outdoor enthusiasts have learned to recognize and respect. It's also true that the Rocky Mountains can be intimidating to people lacking experience in the outdoors. But lack of experience shouldn't stop anybody from getting out to enjoy the Rockies.

People unfamiliar with wild places and things need a basic education to boost their comfort level, confidence and safety skills. Being aware of potential problems is the best defense against them. This knowledge can be attained in many ways. One is to hit the library to scour books about backcountry safety and survival. Another is to choose your partners carefully, ensuring that at least one person you regularly head out with is experienced and knowledgeable. After a while some of that wisdom is bound to rub off on you. A third possible option is the best: take a course.

Unlike many books on the subject, experienced instructors can talk specifically about conditions and situations relevant to the local scene. They've been there, done that, have the T-shirt. They're all former novices in the outdoors. That means they've all made common and not-so-common mistakes that come with being inexperienced. Qualified instructors can help novices make that critical first step that leads to increased confidence and enjoyment of the outdoors. Through classroom lectures and guided field trips, instructors can teach inexperienced folks more in several hours than they could learn on their own in five years.

The University of Calgary outdoor program center and Calgary's Outdoor/Nature Services both offer excellent programs teaching the safe pursuit of a chosen outdoor activity. Courses aren't restricted to beginners. Some are designed for experienced outdoors enthusiasts eager to expand their knowledge.

Knowing about the dangers in the outdoors does more than boost the practical safety factor. It also helps ease the fear that comes with not knowing how to handle certain situations.

Take bears, for instance. Black and grizzly bears live in the Rocky Mountains and in parts of the foothills on the eastern fringe of the mountain region. To many people, bears represent the wildness of the land they love to explore. Seeing a bear in the wild is a thrill, a bonus to being out there. These people appreciate and respect bears.

Some, however, view bears only with fear. They allow this fear to keep them in Calgary or in their vehicles when they venture west. They might take a short hike but are nervous the whole time about encountering a bear. If they ever do see a bear, even 1 km (.6 mi) away, the experience is harrowing, not enriching as it should be. To them every newspaper story about a bear attack reinforces that fear, giving them more justification to stay out of bear country. Yet for every bear attack there are thousands of vehicle accidents, and they wouldn't stop driving on the basis of reading about a traffic accident, no matter how serious.

"The more you can learn about bears adds to the delight of being out there," says Stephen Herrero, a world-renowned Calgary bear researcher and author. "It will make you feel more at home . . . more connected to the woods, not guided by deep, dark unknown fears." The University of Calgary environmental sciences professor, who has researched black and grizzly bears for more than three decades, says knowing about bruins adds to the safety of people and bears alike. Attacking bears injure or kill several people annually in Canada, including Alberta. But attacks and even bluff charges that don't involve actual contact can lead to the death of an offending bear. These bears might be shot by wardens or wildlife officers, or live-trapped and relocated to unfamiliar territory, where survival becomes a question. "Everyone wins by knowing a little more about bears," says Herrero, who wrote the 1985 best-seller *Bear Attacks: Their Causes and Avoidance.*

Indeed, everyone wins by knowing more about potential dangers in the outdoors. You win by not endangering yourself. Park rangers, wardens and other emergency rescue personnel win by not having to risk their lives to save yours. Taxpayers win by having these officials doing more resource protection duties, which are put on hold during rescue operations.

What follows are brief rundowns of the most common perceived fears in the mountains and what you can do about them. They aren't intended to be the final word on the subject. That will come to you through experience and continuing education. The time to start is sooner, not later.

Bears and Other Critters

THIS GRIZZLY BEAR wasn't huge, as grizzlies go. But it was big enough to inflict serious damage to the camera-wielding tourists foolishly standing just 50 m (164') away. A grizzly digging in the ditch for green roots beside a busy highway one spring seemed oblivious to the crowd of people building nearby. As some got even closer, the bear appeared to become annoyed. It faded out of sight into dense bush just beyond the ditch. Disappointed by the grizzly's departure, two middle-aged men remained on the shoulder of the highway, desperate for one last photograph for their holiday albums. As the bear continued to play shy, one shutterbug called it as he would a big, friendly, shaggy dog. "Here, boy. Come on, boy," the man pleaded. Luckily for the tourist the bear didn't "come on." It could have covered the distance to the man in about five seconds—a whole lot faster than the man would have been able to reach the safety of his vehicle.

Incidents like this are all too common in our mountain parks and recreation areas. That more of these encounters don't turn ugly is more good luck than good management. Preventing them is all about respect: many people accustomed to viewing bears only in urban zoos or on television don't respect the wildness of bears in their natural habitat. A national park warden once told me some tourists are genuinely surprised to learn national park wildlife aren't

This sign says it all in K-Country.

just tame animals allowed to roam free. By showing respect for wildlife—its need for space, its power, its place in the natural order of nature—we can avoid most problems with wild creatures in the mountains.

People often ask me where they can go in Banff National Park or Kananaskis Country where there is no chance of encountering bears. No such place exists, I reply, unless you wish to spend all your time in hotel lobbies or golf course clubhouses. The simple truth is that bears live in the mountains and foothills. Like most people they don't spend a lot of time on top of bare rocky peaks. They prefer to forage for food and travel in the lush, vegetation-lined valleys. People tend to develop hiking trails along these valleys, so it's inevitable that the paths of bears and people will cross.

Hikers can reduce chances of a bear encounter by taking several precautions. Stay in a group and make lots of noise by talking, singing or shaking a noisemaker such as bells or a stone-filled can. Never rely solely on small bells attached to backpacks because most bells aren't loud enough to alert bears, especially when you're traveling near flowing water. Ron Chamney, who worked extensively in Kananaskis Country visitor services over two decades, regularly hollers "Yo, bear!" when he hikes. "I like to let them know I'm there so I don't surprise them," Chamney says.

Bears like being surprised as much as people like having a guy wearing a hockey goalie's mask jump out of a closet at them. Some people would react to that experience by fleeing, others by fighting. Bears aren't much different, especially if they're accompanied by cubs. The only predictable thing about bears is their unpredictability. Some will run away when surprised; some will attack. Watch closely for bear signs: tracks, fresh diggings and moist droppings. When hiking in areas where big game hunting is allowed, avoid spots where hunters have made a kill. Bears can be attracted to blood and entrails. Above all, never approach a bear cub or get between a cub and sow, and remember that dogs in the backcountry, even if leashed, can provoke a bear attack.

If camping, don't camp near a bear trail, seasonal feeding ground or where food or garbage have been left. Keep your campsite clean and pack out all garbage. Put away stoves and barbecues when they're not in use. Lock food in vehicle trunks or hang it high between two trees or on a raised pole. Never cook or eat in or near your tent, and avoid using scented cosmetics, soaps and deodorants.

Despite these precautions, people sometimes find themselves face to face with a bear. If that happens, talk quietly while slowly backing up and leaving the area. Don't run. That might spark an attack. If the bear moves toward you, drop your lunch bag, water bottle or anything else that might distract it. Don't remove your backpack. It might protect your back if the bear knocks you to the ground and bites or claws you. Well-aimed blasts of Cayenne-pepper–based bear spray have proven highly effective in discouraging charging bears. Commercially available, bear spray should be used only as a last resort. Although climbing a tree isn't a guaranteed refuge, a bear might feel you're less of a threat when off the ground. If you are attacked by a lone black bear, consider fighting back with all the resources at your disposal: fists, feet, rocks and tree limbs. If it's a black bear with cubs or a grizzly bear, remain motionless with your hands over the back of your head. Often the attack will end once the bear determines you no longer pose a threat to it or its cubs. Remain still until the bear leaves the area. To further educate yourself, read Herrero's book before venturing into bear country.

Elk and moose also should be given a wide berth, especially during spring and early fall. In May and June, cow elk can become dangerously aggressive when protecting a calf or calving area. Several people have been attacked by cow elk in recent years, mainly in and around the Banff townsite. Keep alert, maintaining a distance of at least 35 m (115') from a cow at this time. Cow moose can be equally protective. During the late summer and early fall mating season, bull elk and moose also should be avoided. They, too, can be unpredictable when rutting. An average of six people annually are attacked by cow and bull elk in Banff.

Another animal that demands respect is the cougar. These big cats are wraithlike creatures, tawny and mysterious as they drift quietly and usually unnoticed through shrinking habitat. "Cougars can live under your doorstep and you wouldn't know about it," says Calgary cougar researcher Martin Jalkotzy. Nevertheless, cougars are being seen more and more, especially in the foothills bordering the Rocky Mountains. Several have been shot in recent years after killing dogs or livestock or acting aggressively toward people in farmyards, campgrounds and on hiking trails.

Since a 1982 attack in Waterton Lakes National Park, only one other person is known to have been injured by a cougar in Alberta. That happened in 1994 when a woman on an acreage southwest of Calgary was bitten and scratched by a cougar attacking her dog on the front porch. A University of California study of cougar attacks in the United States and Canada documented 10 cougar-caused fatalities and 48 injuries between 1890 and 1990. Thirty-six attacks occurred between 1970 and 1990.

Most people never see a cougar in their lifetimes. I've been fortunate enough to see three of the big cats so far and the tracks of many others. I always stop to admire the round, four-toed impressions in the mud or snow while wondering how the cougar looked and where it was heading.

Like most encounters with large wild creatures, it's a humbling experience. Just like bears, elk, moose or any other creature, cougars need our admiration and respect, not our fear.

Avalanches

A NYONE WHO VENTURES into snow-covered areas of the Rocky Mountains should be aware of the danger of avalanches, which kill and injure several people a year in Alberta and British Columbia. Skiers, snowboarders, climbers, winter campers and snowshoers should be prepared by knowing how to recognize an avalanche hazard and what to do if they encounter one. "Having the right information and knowing what to do with it is critical," says Evan Manners of the Canadian Avalanche Centre, based in Revelstoke, British Columbia. It's also critical that people not travel alone in avalanche terrain.

Avalanche activity generally increases in high alpine areas from March to May as warmer temperatures break down the snowpack. The most susceptible areas are south and west-facing slopes, especially late in the day. Spring avalanches tend to change from dry slabs of tumbling snow to wet slides flowing slowly down a slope—uprooting trees, dislodging boulders and sweeping away any people unfortunate enough to be in its path. Manners compares this type of avalanche to a train locomotive. "It goes slow, but it's hard to stop," he says.

It's possible to reduce chances of encountering an avalanche by following basic guidelines. Manners recommends taking a course to learn how to "read" snow conditions to know when and where avalanches are most likely to occur. Courses are offered by the University of Calgary and at Calgary Outdoor/Nature Services. They generally fill up early.

Before heading into the mountains, check out current avalanche information by phoning the TELUS Talking Yellow Pages at 403 521-5222, extension 8850. Or you can scan the Canadian Avalanche Association's website on the Internet at http://www.avalanche.ca. It's also a good idea to get a weather forecast for the area you plan to explore. Manners suggests that while driving to your destination, watch for fresh avalanche activity. Note whether most slides have occurred on south, north, west or east slopes. That information could suggest which areas to watch most carefully on your outing. Upon arriving in Banff National Park or Kananaskis Country, check with visitor services centers for current avalanche conditions.

Having the right equipment increases chances of surviving an avalanche. Manners says it's critical every member of the party heading into the backcountry have a shovel, sectional snow probe and emergency locator beacon, which indicates the position of somebody buried in snow. It takes an average of two minutes to dig out a person wearing a beacon. Someone buried five minutes has a 95 percent chance of survival, while one buried 20 minutes has only a 50 percent chance.

Skiers should regard as a danger sign any cracks that develop suddenly in the snow off their ski tips. Another red flag is feeling or seeing snow "whompfing" as it settles. Skiers and other travelers shouldn't assume an area that was safely crossed in the morning will be stable on their return in the afternoon. Wind and heat during the day can make snow less stable than it was hours earlier.

Avalanches sometimes happen so fast there's no avoiding them. If it's apparent you're about to be caught in an avalanche, quickly shed all equipment such as skis, poles and backpack. Then try to stay on top of the sliding snow by making swimming motions with your arms, intensifying effort as the avalanche begins slowing down. As the avalanche stops, stick one arm straight up and put the other hand in front of your nose and mouth to create an air pocket.

Staying Warm

DIEHARD OUTDOOR ENTHUSIASTS don't stay home during extremely cold weather. Nursing hot toddies in front of the fireplace while dreaming of tropical islands and sandy beaches isn't their idea of a good time. They know that bitterly cold Arctic-like weather is as much a part of Calgary winters as are blessed Chinooks. Whether you ski, snowshoe, ice fish, skate, toboggan, snowmobile or just like to wander in the outdoors, there's a simple key to doing it safely and in relative comfort.

"Be prepared physically, mentally and psychologically," says Richard Latis, a Calgary ski patroller and climber. This teacher of wilderness survival, map and compass, and emergency first aid has seen many people get in trouble in cold weather, mainly because they weren't ready for it. Some suffered frostbite, others became hypothermic. A few even died. Hypothermia is a potentially fatal affliction of rapidly dropping body temperature caused by a combination of wind, cold and moisture. It begins with shivering, then progresses to fatigue, fumbling hands, confusion, slurred speech, numb skin and a complete disregard for safety. If any of these symptoms develop, it's time to return to the vehicle or take other steps to get warm. Severely hypothermic people require medical treatment.

It's possible to prepare your body for cold weather outings. You can start by eating right. The body needs proper fuel to operate in the cold. Eat pasta, pizza, potatoes or other carbohydrate-rich foods for dinner the night before. Chow down on cold pizza, cereal or toast for breakfast. Instead of traditional trail mix—which generally promotes thirst because it's dry—Latis suggests carrying high-carbo energy bars like the Coldbuster, Power-Bar and Gobar.

Latis also recommends dressing in layers, starting with polyester, wool or fleece underwear next to your body. These materials will "wick" moisture away from your skin as you work up a sweat. Then add a layer or two of wool or polar fleece, top and bottom. On top of that, don windproof pants and jacket. To check out if clothing is windproof, put fabric to your mouth, make a seal with your lips and try to draw air through it. If air comes through, the garment is merely windresistant, not windproof. Latis preaches an old adage: if your feet are cold, cover your head. More than 40 percent of body heat loss occurs through the head. A warm close-weave knit hat or wool toque reduces heat loss, especially when used in conjunction with a neck tube.

To help keep feet dry, and therefore warmer, Latis suggests sprinkling on a layer of baby powder or Cayenne pepper. Instead of cotton socks, use a blend of polyester, wool and nylon. If your feet get cold, bury them in loose snow, which has a high insulating value, to help retain heat whenever you get a chance.

Calgarian John Dunn is no stranger to cold weather. A veteran traveler by ski, foot and kayak in the Arctic, Dunn lead the first man-powered traverse of Ellesmere Island. When a cold snap grips Calgary, it reminds him of his coldest days in Canada's Far North. One of Dunn's handiest discoveries for keeping warm in low temperatures and high wind chills is a neoprene face mask. Wind and waterproof, it helps keep your head toasty-warm, especially when used in conjunction with snow goggles and fleece hat featuring a nylon outer shell and ear flaps. Dunn says it's not a good idea to try out unfamiliar new boots when the mercury has plunged to -30°C (-22°F). To help keep your feet warm and dry, use insulated gaiters that fit over your entire boot.

If you need to use your hands for cross-country skiing or another activity, Dunn suggests donning a thin pair of insulated gloves inside a heavier fleece mitt or overmitt. Choose outer clothing with big zippers that can be worked by hands protected by mitts or gloves. Above all, Dunn says, don't let a little cold weather stop your enjoyment of the outdoors. "Don't be put off by the weather," he says. "If you've got the right kit and clothing, you'll be all right."

Water Warning

KEITH MORTON, a Calgary outdoor educator, says it's important for hikers and nordic skiers to drink plenty of fluids, preferably clean water rather than fruit juices or pop. Ingesting fluids compensates for body moisture lost through perspiration. Becoming dehydrated on the trail can lead to unpleasant urinary problems, irritability and confusion.

On the other hand, severe stomach ailments can be caused by drinking from a lake, river or creek. "It's like playing Russian roulette," cautions John Pelton, environmental health director with Calgary Health Services. "It may look like an innocent piece of water, but it could contain dangerous bacteria." Such bacteria can cause so-called beaver fever (giardia) and other intestinal disorders. No matter how desperate you might become, never take water out of beaver ponds or streams which flow through them. A stream that appears to be crystal-clear and pure might be contaminated upstream by a rotting animal carcass, manure or other source. Some health problems may not develop until several days after drinking contaminated water. Children and older people are considerably more susceptible.

Packing enough water to sustain all members of your party during a long outing can be difficult. After all, 1 l (3.8 gal) of water weighs about 1 kg (2.2 lb). But it's worth the trouble.

Morton recommends taking a sterile, water-tight container and a good supply of purifying tablets, which must be fresh to be effective. Tablets take longer to work if the water is extremely cold. Since purifying tablets sometimes make water taste funny, Morton suggests adding Tang or other flavoring after enough time has elapsed for the tablet to work. Commercially available portable water purifying filters also can be used. Failing all else, boil the water. At higher elevations, boil it longer than normal to ensure all bacteria are killed. If you are become dehydrated on the trail and can't purify your water supply, drink only from natural springs that can be traced back to their source.

On Thin Ice

A CHILLING SCENE from the movie *Never Cry Wolf* can't help but strike fear in the hearts of anyone who's ever ventured onto a frozen body of water. It starts with our hero, a wolf researcher, plodding over an ice-covered Arctic lake. He stops, listens for some sound only he can hear, then takes another step. Suddenly he crashes through the ice. His heavily laden backpack carries him straight to the bottom of the lake, where he frantically struggles for several seconds. The next scene shows him bobbing on the surface, gasping and shaking but alive. In true Hollywood style he survives.

Anglers at Chain Lakes Provincial Park must be aware of ice safety.

But show biz isn't real life. Fate generally writes a different script. If a person wearing a heavy pack and traveling alone in the Arctic really did plunge through the ice, chances are he or she wouldn't survive. Every year in Alberta, people die after crashing through ice on lakes, sloughs and rivers. That's why learning how to be safe on ice is so important to skaters, cross-country skiers, snowmobilers, tobogganers, ice fishers and anybody else who spends time on frozen water.

The harsh reality is that no matter how careful you are, if you venture onto ice you are gambling with fate. Despite all your precautions, there's always a chance you'll fall through. But risk can be reduced by using common sense and following a few basic safety guidelines.

The Canadian Red Cross recommends ice be at least 15 cm (6") thick for walking on and 25 cm (10") for snowmobiling. Alberta Fish and Wildlife Services suggests that ice be at least 30 cm (12") thick before driving on it. That thickness generally isn't achieved until midwinter. It's important to know that the ice is the same thickness farther from shore as it is close to land because ice always develops sooner close to shore. Ice should be checked with an ice auger or iron spud every time you go out. Keep in mind, too. that ice conditions can vary from lake to lake, and also on different locations on a single body of water. The most treacherous times are late fall, when ice is forming, and in spring, when ice is melting. Weather alternating between bitter cold and warm Chinooks disrupts the development of healthy, solid ice.

The best approach is to err on the side of caution. Don't take chances. It's easy to get too eager to get out to enjoy your favorite activity to let your enthusiasm get the best of you.

Before venturing onto an unfamiliar lake, ask someone who knows it well about the location of thin spots, hidden springs and stream inlets or outlets. Ice near these areas should be avoided. Dark or cloudy patches in ice indicate weak areas. The safest ice is hard and clear blue. Carry a pole, knotted rope or some other rescue device in case your partner falls through. A set of ice claws on a leather thong kept around your neck will help you get out.

Driving on ice is never recommended. But if you do, keep the doors unlatched and open, the windows rolled down and seat belts off. Don't follow closely behind another vehicle because moving "waves" created by each vehicle can break the ice. On cracked and refrozen ice, cross the crack at right angles. Don't park near cracks. If the vehicle starts to sink, jump to safety immediately.

No matter how careful you are, it's critical to know what to do if you fall through the ice. The Red Cross recommends staying calm, facing the nearest shore, stretching out your arms and kicking your feet behind you to keep yourself horizontal in the water. If members of your party take a dunking, reduce the chances of hypothermia by removing the victims' wet clothes and having them don warm, dry ones. Wrap them in blankets and provide them with warm liquid to drink (not alcohol). If they are unconscious, confused or disoriented, take them immediately to hospital.

And always remember: this ain't Hollywood. Few things are less forgiving than unsafe ice.

Ticked Off

Dealing with Rocky Mountain wood ticks that can transmit Rocky Mountain spotted fever is a fact of life when traveling during spring in the mountains and foothills. Although these eight-legged, blood-sucking parasites more commonly feed on wildlife, they will attach to people if they get the chance. The prime season for these flat-bodied arachnids is early April to June. All terrain is potential wood tick country, but extra caution should be exercised on exposed south-facing slopes used by bighorn sheep, elk and deer. Don't sit in these areas, or in meadows and rocky terrain used by grazing wildlife and Columbian ground squirrels.

To avoid ticks, spray or rub your clothing with a DEET-based repellent and pull your socks over pant cuffs. Check yourself, companions and your children thoroughly after each outing. Pay particular attention to your head, neck, armpits and crotch areas. Pets also should be checked.

If a tick gets attached to you, remove it gently with tweezers to ensure it doesn't break. Treat the bite area with antiseptic. See a doctor if you can't remove the tick, if inflammation occurs after removal or if you experience a fever or headache.

Recommended Reading

Alberta Forestry, Lands and Wildlife, *Alberta Wildlife Viewing Guide*. Edmonton: Lone Pine, 1990.

Acorn, John and Chris Fisher. *Birds of Alberta* Edmonton: Lone Pine, 1998.

Beers, Don. *Banff–Assiniboine: A Beautiful World*. Calgary: Highline, 1993.

———. *The World of Lake Louise: A Guide for Hikers*. Calgary: Highline, 1991.

Bullick, Terry. *Calgary Parks and Pathways*. Calgary: Rocky Mountain Books, 1990.

Calgary Field Naturalists' Society, *Nose Hill: A Popular Guide*. Calgary: Calgary Field Naturalists' Society, 1988.

Cameron, Ward. *Kananaskis: An Altitude SuperGuide*. Canmore: Altitude Publishing, 1996.

Copeland, Kathy and Craig. *Don't Waste Your Time in the Canadian Rockies*. Riondel, British Columbia: Voice in the Wilderness Press, 1998.

Corbett, Bill. *Best of Alberta: Day Trips from Calgary*. Vancouver: Whitecap Books, 1984.

Corbett, Bill. *Best of Alberta: Outdoor Activities in Alberta's Heartland*. Vancouver: Whitecap Books, 1993.

Daffern, Gillean. *Kananaskis Country Trail Guide*. Calgary: Rocky Mountain Books, 1996.

———. *Kananaskis Country Ski Trails*. Calgary: Rocky Mountain Books, 1992.

———. *Short Walks for Inquiring Minds: Canmore and Kananaskis Country*. Calgary: Rocky Mountain Books, 1994.

Dawson, Chris. *Due North of Montana: A Guide to Flyfishing in Alberta*. Boulder: Johnson Books, 1996.

Dodd, John and Gail Helgason. *Canadian Rockies Access Guide*. Edmonton: Lone Pine, 1998.

Edworthy Park Heritage Society. *Early Days in Edworthy Park*. Calgary: Edworthy Park Heritage Society, 1994.

Elphinstone, Dave. *Inglewood Bird Sanctuary: A Place for All Seasons*. Calgary: Rocky Mountain Books, 1990.

Elton, Heather. *Banff's Best Dayhikes*. Edmonton: Lone Pine, 1997.

Finlay, Joy and Cam. *Parks in Alberta: A Guide to Peaks, Ponds, Parklands and Prairies for Visitors*. Edmonton: Hurtig, 1987.

Gadd, Ben. *Handbook of the Canadian Rockies*. Jasper: Corax Press, 1995.

Hallworth, Beryl and C.C. Chinnappa. *Plants of Kananaskis Country*. Calgary: University of Calgary Press, 1997.

Herrero, Stephen. *Bear Attacks: Their Causes and Avoidance*. New York: Nick Lyons Books, 1985.

McLennan, Jim. *Blue Ribbon Bow: A Fly-Fishing History of Canada's Greatest Trout Stream*. Red Deer: Johnson Gorman Publishers, 1998.

——. *Trout Streams of Alberta: A Guide to the Best Fly-Fishing*. Red Deer: Johnson Gorman Publishers, 1996.

Pole, Graeme. *Walks and Easy Hikes in the Canadian Rockies*. Canmore: Altitude Publishing, 1996.

Potter, Mike. *Backcountry Banff*. Banff: Luminous Compositions, 1992.

——. *Central Rockies Wildflowers*. Banff: Luminous Compositions, 1996.

Potter, Mike. *Hiking Lake Louise*. Banff: Luminous Compositions, 1994.

Robertson, Anna. *Fish Creek Provincial Park: A Guide to Canada's Largest Urban Park*. Calgary: Rocky Mountain Books, 1991.

Van Tighem, Kevin. *Bears*. Canmore: Altitude Publishing, 1997.

——. *Wild Animals of Western Canada*. Banff: Altitude Publishing, 1992.

von Hauff, Donna. *Alberta Parks: Our Legacy*. Edmonton: Alberta Recreation, Parks and Wildlife Foundation, 1992.

Schaupmeyer, Clive A. *The Essential Guide to Fly-Fishing*. Red Deer: Johnson Gorman Publishers, 1997.

——. *Prairie Oasis: Kinbrook Marsh*. Brooks, Alberta: Clive A. Schaupmeyer, 1991.